25 Years of the Earl of Seacliff

Michael O'Leary and Mark Pirie

Published by Michael O'Leary, 2023.

Earl of Seacliff Art Workshop
Paekakariki

The Earl is in...
25 Years of the Earl of Seacliff
A to Z

Michael O'Leary, the Earl of Seacliff by John Girdlestone

Michael O'Leary by Michael O'Leary

I was beamed down by the Mother- ship in October, the month of our Lady, 1950 the Year of the Tiger. As a Libran I am a well-balanced person who is continually being thrown off-balance. I chose Auckland as my birthplace (i.e. let down centre) because of its thunderstorms and movie theatres. I am at present touring the South Island in an attempt to contact my spaceship (the air is clearer). I have been in Dunedin six years waiting for a sign. I have so far only discovered an advanced colony of Aliens from the galaxy of Oamaruvia but I'm still searching.
Thank you for being so polite.

Foreword by Peter Olds

The Earl of Seacliff Art Workshop published my book *Music Therapy* in 2001. It was my first since *After Looking for Broadway* appeared in 1985. In-between time I had been bumming around the North Island fishing, drinking and living with my parents in Omokoroa. Later, I settled in Seacliff; in a hut, with chooks, pinecones and candles. I already knew Michael O'Leary from the Cook days ('70s, early '80s). After Seacliff I moved back to Dunedin and caught depression. Bryan Harold and Michael were running a bookshop in the Octagon called O'Books. It became a meeting place for would-be-poets, drifters and Dylan look-a-likes. About this time Michael asked me if I'd like to publish with The Earl of Seacliff - which he was beginning to crank up and was looking for manuscripts. I hadn't written anything of note for years, so I said maybe; and went away to think about it. Five bloody years later (and one dead chook) I came up with *Music Therapy*. Since that publication, ESAW has published three more books of mine, *The Mad Elephant, Reaching for the Baxters* and *Graffiti*. I'm very happy to be associated with Michael and ESAW; and I still hold out hope that Pete Best will come out of retirement and join our combo when we go into the studio on Friday to lay down the tracks for our new retrospective: 'Private Hotstuff and his Gregarious Stomach-churning Social Group'. Congratulations, Michael, and the Earl of Seacliff Art Workshop.

Peter Olds

Foreword by David McGill

Michael O'Leary was as usual metamorphosing. The venue was his Kakariki Bookshop tucked in to a shady side of a side street of central Paekakariki. The date was significant, a conjunction of three sevens on the cusp of the Matariki calendar. It was the seventh day of the seventh month of year 7 of the new millennium. It was Ringo's Birthday. Many disparate folk were packed in to Michael's wee bookshop to launch my pop music memoirs, *The Treadmill Tapes*. By some magical mystery turn, there were people - who had never met - lustily singing, 'Happy Birthday to you / Happy Birthday to you / Happy Birthday, Dear Ringo / Happy Birthday to you.' I could have sworn Michael was happy drinking red wine. I saw no signal from him. I did not hear him start off the singing. It seemed spontaneous. I think he induced by beneficent thought processes a desire for the mayor-to-be of Kapiti, a wind gardener from Wellington, a mead mistress from Wellington, a strategic pay executive from Auckland, a former Dutch chef from Otaki, a chippie and a food refuge administrator, a professional entertainer from Island Bay, a scriptwriter from Raumati, a seamstress from Brooklyn, a Christian folksinger and designer from Paraparaumu Beach, a children's illustrator from North Shore City, a displaced retirement home occupant and a number of folk who wandered in off the street - Michael induced all these people to sing Happy Birthday to Ringo. Michael has a knack for achieving the metastable condition of passing so slowly to another state as to seem stable through his talent for metathesis. I observe this frequently as we circle the Beatles' songs on a weekly basis as if we are shepherds rounding up our precious sheep so we can count them awake. Michael has metamorphosed through many locations, making all familiar with his epicentric good cheer. We were born in Ōrākei, we have travelled by train many times around the country and written about our adventures, and our trains have stopped at Paekakariki, where we reside within the sound of train clacking old and new, for the steam trains also travel out of here to spread the good fellowship that is such a distinctive characteristic of ex-railway worker and Paekakariki poet laureate and Earl of Seacliff Art Workshop 25th birthday boy Michael O'Leary. Happy Birthday, Dear Michael, happy birthday to you. — *David McGill*

Introduction

1

I first spoke to the Earl of Seacliff, Michael O'Leary, in 2000. He had phoned me to follow up on a questionnaire he was sending out to small press publishers for his MA thesis at Victoria University of Wellington. Having recently returned from Dunedin and completed my own MA thesis at the University of Otago, I was sympathetic to the work involved and the idea about which he was gathering information.

I wrote my responses to Michael's questions[1] about my publishing company HeadworX and they were included in his thesis. Steele Roberts in Wellington eventually published the thesis in book form in 2007.

One of the key ideas about small press publishing that emerged from the responses to Michael's questions was that given by Alan Brunton (Bumper Books). Alan's reasons for starting his own company were:

> The example of rock and roll artists controlling their own labels, e.g. the Beatles with Apple, Lewis and Pound with BLAST, Ferlinghetti with City Lights.[2]

This 'rock and roll' idea was also the major influence on Michael starting his Earl of Seacliff Art Workshop in 1984.

Michael is a publisher interested in work outside the literary 'mainstream', including work from other cultures.[3] He has promoted writing by those often seen as unacceptable or old-fashioned to 'mainstream' publishers, literary editors and the more fashionable academic cliques. The very sign of his success as a literary editor is the number of well-established writers/artists who earlier in their careers worked with him, e.g. David Eggleton, Andrew Johnston, John Pule, Gregory O'Brien, and others. But, in that 'rock and roll' sense that Alan mentioned, Michael has also published his own experimental novels and writings (like the Beatles with Apple) keeping control of the production and the form of his words on the page. Michael's use of language and puns has always been idiosyncratic and it has been necessary for Michael to keep control of his work, just as a band keeps control of the production of their songs at an independent level.

In Raewyn Alexander's essay, 'Relegated to oblivion: *poetry and the media*', she comments on the way some poetry publishers outside the 'mainstream' are treated here and uses myself as an example:

> Mark Pirie ... has a profound understanding of contemporary New Zealand poets and their audience and as editor and publisher of *JAAM (Just Another Art Movement)* and founder of the publishing house HeadworX, has shown longer established publishers how they should be doing their work.
>
> Pirie's initial forays into invigorating the world of poetry and magazine production met with fierce opposition - an opposition that charitably, could be considered as nothing less than protective as a number of established writers and publishers barely acknowledged what he was doing and in some cases, opposed it. Less kindly, it might be said that some of these literary aficionados believed poetry properly belonged only to an elite of themselves, their colleagues and associates. Such beliefs conform to the perennial practice of the powerful doing everything possible to maintain control of their local and overseas monopolies. Those they exclude sometimes go underground and form groups of their own, which those who have forced them into this position invariably denigrate and identify as subversive.
>
> Pirie is an example of someone who believes in what he's doing and perseveres despite adverse criticism levelled at him. Literary community insecurities and biases produce chilly responses. The climate poetry encounters is sometimes so adverse that it hinders rather than helps its development.[4]

Change 'Pirie' here for O'Leary and 'HeadworX' and *JAAM* for ESAW in the 1980s and you might get the same story. O'Leary has 'persevered' for 25 years in this country and lasted the distance. The sheer size of this book is a tip of the hat to the Earl. His large output and success requires the acknowledgement this book offers.

2

In the last nine years, the continuing friendship between Michael and myself has formed the basis for a strong working relationship on a collaborative level. I have typeset a number of Michael's ESAW publications as well as my own books he's published, edited ESAW books (like the Winter Readings anthologies, Meg Campbell's *Resistance,* Will Leadbeater's *Jubal's Lyre* and Jill Chan's *the smell of oranges*), we have produced a cover photo series together, co-authored a book of sonnets and co-organised a series of reading events in Wellington. Michael, more than any other, has responded to my work in a warmth of manner that is unusual in literary circles. Since 2001, when I published my first chapbook with Michael, *The Blues*, I have gone on to be the most prolific author of ESAW with around twenty publications (my own books as well as anthologies I've edited). This case of like-minded collaboration, however, is not peculiar to me alone. The large number of writers who willingly gave of their time to contribute to this book indicates the warmth and aroha given between Michael and his authors. As Heather McPherson writes (of her experience working with Michael) in her essay 'Writing in the Book of Aotearoa':

> Over my own work and especially with final proofs I'm slow, dithery and indecisive. Michael was patient and supportive through the many phone calls; in the exciting week before the MS went to print I stayed with him.

Or as Elizabeth Smither comments in 'Gorilla/Guerrilla':

> You've got to be at a distance to see faith and genius, and that's what is obvious now about Michael O'Leary and the Earl of Seacliff Art Workshop productions. Publishing is not what it was but Michael represents what it should be, what it is in every writer's heart of hearts. Books produced without fuss or flourish; not a meddling accountant in sight. Just good friends, word of

mouth, faith in literature ... And the presiding generous spirit of an alpha gorilla.

Michael's way of working with people, then, and his respect for people in the world has created an original way of working with authors, which is very different to mainstream editors' treatment of their writers.

3

After doing my research, soliciting and collecting all the articles, I started to think of a way to put together a book on the Earl. I had several ideas: one was doing a kind of 'rock star' presentation of the Earl as the best way to bring out his distinct personality and qualities as an artist, writer, performer and bookshop/art gallery proprietor as well as highlighting the wide range of interests throughout his life. Secondly, there was a desire to put together a type of 'literary companion' to Michael. Sometimes critics denigrate his writing to the effect that is often misunderstood. Many of the pieces chosen on his novels for instance will help to treat the work more seriously and provide scholars and researchers starting points for further discussion of his work. The final idea was doing a book in celebration of the Earl and his life (on the 25th Anniversary of his publishing company).

The 'rock star' *A to Z* approach also seemed to be the best way to maintain a focus on the texts at hand as well as inclusiveness (a hallmark of Michael's publishing approach). Unfortunately, not every book published by ESAW could be included and in some instances the 'rock' theme behind the book helped shape the selection with a majority of the books and poems discussed here having some crossover between literary culture and pop culture.

Overall, I selected the best or most informative pieces of writing I could find on the books included. In some cases, some of the reviews and articles here may not be entirely flattering of Michael's work or the books he has published, but that is the point of criticism, and it was not my (or Michael's) intention to have a book solely consisting of one- sided praise and grandiose entries. As well, I have included biographical and other information concerning the composition of some of Michael's key poems and literary works. This may further give valuable background to Michael's writing to scholars who wish to study his works in a longer form or in detail.

I enjoyed putting this book together, tracking down and researching the historical articles. I think the book offers a comprehensive guide to the Earl at this point in his writing life as well as offering an innovative approach to literary criticism in this country. The Earl is a unique writer and one of the liveliest characters on our Aotearoa literary scene in the last 30 years. It is hoped this book will aid the recognition of his literary work in the years to come.

Mark Pirie
Wellington
30 April 2009

Notes

[1]The set of questions Michael sent to publishers are in Michael's unpublished self-questionnaire at the back of the book as an appendix.

[2]Alan Brunton/Michael O'Leary, 'Questionnaire for Alternative Small Press Publishing in New Zealand (1969-1999)', *brief 28* (Spring 2003), p. 42.

[3]ESAW has published a diverse range of international writers, including work by Moshé Liba (Israel), Richard Berengarten (UK), Basim Furat (Iraq), Aucklander Jill Chan (formerly of the Philippines), African-American jazz poet and Wellington resident L E Scott as well as Māori and other indigenous Pacific writers.

[4]*Poetry NZ 27* (September 2005), pp. 100-101.

Ka Tahuri Au

Ka tahuri au
Ka kite aki au
Ngā pomairangi
E heke ana mai
Ki runga o Aoraki e
Tau iho ki runga
Ngā mokopuna e
No te Waipounamu e
He Iwi e

Winsome Aroha

(Sung by Winsome Aroha on Bloomsday 2002 at the launch of *Unlevel Crossings*, a novel by Michael O'Leary, which is inspired by and dedicated to her by the author.)

On ESAW's 25th Anniversary

for Michael O'Leary

Today, you look forward
to all the futures
you'll get to.

Every book yet to be bound,
to be made
into being.

For now,
you're laughing
away the afternoon.

The years look at you
longingly,
full of memories
somewhere written.

Jill Chan

The Earl's Timeline: 1984-2009

1984 was a year made notable by George Orwell: it was also the year Michael O'Leary turned 34, was working for the Auckland City Council and found himself commissioned to write books on two Auckland cemeteries. At this time the idea of setting up an 'art and writing factory' had been turning over in his head. Having been to art school, he imagined a place busy with artists and writers who could come in and work anytime day or night, similar to the labouring and factory jobs he'd worked in most of his life. It was a fanciful notion he later admits somewhat akin to Andy Warhol's Factory.

However, the experience and knowledge gained from the publishing of those two books gave him the impetus to set up the Earl of Seacliff Art Workshop.

Why start his own press? The realisation that his original and idiomatic writing style would not be acceptable to mainstream commercial publishers, coupled with a strong desire to publish other poets and writers who may struggle to get their work published.

The name Seacliff came from the small settlement north of Dunedin where he lived for some time in his twenties. He first saw Seacliff from the Southerner while travelling south to Dunedin in 1974. 'I can always remember it; a thick fog shrouded the whole town. All I could see were church spires poking through, and roads leading into the fog. In my mind it connected with Heathcliff, and the atmospheric beautiful- spookiness of *Wuthering Heights*.'

Trains and railways are another lifelong passion and are threaded through much of his writing, particularly the novels. At Seacliff, with friends Peter Olds and Bryan Harold, he stood in the middle of the track causing the train to slow right down and stop. They were protesting NZ Railways' decision to discontinue the service there. The service was resumed sometime afterwards.

He spent the '70s in and around Dunedin working on the railways track-gangs and other similar occupations. During 1980 he travelled to Auckland for ten days. Ten days became ten years. During that decade (among other things) he worked as a drain layer and concrete landscaper during the hectic refurbishing of Queen Street. Often this was done in 12-hour night shifts while working at his Parimoana Bookshop in Kingsland during the day.

After establishing the Earl of Seacliff Art Workshop he collaborated with and published writers and artists such as Elizabeth Smither, Nigel Brown, John Pule, Gregory O'Brien, Iain Sharp, Sandra Bell, Grant Duncan, and David Eggleton, with whom he had earlier produced artefacts in their 'mini-factory' for sale on Queen Street with one eye out for council officers. O'Leary participated in many live readings in the 1980s, in particular the Globe Hotel evenings organised by poet David Mitchell. During this time he wrote his novel *Out of It,* which seemed to sum up the times aptly.

Back in Dunedin in 1990 he and Bryan Harold opened a new bookshop, O'Books, and an art gallery, O'oops Art Gallery, named after the dodgy staircase, which held exhibitions for many local artists and became a venue for performance poets. During this time he completed a BA in English at the University of Otago. Then, back to Wellington in 1997 where he established ESAW bookshop. He kept the wolf from the door by engaging in a variety of pursuits, including a spell as a creative writing tutor, being an extra on *Via Satellite* and Peter Jackson's *Lord of the Rings* and proofreading for Huia Publishers and the Te Puni Kokiri newspaper. He began studying for his MA at Victoria University. His thesis, 'Alternative Small Press Publishing in New Zealand (1969-1999)', was completed in 2002 while running Pukapuka Bookshop at Paekakariki. O'Leary then wrote a couple of Waitangi Tribunal reports and had a brief stint at 'Te Ara', the online encyclopaedia.

Currently he is studying for a PhD on New Zealand women's writing through the Victoria University Gender and Women's Studies Department and co-runs a new shop Kakariki Books in the Paekakariki Railway Station. With Wellington poet and publisher Mark Pirie, of HeadworX, he co-edited the "Greatest Hits" edition of *JAAM* literary magazine and co-produced an anthology of their sonnets. They both organise the annual poetry event at the City Gallery in Wellington called 'Winter Readings' usually done as a music/poetry tribute based on a well-known pop album. Last year's event was based on the Beatles' White Album.

Another collaboration is with playwright and novelist Brian E. Turner, of Otaki, who helps with technical aspects such as typesetting, proofreading and maintaining the ESAW website. Niel Wright has also had many collaborative projects in conjunction with ESAW and O'Leary.

Rob Hack

"A Sonnet to Ché Guevara"

Date of Composition: 1997
Collection: *Paneta Street*
Anthologised in: *Ché in Verse* (UK)

'A Sonnet to Ché Guevara' was written in 1997 when Guevara's body was exhumed from its communal grave in Vallegrande and returned to Cuba. The 30th anniversary of his death was celebrated across Cuba. Ché died on 9 October 1967, John Lennon's 27th birthday, both men being an influence and an inspiration in the Earl's life. When O'Leary heard that there was going to be an international anthology, *Ché in Verse*, published to commemorate the 40th anniversary of the death of Ché he decided to put his poem forward. Having it accepted was great but when he received his contributor's copy O'Leary was amazed to find his name alongside Pablo Neruda, Hans Magnus Enzensberger, Derek Walcott, Yevgeny Yevtushenko, Adrian Mitchell, Lawrence Ferlinghetti, Thomas Merton, Robert Lowell and Allen Ginsberg.

After Tokyo

Date of Publication: 1987
Publisher: ESAW
Category: Fiction

Life seen at street level

The 'mad Kiwi ranter', David Eggleton, renowned as a performance poet in the John Cooper Clarke style is widening his repertoire to include short stories. Eggleton, who first started performing poetry in the early 1980s, is now second only to Sam Hunt in the number of performances he gives each year.

His first book, *South Pacific Sunrise,* established his reputation as a poet. His second, *After Tokyo,* published by the Earl of Seacliff Art Workshop, contains 33 stories that take a savage, satirical look at life in New Zealand.

'A third is set in Auckland, a third in Dunedin and a third in some futuristic zone,' he says. 'My fiction is intensely episodic. Incidents pass by in a kaleidoscopic whirl. I aim for a kinetic, fluid style.'

He sees his work as having connections with the surrealists of the 1930s, the Beats of the 1950s and the 1980s punk movement.

'I am writing in reaction to the mainstream of New Zealand literature which is so often serious and dull.'

Originally published in 'radical, alternative, anarchist underground' magazines, Eggleton now commands space in *Craccum, Tango, The New Fiction* and *Rambling Jack.*

'What Barry Humphries has done for Melbourne kitsch I would like to do for Auckland's bad taste scene,' he says. 'There's a lot of colourful activity in New Zealand not reflected in the writing.'

Eggleton admires local writers Russell Haley and Ian Wedde.

Rapier-like thrusts of his own satire surface in stories such as 'Party-Going' which features Gaylene 'toting her bubble cut hairdo' and Max Crax, the personality, Barf Chompson, theatre director, Zing Zillions, teen idol, Ray Gurgitate, an elderly pop star and Strewth Brawn, Kiwi solo actor.

Eggleton takes the stance of a neutral observer.

'I am not present in any of my stories,' he says. 'I try to pick up on the groundswell, write to the street.'

Some of his stories are inspired by the violent urban changes taking place in New Zealand. 'Golden Block', set in Dunedin, was provoked by seeing an incongruously gaudy shopping mall being constructed amid rundown Victorian architecture.

His work is concerned with surfaces and the powerful influence of images in our culture. He also uses a female point of view. 'Instead of looking at New Zealand through macho eyes I am looking for a different angle of vision, a new perspective on local behaviour.'

Eggleton, who comes from Mangere, lived in Dunedin in the late 1970s before returning to Auckland. Recently back from a highly successful reading tour in Denmark, Holland and England - where he won the Covent Garden Street Entertainers Festival Award - he performs regularly in schools and cafes. Robyn Conway's black-and-white drawing inside the cover of Eggleton's book shows bees and cockroaches scuttling along a clover leaf highway - 'Insects skitter away like a nuclear exodus rehearsal...'

'I guess I could be seen as a punk writer,' says Eggleton. – *Michael Morrissey*

(From Auckland's *Inner City News* c.1987)

Alternative Small Press Publishing in New Zealand (1969-1999)

Date of Publication: 2007
Publisher: Steele Roberts
Category: Non-fiction

This book on small press literary publishing in New Zealand in the last thirty years began as an MA thesis and was published by Steele Roberts in 2007. That the 1960s cultural 'revolution' influenced the small press movement is a major theme, a fact borne out time and again from the primary source material. This thesis recognises people who dedicate so much time and resources to ensure that our literature is vibrant and alive. The protagonists from the 1960s era who had a profound effect on the 'youth culture' like Bob Dylan and The Beatles are shown to have had a significant influence by simply showing that 'You can do it'. That waiting for official sanction was not necessary, a major underlying catalyst to those involved in small presses. O'Leary's book challenges the myth that self-publishing is somehow inferior, asserting that small press publishing allows the artist control over their work, and that this is a positive and desirable thing.

The Angel Bus

Date of Publication: 2004
Publisher: ESAW
Category: Song Lyrics

Popular music has had a major influence on many New Zealand poets writing since the 1960s. Mark Pirie's collection of lyrics, *The Angel Bus,* reproduced a selection of the many songs Pirie composed in his late teens. At the time (1992-1994) he was involved in various bedroom bands such as Hydraulic Sidearm, whose 4-track demo included a cover of Napalm Death's 'Unchallenged Hate'. The book shows Pirie's initial inspiration for writing poetry was as a songwriter and he was influenced by many bands and performers such as The Doors, Henry Rollins, Ice T, Pearl Jam, the Sex Pistols, blues musicians and others. The cover drawing by Michael O'Leary was after the American writer Ken Kesey's magic bus. Kesey died in 2001, but remains an inspiration for Pirie and many others with his colourful writings such as the novel *One Flew Over The Cuckoo's Nest* and his tours with The Merry Pranksters.

The Arraignment of Dr Ley

Date of Publication: 1989
Publisher: ESAW
Category: Satire/Humour

The Arraignment of Dr Ley was a satirical piece written by O'Leary and Iain Sharp in response to an article about the Auckland poetry scene in the 1980s by Graham Lay for the *New Zealand Listener*. O'Leary comments: 'We found a photo of the Nazis on trial at Nuremberg and tipped in Graham's image where the labour minister, Dr Ley, was in the photo. I found this great quote from Goebbels about Ley being "not the sort of man we want writing in the press". My next-door neighbour in Mt Albert was teaching at the same school as Graham so I surreptitiously had her put a copy in his letterbox at work. Warwick Jordan, of Hard Echo Press, hand-printed it and Nigel Cox, who ran Unity Books in Auckland at the time, liked it so much that he ordered an extra 100 copies.'

Auckland years

Early Sightings of the Earl

The first time I clapped eyes on the Earl he had not yet laid claim to his earldom. He might not have known where in the world Seacliff was. I certainly didn't. This was in 1962 or thereabouts, and I was nine years old and Michael O'Leary eleven. Both our fathers are dead now, but they were alive back then and in their bibulous prime. They both drank at the DB Onehunga on Saturday afternoons when they were supposed to be looking after their young sons. They both had the same routine. Michael's dad would give him a shilling to buy a milkshake at the dairy next to the State cinema, across the road from the pub, and say, 'I'll just be a few minutes.' So would mine. They were lying, of course. Their boozing always lasted at least an hour while Michael and I stared at the posters and photographs in the State's lobby, advertising current and forthcoming movies, and then mooched around the DB Onehunga's carpark.

You might imagine from this that I knew Michael quite well as a boy. In fact, I never spoke to him. I was a shy, suspicious and antisocial kid. I would wait outside the dairy, watching until Michael had finished his milkshake, before I ducked in for mine. I remember him smiling at me on a couple of occasions, though, as we passed in the dairy's entranceway.

I've often wondered whether our fathers knew each other. They might have done. I inherited my shyness from my dad. Sober, he barely said a word. With a few whiskies inside him, however, he became everybody's pal and wanted to sing. I imagine him slinging an arm round Michael's father, whom he would have identified only as 'Paddy', and the pair of them duetting on 'Danny Boy', 'Galway Bay' or something similar. Michael's dad would have identified mine, who was born in Glasgow, only as 'Jock'.

Years passed. My father switched his allegiance from the DB Onehunga to the Ellerslie Hotel. The next time I recall seeing Michael was at Auckland University in early March 1974. I was an MA student at the time, studying English and New Zealand literature. I'm not sure whether Michael was formally enrolled or just in the habit of occasionally spending time on campus. Early in the academic year, the English Department organised a special seminar on Janet Frame's novels and stories. Frame herself wasn't there and wasn't even in the country, having been awarded the 1974 Katherine Mansfield Fellowship at Menton on the French Riviera, but the guest of honour was her sister, June Godfrey.

Michael, then at the height of his hippie phase, sauntered in, long-haired, barefoot and dishevelled, and immediately gave June Godfrey a kiss and big warm hug. 'Who the hell is this guy,' I said to myself and straight away jumped to the wrong conclusion. Thinking he must be part of the Frame family - I convinced myself he was Janet's illegitimate son. When I whispered this suggestion to some of my MA classmates sitting nearby, they quickly and excitedly concurred.

I finally spoke to Michael a couple of months later. I was having a coffee in the student cafeteria, after a tutorial on Shakespeare's *Troilus and Cressida* or something similar, with a friend, John Curry, who has faded from the limelight in recent years but was once regarded as one of the country's most promising young stage directors. When Michael came into the cafeteria, I leaned across the table and said to John, *sotto voce*, 'Don't look now, but see that bloke over there? He's Janet Frame's bastard offspring.'

'And I'm the pope's daughter,' John snorted and retorted. 'That's not a Frame offshoot. That's Michael O'Leary. I know him quite well.'

He called Michael over to our table. Almost as soon as he sat down, Michael pulled a wad of hand-written poems from his satchel and passed them to John and me to read. One of them contained a reference to a milkman wearing a derby hat. 'That's like the Dylan song *On the Road Again*,' I suggested.

'Yeah,' Michael conceded, a bit on the defensive, 'but the other images are my own.'

Which, indeed, they were. I wasn't trying to catch Michael out on a bit of plagiarism anyway. I was more impressed that he knew the lyrics to one of Bob Dylan's more obscure efforts. I've long since come to the conclusion that there isn't *any* song from the 1960s or '70s that Michael doesn't know. Give him a half a line and he'll finish it for you, whether it's from the Beatles or David Bowie or something one-off and demented, like 'Let it All Hang Out' by the Hombres and 'I am a Mechanical Man' by Bent Bolt and the

Nuts. He's capable of speaking for hours on end, using only song titles and quotations.

More years passed. Michael moved to Otago, living first in Dunedin and then about twenty kilometres up the coast at Seacliff, site of the old mental hospital, now in ruins, where Janet Frame had been subjected to electro-convulsive therapy in the late 1940s. In claiming Seacliff as his fiefdom, I'm not sure whether Michael became Frame's bastard heir or the illegitimate landlord of her mental landscape.

We next met in late 1981 at one of the poetry readings organised by David Mitchell at the Globe Hotel in Wakefield Street, Auckland. Michael had shifted again and was now living with flatmates in Patey Street, Remuera. This was more or less on my way home to Ellerslie, so I offered to give him a lift at the end of the reading. While I drove, he asked me if I could give him $500 to publish his first poetry book. This ploy would not work nowadays, when I never have more than a few cents to rub together, but back then I had some money saved. There was something about the cheeky directness of Michael's request that appealed to me and I agreed.

Besides, the book that Michael had planned did not contain just his own writing but that of two of his cronies from Seacliff days, Sandra Bell and Brian Hare. As it happened, I knew Brian quite well because we were at high school together. Even as a teenager I recognised that Brian was much cleverer than I was in terms of native intelligence, but I scored far better than he did in exams and so forth, largely because his disastrous family history inclined him to not give a flying shit about such matters. His father was dead and his mother was confined to a Seacliff-like mental institution, a hopelessly degenerative schizophrenic. Brian lived with an older brother. Several times a week, he wagged school to go to the racetrack, either to bet or to study form. He had a huge physique, even in his teens, so his age was seldom challenged by racecourse officials.

Poor doomed Brian! He ended up as mad as his mother. Whereas Michael enjoys playing the part of the Earl of Seacliff, Brian came genuinely to believe he was the Prince of Ireland. Worse, he also believed with equal sincerity of conviction that many of his erstwhile friends were, in fact, agents of Satan. He would charge at them like an enraged rhino, intent on righteous eradication.

In 1981, however, Brian was still lucid and I was keen to help him as well as Michael. Their book was titled *Surrogate Children*, which amused me, given my earlier misapprehension about Michael's maternal progenitor. It was not an Earl of Seacliff Art Workshop production. The imprint was 'Lancaster Publishing', run by Auckland anarchist Bruce Grenville, a colourful and rather strange character, most famous for issuing a series of postage stamps from an imaginary sultanate located at Occussi-Ambeno, on the western half of Timor. I've always thought that 'Lancaster' was a disappointingly staid brand-name for the personnel involved. The Sultan of Occussi-Ambeno's Art Workshop would have had more zing.

ESAW had its origins a couple of years after *Surrogate Children* appeared. In its earliest incarnation it really was an art workshop. Because they were hard-up, Michael, his old friend from Otago days David Eggleton, and the Niuean poet John Pule, whom they had met at the Globe Hotel readings, did quick watercolour and crayon drawings on cardboard and sold them on Auckland streets. It amuses me, now that paintings by Pule routinely sell for $30,000 or more, to recall the time when he was happy with a few coins for beer money.

The ESAW artisans' base, if I remember correctly, was a peculiar little shop in Symonds Street called the Proutist Universe, which was once again run by Bruce Grenville. 'Prout' is short for Progressive Utilisation Theory, a system for redistributing the world's economic resources, devised in 1959 by the Indian savant Shrii Prabhat Ranjan Sarkar. I guess Bruce was an admirer. The shop sold pamphlets advocating Proutist philosophy, but in 1980s Auckland the demand was not brisk. The store lasted only a short time.

Knowing how busy Michael now is with the publishing arm of ESAW, I realise my impertinence in suggesting further titles for him to issue or reissue. Still, I reckon that for nostalgia's sake and in recognition of his Proutist roots, he should publish some of P.R. Sarkar's *Songs of the New Dawn* (there are 5018 in total, I'm told). If I ever get round to writing another ESAW book myself (providing, of course, that the Earl permits me), I plan to call it *Onehunga Milkshake. – Iain Sharp*

Early Days

In a row of shabby shops in Kingsland, a bright yellow sign [painted by Greg O'Brien] points the way to Parimoana Book Shop - New and Used Books. Inside, Michael O'Leary, Earl of Seacliff, sits behind a huge desk. He is a big man, with an earring dangling from his left ear, a heavy beard and long hair. The predominant feature is his dark eyes, which seem to be laughing at a personal and cosmic joke.

On the back wall are crayon drawings of insects, and a column in the centre of the shop is being transformed into a lively totem pole - pots of paints, rags and brushes sit on the floor waiting for the next appearance of the artist. It's a work of intricate and beautiful design (by John Pule).

A young man goes to the counter to buy a book. It's a ten dollar sale, but O'Leary doesn't know how to ring it up on the old-fangled till. Slow-moving, he's quick to laugh. The customer gives advice, but the sale is rung up as $1. Then there's a struggle with the change.

Teething problems, but it's early days. Today is Parimoana's first day in operation. Michael O'Leary is in business.

Born in Auckland, O'Leary grew up in Ōrākei. It was a good place, he says, because people are more free-and-easy in a state housing area, and it was close to Ōkahu Bay where he went swimming.

'Being brought up a Catholic is like being brought up in Disneyland,' he says, 'except everything is painted black. It leaves you with a melancholic nature. The discrepancy between what you learn as a Catholic, and what you experience in real life is so great that you either become really straight, or you're really out-of-it. Seventy per cent of alcoholics are Catholics, a lot of homosexuals and prostitutes. We're a weird mob,' he hoots with laughter.

'With a name like Michael O'Leary, I had to be either a writer or a navvy. I became both.'

By 1971 he was at Auckland University part-time. At first he enjoyed it immensely. 'In those days there were a lot more working-class people at university. Now it's become elitist again. Basically, university is a job-training scheme for the rich and powerful in society. But at that time it was liberating.'

In 1974, he decamped to Dunedin, where his creative urges became channelled into writing. He lived at Seacliff, across the road from the mental asylum, which was an inspiration. 'It's an amazing area, like *Wuthering Heights*. Very spooky. The grounds are beautiful, run by Lands and Surveys now, with sheep and cattle grazing around the trees. I was on a work scheme for a while that kept the grounds tidy. I also worked on the railway lines around there.'

He adopted the title Earl of Seacliff, 'I'm an Irish earl, and that makes a difference. Theoretically, they're extinct.'

After six years it was back to Auckland. O'Leary and David Eggleton got together that Christmas to paint. They sold their work in Vulcan Lane, working three days a week on painting and three days on selling. Just for a laugh, O'Leary called the enterprise The Earl of Seacliff Art Workshop.

'I like the idea of art and literature not being precious. That's why I called it the Art Workshop, because it sounds like a factory. One of my aims for the Art Workshop is for it to be a factory in New Lynn or Panmure where people make art instead of stoves. There'd be a place for literature, a space for the actual writing, and then the printing. But that's a long way off,' he laughs, 'on the 20-year plan.'

From PEP work putting together booklets for the city council he gained the expertise to publish a book. He decided to make money out of publishing. Had he turned commercial? 'Well, yes, if being commercial is making a living out of your talents. It's better than spending eight hours a day earning a living at something you don't like. I'm now making a living at what I do like.'

Writing poetry, he says, is particularly intense. 'You never know when it's going to hit you, and you have to do something about it, right then, whether it's 4 am or 2 pm. That's not conducive to being in the everyday world. It's always a dilemma I've faced - having to earn a living and be creative. My latest novel deals with that. In the past two years I've turned away from poetry and tried to make everything more tangible to give me some distance between myself and the person I've created. So I can go home at the end of the day and no longer be a poet, or the Earl of Seacliff. Your private life really suffers when you become too involved with the idea of what you are. It's hard to have a relationship, for example. It's all right to be Brendan Behan, but who wants to be his wife?'

Up until November 1986, O'Leary published only his own work, but in the last few months, he's published four other writers: Grant Duncan's *Away With Words; Gorilla/Guerrilla* by Elizabeth Smither and illustrated by Greg O'Brien; Ron Riddell's *Elegy in Memory of Barry Mitcalfe,* and a Tongan colouring-in book, written by O'Leary and translated by Kahoa Corbett.

When the publishing house was just an idea, O'Leary didn't know how he was going to get the printing done, but as he says it's funny how things fall into place. He was in the pub one night and met a woman he hadn't seen for 10 years. He told her about his publishing plans. She told him she was setting up a women's printing collective.

Would they do the printing for The Earl? Yes! The poetry typesetting is done by the collective in Auckland, but the prose is sent down to Dunedin where it's cheaper. The Workshop is hoping to develop more into prose - it sells better than poetry. O'Leary himself is concentrating on prose these days, with his novel, *Out Of It,* coming out soon.

'We do a print run of 200-250, and we break even on that. In Auckland I distribute the books personally to bookshops. We've had good reviews. And there was an item in the *Listener* about the way I'd used the work scheme to do something creative, after all the talk about the gangs abusing the scheme. That created some interest. We are getting by.'

But it did become apparent that the publishing enterprise needed a firmer financial basis, a source of income. 'I noticed that this shop was empty. It had been empty for months. I had a shop for a while in Mount Albert at the back of another shop, but that was really storage space. It wasn't designed to work.' He laughs. 'You don't expect to find a book shop at the back of a barber's.'

The five-year plan is for the bookshop and the publishing business to be financially viable. On the 20-year plan is a Pacific Bookshop in Sydney - and marriage. 'The Irish always marry late. And drink a lot. I'm not married, and I drink a lot. It's the old influence. But for now, being in business and running Parimoana absorbs me.' – *Joan Rosier-Jones*

(From *Metro*, August 1987)

"The Ballad of Courtney Love"

Date of Publication: 2004
Publisher: ESAW
Category: Poetry broadsheet

'The Ballad of Courtney Love' is a broadsheet poem printed as a free gift inside Mark Pirie's collection, *Bullet Poems* (2004). The poem is based on Lawrence Durrell's 'Ballad of the Good Lord Nelson', and features a repreated refrain *'Aboard the dream, the dream of rock O!'*. 'The Ballad of Courtney Love' was Mark Pirie's first attempt at the ballad form. Rock celebrity couple Kurt Cobain and Courtney Love were significant influences on Mark Pirie's stage persona at the time. Pirie appeared in drag at Winter Readings, Tupelo bar, dressed in a petticoat, playfully mimicking Cobain's stage persona and Love's dress sense. In Iain Sharp's *Sunday Star-Times* column, he misreported Pirie's outing, saying he had appeared at the Prime Minister's Awards in drag, which led to interest from journalists. However, an article to be written on Pirie in the *Sunday Star-Times* entertainment pull-out section was pulled after the editor learned of this error in fact. Some- how Pirie was no longer as interesting!

'...having seen him perform his "Ballad of Courtney Love" in full drag, I can testify to the terrifying strength of [Pirie's] determination to link staid old New Zealand poetry with the more flourishing pastures of rock music.' — Jack Ross, *brief*

Nigel "Booga" Beazley

Nigel Beazley (aka Booga) was the lead singer for the influential '90s rock band Head Like a Hole (HLAH) from Wellington. HLAH quickly rose to prominence in New Zealand through their unusual stage performances that sometimes included the members appearing naked or caked in mud on stage. In the early Noughties after the band had for a time disbanded, Booga was playing cricket for Hutt District Cricket Club and met the poet/publisher Mark Pirie. Pirie was his teammate that season (2002-03). Both were handy bowlers for their team but often struggled with the bat. Pirie asked him to appear on the cover of the *JAAM 21 "Greatest Hits"* collection with the Earl of Seacliff. Booga played George Harrison (far left) on the *Abbey Road* remake cover. The Earl was John Lennon (far right), Pirie was Paul McCartney and Niel Wright was Ringo Starr. Later in the season, Pirie broke his wrist diving in the field to stop a run. Within an hour or so, Pirie returned to the ground from Hutt Hospital, all fixed up with a cast around his arm and attempted to resume his part in the match by taking over the scorebook. Booga later helped drive him to the captain's house after the match, and stopped at the dairy to buy Pirie some lollies for his troubles. Who says cricket's not a dangerous game.

Becoming Someone Who Isn't

Date of Publication: 2007
Publisher: ESAW
Category: Poetry

Review of Jill Chan's Becoming Someone Who Isn't

'Exile, in the words of Wallace Stevens, is "a mind of winter" in which the pathos of summer and autumn as much as the potential of spring are nearby but unobtainable. Perhaps this is another way of saying that a life of exile moves according to a different calendar, and is less seasonal and settled than life at home. Exile is life led outside habitual order. It is nomadic, decentered, contrapuntal; but no sooner does one get accustomed to it than its unsettling force erupts anew,'

concluded Edward Said.[1] Reading Jill Chan's first collection, *the smell of oranges* (ESAW, 2003), it was easy to see how much the author concurred with Said's astute reasoning about exile as a disruptive state. Poems such as 'Understanding', 'Here I Am Taking Leave' and 'In the Next Room' spoke in tight form and tighter intimation about being, as Said puts it, decentred and contrapuntal.

    it's time to ease
    this hand
    into a different pocket, (p. 42)

Chan wrote in 'Here I Am Taking Leave'. Time and again in *the smell of oranges*, the classy poems felt like they were backed by shadows of meaning which the reader drew upon as heavily as they did its language. Set against her first offering, Chan's latest collection, *Becoming Someone Who Isn't* constructs a similar picture from a similar amount of inference. Again the territory - a poetic navigation through the existence of the outsider - is the same; and again, more often than not the poems are allusive in content. Where *Becoming Someone Who Isn't* is concerned, the result is a body of work which, like its predecessor, is shrouded in suggestiveness and atmospheric import. Not that *Becoming Someone Who Isn't* is merely *the smell of oranges - Part 2*. Rather, it both deepens Chan's existent analysis with the fraught process of immigration and strengthens the connections between such analysis and Saidean ideologies.

> Home is where
> I fail to return (p. 27)

Chan writes in 'Cartography', a sense of belonging that exists beyond the grasp of the narrator is everywhere prevalent in *Becoming Someone Who Isn't*. 'The Night', 'All the Things I Say', 'Stars' and 'Must I Follow': here are poems that evoke senses of division (between protagonist and someone or something else), co-existence, duality and extrication. Take the former, for instance. It opens with immediate detachment:

> Sometimes the things
> we belong to
> don't belong to us. (p. 13)

Thereafter, chronology, in the form of night - symbol of all that's covert and threatening - becomes something exclusive.

> The night is there
> for all
> but some
> only see it
> if they stop pretending it is theirs...

In essence, through such poems, there's a repeated desire to belong to something which is hostile to the desirer. If it's a stifling portrayal of exile, it's one that's embellished by Chan's poetic exploration and deconstruction of silence.

Silence is wound.

It cries like a wound
would cry
if it were silent all its life (p. 25)

she writes in the emblematic verse, 'Silence'. Here silence is anthropomorphized into an anonymous woman who is brutalized by the world because of her inability (or is that refusal?) to speak. There's a clear sense here of victim-hood being visited upon the victim twice- over: once through their muteness and then through the world's treatment of their speechlessness. Even so, silence becomes something special, something only the silent hold. This is made clear by poems such as 'Diver' and 'When Here'. The latter, especially, makes a most advantageous case for silence:

Silence has to be saved
from its depths.
To be plain and silent.
That needs care (p. 33).

Even so, silence remains an adversity, a vantage point which even when it marks the bearer out as special nevertheless deprives them. As Chan writes in 'Diver':

I have been keeping my silence tucked inside the mustn't-haves (p. 62).

If this sounds more than a little bleak, the mute poet-emigre's sole salvation lies in the act of writing.

A white page
is the origin of wakefulness, (p. 54)

intones the author in the collection's titular poem. As with *the smell of oranges*, *Becoming Someone Who Isn't* posits that the formation of a poem grants the kinds of spiritual and actual freedoms migration denies. In *the smell of oranges*, poems such as 'Writing Bad Poems' and 'Life as Poetry' established this line of authorial reasoning. In *Becoming Someone Who Isn't*, it's left to the section 'Journal' and verse such as 'Art Gallery' to perpetuate it. In the case of the latter, as with the titular poem, we're offered writing as an act of stimulus:

> words on paintings
> the cursive waking
> how the eye steadies
> the hand steadies
> the soul (p. 18).

To be a scribe, then, is to find one's whole self brought to life, Chan tells us. And yet, there's something about the use of that word 'waking' which, as with the word 'wakefulness' in the titular poem, invites closer scrutiny. For 'to wake' is not only to be invigorated, but also to mourn. Herein lies Chan's deeper import: writing not just as liberation, but as a symbolic loss (of thoughts transferred to page) that thence permits renewal. The same message is imparted in 'Journal' through the entry, 'Summer':

> ...you showed me the most sensitive and forgiving things anyone
> has written about winter: betraying oneself and feeling worthy of
> saying it (p. 61).

Again, the line of reasoning is: writing as a dangerous act which brings merit nevertheless. As with Chan's analysis of exile, we're talking once more about duality, extrication and division. And as with Chan's feelings for migration, these points are also delivered through chronology and its associated ciphers: here, summer and its arch-rival, winter. In this, we're returned not only to Said's argument about the exiled being motivated by a different calendar, one beyond the normal order, but to seeing how valid a Saidean analysis of Chan's poetry is.

Reading *Becoming Someone Who Isn't*, I'm reminded of numerous second collections by New Zealand emigre-poets. Peter Bland's strident *Domestic Interiors* (Wai-te-ata Press, 1964), Harry Ricketts' *Coming Under*

Scrutiny (Original Books, 1989), Kapka Kassabova's weighty *Dismemberment* (AUP, 1998): here are books which, like *Becoming Someone Who Isn't*, forlornly but accurately voice the travails of immigration and resettlement. And yet there's something different about Chan's second collection. It's true, it doesn't hold the consistent gravitas of Kassabova's book or the lucidity of meaning of Ricketts' collection, but nor is it as unremittingly grim as Bland's. Rather, even though its author uses the same canvas as the writers of these other second collections, *Becoming Someone Who Isn't* paints a different picture: the picture it paints is of expatriate existence as an allusive, rather than definitive undertaking. As an emigre-writer, I understand and empathize with such reasoning. Given New Zealand readerships long engagement with the works of migrant-writers such as Chan, I'm convinced that *Becoming Someone Who Isn't* will find a welcome and enthusiastic following amongst the poetry-loving audience. – *Siobhan Harvey*

Notes

[1] Edward Said, 'Reflections on Exile', in *Reflections on Exile and Other Essays* (Cambridge, Massachusetts: Harvard University Press, 2000), p. 186.

(From *Poetry NZ* 36, March 2008)

Before and After

Date of Publication: 1987
Publisher: Miracle Mart Receiving
Category: Poetry/Fiction

(See under *Out of It*)

Richard Berengarten

Richard Berengarten (aka Richard Burns) is a European poet who writes in English and lives in Cambridge. He was born in London in 1943 into a family of musicians. He has lived in Greece, Italy, the UK, the USA and former Yugoslavia, and has travelled widely in other countries. He has published more than 20 books. In 1975, he launched and co-ordinated the first international Cambridge Poetry Festival. As a theorist, he is especially interested in poetry universals. His poems have been translated into 21 languages. He is a Bye-Fellow at Downing College, Cambridge and Preceptor at Corpus Christi College. ESAW has published three excerpts from his long poem *Manual*, a sequence celebrating human hands, in their poetry mini series.

The Bibliographical Novel

Michael O'Leary and the Bibliographical Novel

There is a type of book recognised as a genre written by and intended to interest bibliophiles, bibliographers and book traders. There are even novels written in this genre.

Michael O'Leary, the poet, novelist, research writer, reviewer and publisher, has throughout much of his adult life been a second-hand book dealer/seller. It is not surprising then that his fiction conforms to the bibliographic genre: 'The Bibliographical Novel'.

His novel *Straight* conforms to the conventions of this genre, the chief of which is that books themselves have a high significance in the novel.

This genre entails the type of story that you would expect from or to interest a person whose private and professional life takes place inside book collections, such as libraries or bookshops, whose contents continually impinge at random on that person. Of course it is fairly to be pointed out that my own 2007 novel, *Weston Burley's Business in Great Waters,* also falls within the bibliographical genre as just described.

An aspect of *Straight,* as well as O'Leary's other fictions, is that (except incidentally) they are not narrative-driven and do not show great narrative drive as a regular feature.

In *Straight,* on the one hand, there are a series of fictionalised but recognisably autobiographical flashbacks (in the 2007 version this is printed in italics). The other story line is not so much narrated as simply reported by an academic who finds various published accounts in journals and books that understood together provide an outline and provide some detail.

In effect the novel *Straight* is presented as a set of found narratives, found that is in already-printed material available to bibliographical research.

In other fictions of Michael O'Leary, the impact of books is felt and reflected as the Dada technique of structuring a new writing on random references to existing books, for instance encyclopedia headings or selective or arbitrary words found in some other text (e.g. Shakespeare's *Richard III*).

Of course what are described here are just practices of intertextuality of which there are many, some showing in every book under the sun since the year dot. Authors of books one way or the other reflect books in every book they write. I am no exception either to that general rule. – *F W N Wright*

Blackthorn

Blackthorn was a Dunedin-Irish Celtic band that included Celtic musicians Paul Ryan and Patsy Ryan. Blackthorn was around for 10 years from the 1980s till the 1990s. They were popular in Dunedin and helped advance Celtic music in New Zealand during that period. Blackthorn recorded and regularly performed several of Michael O'Leary's song lyrics. Two songs of Michael's arranged and composed by Blackthorn appear on O'Leary's CD release *Toku Tinihanga*. One of Michael's other songs that Blackthorn arranged is 'Potatoes, Fish and Children'. John Dolan wrote in *Glottis* 7 (2002) that: 'One of the few really good songs about the Māori wars is Michael O'Leary's 'Potatoes, Fish and Children', about an Irish soldier deserting to the Māori on realising their likeness to his own kind.'

The Blues

Date of Publication: 2001
Publisher: ESAW
Category: Poetry

Review of Mark Pirie's *The Blues*

This small collection is a young poet's juvenilia written between the ages of 18 and 20. The inspiration for much of the work was the singer, the late John Lee Hooker. But the centre of interest is actually a writer of poems musing about the writing of poems. There's even a mini manifesto in the criticism of the poet 'who thinks every poem written / should be well-thought out, / have a specific style, / affect a particular audience / and challenge the use of language.' ('Averages'). There are also pastiches of various styles, including that of the song lyric, a successful emulation of Sam Hunt ('Early Morning Blues'), a nice haiku: 'through the trees / paddy wagon follows/ "the kids"', an Eggleton version which actually sounds in parts rather like some of Michael O'Leary's early satires, and various others. And all the way through the poems are the allusions to music. The poems are on the whole, as might be expected, rather slight. But there are some very strong lines pointing ahead to the accomplished poet-in-the-making: 'these days there are constant reminders that / all your best truths and maxims / are walking, / inching along a tightrope, and / one day, without warning, they'll vanish ... / ... like you, no longer part of this world.' ('Reluctantly refuting a Billy Collins' poem'). And intriguing images 'she crosses the road, moves up the street, / and soon her image chops apart, / vanishes under the ledge' ('The Orphan'). The language and its rhythms are assured and apt. Yet I think Mark Pirie was right not to include these in his recent substantial collection - and certainly he has more sense than some well-known poets who try to persuade us that their youthful poetic attempts helped to shape the course of Kiwi poetry. This is a collection in which it's interesting to watch the younger Pirie flex poetic muscle, look for the kinds of voice that fit him, and try out a variety of poetic purposes. The one that appealed most to me is 'The Dream' which in setting down the leaps of the thinking mind produces an effect close to the post-modern. Having read this book, I don't think my own juvenilia would come up to scratch. The publisher, Michael O'Leary, provides a book that is simply but very attractively produced and fits the poetry well. I think many people will enjoy this small book. – *Bernard Gadd*

(From *Southern Ocean Review* 23, April 2002)

> **" "**
>
> 'The number of poems represents the number of years the author has lived. These hard-hitting, sometimes lonely, sometimes sad poems affected me deeply. A talent to keep an eye on.' – Frances Cherry, *Booknotes*

> **" "**
>
> 'Plenty of grunt in these poems ... Pirie brings personality back into poetry - plus political comment, satire, passion, humour and very good poetic craft to enable it all. The sort of stuff that would leave Creative New Zealand in a bit of a tizz ... Pirie is not only a good poet, but an enthusiastic publisher who is promoting the very worthwhile work of others. At 26, Pirie is going to serve New Zealand literature very well in the decades to come.' - Trevor Reeves, *Southern Ocean Review* 22
>
> '...at a relatively early age [Pirie] was producing a quality and quantity of poetry that many older and long established writers would have been pleased to emulate.' - Alistair Paterson, *Poetry NZ*

Book of Aotearoa

Writing in the Book of Aotearoa - Michael O'Leary

Michael on the phone said a friend was getting something together to celebrate 25 years of the Earl of Seacliff, would I write something. *Something* can resemble anything from a smoking beehive to a bumper sticker so I disappeared into one of those silences that keep opening up like a rip in the surf sweeping you further out every second and then he added casually, like how we got together to do the book ... and the rip let go and my feet touched sand and I huffed inshore.

Sure, I said, and after hanging up wandered about till I found my book Michael published - goodness - is it really five years ago? Uh, there's the date: 2004. Last year I talked to Michael about doing another book but then I got sick and this year I've suggested a different book but with a moveable deadline so that project's in the process of becoming ... I thought back.

I was staying in Paekakariki and my friends talked about their eccentric village bookshop. So I duly meandered down and the first couple of times it was closed so I could only peer through telescope hands into the dim. It wasn't quite The Old Curiosity Shop, though it could have winged out of that volume, a small elderly building with an air of past ages stacked and slipping, teetering and unravelling behind it, kites and balloons full of words floating about and pigeon posties flying through a shadowy window into a shadowy interior of shelves and stacks of books, variations on the familiar, rare and arcane Book of Aotearoa. Treasure!

The day it was finally open I stepped into a quietness - who was it who said full of those profundities that hover where someone's oblivious to presences other than the performers on the page, who erupt and strut behind the eyes fixed on the page? I crept about greedily eyeing the books. Behind the counter, almost part of the fixtures - or fictions, maybe - a motionless bent head blended happily with the books, a dark mop of candyfloss hair, a big man with a beard and a gentle giant image. (My first Harry Potter movie I was distracted by a similarity of one Hagrid to one M. O'Leary and in fact his

- Hagrid's - appearances I remember most clearly possibly because I already had an internal visual template. Though Michael's better looking.)

I'd love to say Michael and I were an immediate hit and talked nineteen to the dozen, but both being probably more introverted than we look it's truer to say we struck up a warm interest. I liked the vision and breadth of his shop, how he cares about many writers and writing. I liked the production of his books, their design, their accessible paper and print, the way they sit easily and invitingly in my hand. I found his rich prose style vivid and evocative and some of his poems haunting. What also endeared Michael to me, along with the diversionary gentleness of his personality, was that on a shelf among the millions was a copy of my book, an unexpected compliment, and that he knew who I was other than being just a writer in stock. At the time I hadn't published for years, had recently had a collection turned down by AUP and wasn't sure where to turn next.

So, we kept in touch and - the next year was it? - we began talks about doing a book together. Over my own work and especially with final proofs I'm slow, dithery and indecisive. Michael was patient and supportive through the many phone calls; in the exciting week before the MS went to print I stayed with him.

Michael lives simply, frugally, intensely, on the edge of the coast, on the edge of health, on the edge of poverty, on the edge ... and also in the centre of his life, his consciousness, his poems, his beliefs, his environment, his family, friends and his industry - in the sense of productivity, meaning writing, publications, and currently his PhD study.

This latter, he says, is a struggle and 'a bit of a changeover ... instead of writing your own thoughts you're distilling other people's ... like whisky – and you get the same hangover...' Well, maybe, though I've heard independently he's doing fine.

Unsurprisingly Michael prefers, he says, to 'dance to [his] own tune' – which with this handsome man could suggest the Pied Piper, but from discussions during my stay I think means an almost mystic vision of the writer's role as a Baxterish seer-figure and outsider, who writes as a compulsion and as an 'expression of my time on this earth'. Michael pursues and records the fractured pieces of psyche of a not so ordinary narrator through a musing and amused slippery consciousness, tripping in and out of the complex beings he and his characters become in a Kiwi cultural Māori-Irish mix; his books have pace, richness and zest and are unlike any others I have read.

Between Michael and his helpful printer we completed my *Travel and Other Compulsions* – a handsomely designed, typeset and produced package, with a dramatic cover. It sold well (eventually it sold out). But, says Michael, that doesn't mean it recouped its costs. Nor does it mean that Michael has received any more Creative New Zealand grants since. It's not surprising if sometimes his phone calls are shot through with a little discouragement, but briefly: Michael has wellsprings of vitality and prefers to spend energy on being optimistic.

Thank goodness, thank Goddess. Because Michael and the Earl are held in great affection by those who without him would have no voice - who may not interest mainstream publishers, who represent an appreciative, alternative, local consciousness. A mentor producing, in his own and others' books, original and picturesque work, Michael creates for the Earl of Seacliff a distinctively quirky place in small press publishing, part of a wonderful pedigree starred with Bob Lowry, Caxton, Spiral...

Thank you, Michael, for your stamina and integrity, warmth and charm, and for dedication and vitality in your first 25 years. May your name shine in the Book of Aotearoa. – *Heather McPherson*

Bookselling

The Earl of Seacliff

Waikouaiti on a Sunday afternoon
Was as bleak and cold and desolate
As my heavy heart
Ye Gods, it felt like the ends of the earth
"OPEN," said the solitary sign
Outside the only store brave enough
Or lonely enough
Or just too goddamned lazy
To close the doors and go home

Did you say "Oh God, not another one"
As I stepped through the door
I looked and thought
"What a bear of a man, he has eyes that listen"
We talked of poetry
And my beloved early school readers
And smiled smugly as we rubbished
The bureaucratic sabre-rattling
Of the powers that be

Later I saved the best books for you
On your trips to Oamaru for bargain buys
Though the library staff frowned
With disapproval of a relationship not understood
Should they not have known
As I was crushed in your bear hugs
That the love of your life was the written word
Now you are famous and I am old
Do your eyes still listen?

J D Bowen

Michael O'Leary's Bookselling Influence

Michael and I met in the late 1980s when he visited his family in Wellington, contemplating moving here. Sharing fantasies of Irish life and literature, we enjoyed talk of very many things we carried in our heads. He dumbfounded me when he revealed he'd written and published the *Irish Annals of New Zealand*. He was the figure who had appeared at a book auction a couple of years earlier, bidding on behalf of his local university. A principal of O'Books of Dunedin, he had earned the confidence of librarians and, as I recall, he secured some serious material for them.

Settling in Wellington in the early 1990s, Michael quickly found the company of Rowan Gibbs (of Smiths Bookshop), Niel Wright, Martin Schanzel and other book-loving folk. We all hoped for the success of the shop he opened in Featherston Street. (Opening bookshops is one of Michael's strengths, and this one displayed very well his talent for creating atmosphere and charm.)

In those days, book-dealers' conversations often centered on the mysteries of GST, the banana box issue and foibles of the trade. We were working in a trade unchanged for a century or so. Bibliographies, other reference works and a store of stories, facts and apothegms received at the feet of older dealers equipped us to deal with most of what surfaced.

Something was looming out there though that we had no inkling of. When Michael began his computer project we could only wonder. Thinking now of his foresight, it amazes me still. Somehow he acquired a suitable machine, found expert advice and enrolled himself (and his friends) on Bibliofind, an idealistic communal site that sold books. Soon the first order from overseas arrived, miraculously.

When Michael closed the Featherston Street shop, Rowan took over the computer. Since then the internet has progressively become the main means of selling books overseas, and it is now crucial to the trade. Building on Michael's beginning Rowan and I in our different businesses have been able to survive the biggest change since Gutenberg.

In confabs these days we praise the internet, and the name Michael O'Leary is often on our lips. *– John Quilter*

Bullet Poems

Date of Publication: 2004
Publisher: ESAW
Category: Poetry

Review of Mark Pirie's *Bullet Poems*

Mark Pirie's *Bullet Poems,* according to its jacket blurb, 'takes aim at a wide variety of contemporary issues, particularly war, politics and world events'. World events being what they are of late, one could be forgiven for concluding that Pirie is a lousy shot. But this criticism could also be applied to Eminem and P Diddy who failed to turn the US [2004] Presidential election, despite their very public efforts and considerable media clout. As I mentioned, this is a subjective review, and to qualify my subjectivity here I have to confess that when it comes to Ice, I have difficulty distinguishing a T from a Cube. So much poetry, so little time.

Subjectively, then, Mark Pirie appears to speak from a space somewhere between academia and pop culture, and with a voice that draws equally from both. When it works, his heavy use of quotation and cultural reference, driven by an urgent hip-hop sensibility, produces a powerful effect.

When it doesn't, the effect seems merely art referring to art referring to art. The failing, of course, is probably mine sometimes I just don't hear that boom-box. Specifically, 'Bullet Poem', which sneaks in with a *faux* macho swagger to make its chilling point is superb but 'Table of Casualties in the Iraq War', for all its ghastly cold statistics, never rises above its cut-and-paste origins. In contrast, 'Senseless Sonnet', a very tidy fusion of facts and verse, works beautifully. When being overtly political Pirie is never strident, and he can be engagingly self-deprecatory, as in the wittily autobiographical 'Lifestyles of the Rich and Infamous', where he refers to his 'wigga' ('for a bit') past.

Despite its title, around half the works in *Bullet Poems* are personal and reflective, but the political dimension is never far away. In such heartfelt poems as 'The Western Approach' (for Howard Nemerov) and 'For Osip Mandelstam', where he directly addresses his influences, there is a sense of the poet paying his dues. For this reason these sort of works, although highly accomplished, appear to be something of a necessary and passing phase.

Mark Pirie's writing is impressive in its honesty, wit and passion. His willingness to experiment is admirable, although I do feel that the world needs a mildly satirical poem about Courtney Love about as much as it needs, um, a five-wheeled car. Not many have succeeded in forging a convincing voice from such disparate elements and I look forward to reading more of his work. – *Joe Wylie*

(From *Takahe* 53 (2004))

Cognac

A favoured drink of the Earl that is mentioned in his poem 'The Earl's Progress' and in his sequence 'Station to Station: a cognac for David (Bowie)':

The Earl's Progress

So drunk that he could live without love
So drunk he pissed against a car in the main street
He stole, and disobeyed other commandments
He accosted perfectly decent people with his story
He lied to himself about poetic licence

But as he stumbled to the final bar that night
He summoned all his aristocratic nobility
And with neither rhyme nor reason, nor recognition
nor recollection of anything
The Earl uttered with a religious fervour
that sublime word, 'Cognac!'

Michael O'Leary

Count Potocki de Montalk

The Earl of Seacliff met Count Potocki de Montalk, the writer and pretender to the Polish throne several times. The Count is considered by the poet and critic Niel Wright to be the 'all time bad-boy of Aotearoa letters'. His published poetry includes *Prison Poems* (1934) and a book of reflections on his fellow poets. He is yet to be forgiven for his neo-fascist sympathies, unlike Ezra Pound. O'Leary, writing humourously of his meetings with the Count, says: 'My reflections of my fellow poet and aristocrat, Count Potocki de Montalk, are somewhat dimmed and obscured by copious amounts of alcohol. The venue was a restaurant in Auckland in 1983 with the good Count, myself, his publisher Donald Kerr of Prometheus Press, and another fellow poet and Seacliff Family member Iain Sharp present. There may have been others, but as I said I was ... We were celebrating the launch of the Count's (whom we often drunkenly and jocundly referred to as a 'Silly Old Count') memoir *Reflections of My Fellow Poets* during his first visit to his homeland in 55 years. As the evening raged on he and I got into an argument over the Holocaust, of which he was a fervent denier. We yelled and screamed - remember I'm a Nice Nazi - as he came out with one outrageous anti-Jewish outburst after another. Finally, however, the fact that I was an Earl and he a Count won the day, and being fellow poets to boot, we embraced and wished each other salutations and long life in the manner of the Turk.'

Cover photo series

Cover artists

They are one of the highlights of the New Zealand publishing year - every time you open a package of books from the various ventures of poets Mark Pirie and Michael O'Leary, you ask yourself the same question: 'Which album will they have done this time?'

Starting in 2004 with a pastiche of The Beatles' *Abbey Road* cover – for an anthology of writing from the literary magazine *JAAM* - Pirie and O'Leary, working with photographer John Girdlestone, have produced a succession of increasingly elaborate and playful reconstructions of album artwork.

Calling upon friends such as fellow poets Iain Sharp and Niel Wright, writer Geoff Cush, *Dominion Post* art critic Mark Amery and bookseller John Quilter to take cameo roles, they have restaged everything from the Rolling Stones' *Aftermath* to U2's *The Joshua Tree,* from the Doors' *Morrison Hotel* to Oasis's *(What's the Story) Morning Glory?* - retitling them *Poetrymath, The Manuka Tree, Tupelo Hotel* and *Poetrywall.*

Each exercise - more often than not for publicity and publications associated with Pirie and O'Leary's Winter Readings series of events - is lovingly rendered, with the devil in the detail: the precisely posed actors, the immaculate imitations of typeface and photographic technique.

Used to working to the high standards of the film industry, Girdlestone, a production designer, views the covers as rough and ready. But to the less tutored eye, and taken for what they are, each is a little marvel. What really sets them off is the sly variations, best enjoyed by those with a degree of musical literacy and a knowledge of the Greater Wellington scene, both literary and geographic.

Just where is that path where they shot *Sounds of Sonnets,* their take on Simon & Garfunkel's *Sounds of Silence?* And what about the rail tracks for *JAAM Tracks,* inspired by *The Complete Animals?* Those rail tracks are actually the tram tracks in Paekakariki's Queen Elizabeth Park.

Indicating the fine-tuning that goes into the photographs, Pirie points out that on the original cover The Animals' Eric Burdon is wearing an ammo belt with real bullets on it - 'so my ammo belt is made up of pens'. 'Mightier than the sword,' chips in O'Leary. Paekakariki and the area around it provide many of the settings for the photographs, that being where O'Leary and Girdlestone live. (Pirie is a Wellingtonian.) *Sounds of Sonnets* was shot in Waterfall Road, *The Manuka Tree* in a different part of Queen Elizabeth Park.

Tupelo Hotel was done at Wellington's Tupelo Bar. 'Because that was where I used to go every week for drinks,' says Pirie. 'Also,' says O'Leary, 'Tupelo has the other pop connection, with Van Morrison *[Tupelo Honey]* and Elvis [born in Tupelo, Mississippi]. So it's a kind of mixture of things.'

Cuba Street stood in for London's Camden Town for *Poetrywall,* and for *Greatest Hits* Salamanca Road by Victoria University became Abbey Road.

'It's also slightly satirical in having it with the university in the background,' says O'Leary. 'It's a bit of an in-joke in saying 'f... you' to the establishment, the people who get the literary credence in this country - you've got to go through the creative writing courses to get anywhere.'

Pirie adds: 'There's a coterie of Wellington writers that is well known. The impression they give to people is that they are the only writers of note in the country. Walking across a pedestrian crossing near the university is a way of saying there's more to NZ literature than that.'

From the off, the team has had their eye on the small things. Their footsteps are, of course, the same as The Beatles, but more than that, says O'Leary, 'if you look at the original *Abbey Road,* there's a guy standing up the road. Well, in ours that's John Quilter. And you know the Volkswagen on the *Abbey Road* cover that had the number plate 28IF and it was around the time that Paul McCartney was supposed to have died and if he had lived he would have been 28. Well, Mark made a new number plate for his car, 29IF – "if I lived".'

Pirie, in particular, has become quite a performance artist during the course of the shoots, wearing his hair short for *Tupelo Hotel,* growing it long for *The Manuka Tree* and to be one of the Mahones for *It's Time to Go!,* the poets version of The Ramones' *Hey Ho, Let's Go! '*That one is actually a bit more detailed,' says Pirie. 'I cut up a pair of jeans for it to make it look more punkish, and I got a studded belt and hired leather jackets for everyone.'

Pirie's, finest hour, however, was when he took on the mantle of John Mellencamp (or John Cougar as he was then) and the *American Fool* album, retitling it *Wellington Fool.* 'At that stage, I was supposed to go solo for a collection [in the Earl of Seacliff Art Workshop mini-series]. So I had to pick something I could go solo as. I actually quite like John Mellencamp's lyrics. Back then, he was Johnny Cougar and had this James Dean, Harley-Davidson idea going on. So I thought it would be really good for a pastiche photo. Everyone knows I drive a Honda City and don't have a Harley-Davidson. It looks so preposterous standing their in the leather jacket and sexy gloves next to this Honda City.'

'Pastiche' is the word Pirie and O'Leary are insistent on when talking about the covers. 'Even though we are playing these roles and all that, we are not really trying to be them,' says Pirie. 'We are trying to give an impression of what their album covers are like as a tribute to them rather than just a straight-out parody. It could easily degenerate to that student capping level if you made it a parody and I just don't think it would be as funny.'

Initially inspired by the influence of pop music on their writing and a desire to make their Winter Readings more inviting to those not normally interested in poetry, Pirie and O'Leary's ongoing project has taken on a life of its own. 'We get people sending us ideas for album covers now and friends who want to be in the next shoot,' says Pirie. 'Geoff Cush has been hassling me to do this Cream cover, *Fresh Cream.* It's a Cream cover with fresh cream, We've also got ideas to do The Kinks. There's always going to be album covers we can do.' – *Guy Somerset*

(From *Dominion Post*, Saturday, 5 January 2008)

Doomsblay

Date of Publication: 2004
Publisher: ESAW
Category: Poetry/Fiction

Next to John Lennon, James Joyce has been the major literary influence in O'Leary's life as an artist. An interesting link between the two came from a comment by Yoko Ono he read recently in which she compared Lennon's writing with Joyce's, concluding that Lennon's was better because of his humour! She obviously hasn't read *Finnegans Wake* aloud in an Irish accent whilst drinking a bottle of whiskey, as O'Leary has. This small eight-page publication was put out in a signed and numbered edition of 50 copies to celebrate the 100th-year anniversary of Bloomsday on the 16th of June 2004. It was typeset, designed, printed by Mark Pirie on his home computer, who also hand-bound it. It included two dream sequences from *Unlevel Crossings* plus a poem titled 'Doomsblay: One Hundred Years of Desmond and Molly, Ha Ha Ha.'

Dreamlander Express

Ticket to Ride with Michael O'Leary

(Launch speech for Michael O'Leary's *Straight*)

The political pundits are saying 2002 was the high water mark of Helen Clark's success as prime minister.

For my literary associates 2002 was also a high water mark. It was the year when Michael O'Leary's novel Unlevel Crossings was published by Huia. I launched Unlevel Crossings here at Paekakariki on Bloomsday. In my remarks I ended by saying, "If you need further help to understand what Michael O'Leary is on about in this book Unlevel Crossings, read his other books, because all his writings hang together."

From 1996, as a publisher, my aim was to get Michael O'Leary's writings into print or back in print, and this we did, but it meant that writings that hang together in reality still had to be looked for in a dozen different publications. So the next step had to get them all together under a single heading as a trilogy of novels.

This is a truth that Michael O'Leary thoroughly understands himself. He sees *Unlevel Crossings* as the start of a trilogy, the second book of which, *Straight,* we are launching as such here today five years later.

In *Straight,* as we have it today after ten years of talking about what was required, Michael O'Leary has brought a novel (which always had links with *Unlevel Crossings*) into tighter integration with it as the second book in the trilogy. *Straight* is Ponsonby Gothic set in the 1980s. The hero Calvert lives in the anxious present but like most of us spends much of his time in thoughts of the past, which is perceived as the dreamtime. Within this structure the novel is well-written and straightforward enough. Michael O'Leary is an economical writer. A straightforward book that makes its point in few words is just the ticket to ride on Michael O'Leary's dreamlander express.

Also of interest, Michael O'Leary is right now putting the finishing touches to the third part of the trilogy *Magic Alex's Revenge,* so we are now in sight of having all Michael O'Leary's prose narrative and much of his verse narrative brought together as a unity in a trilogy of novels.

It gives me great pleasure to launch *Straight* here today because of the three books in the trilogy, this is the one that readers will find most ready to get into with appreciation. In *Straight,* Michael O'Leary's talents are openly on display. With this assurance, you are well placed as a reader or critic or reviewer to turn back to *Unlevel Crossings* and find there also the merits that may be less obvious if you come to it by any other route.

But the trilogy needs *Straight* as its middle novel, because - when you get to the last book *Magic Alex's Revenge* - there, much of Michael O'Leary's finest and most appreciated writing, is on show, and you need to approach that book in the confidence that a master is at work at the height of his powers.

So read this book *Straight*. Buy it, borrow it or steal it, but read it. And thereafter it will be your *vade mecum* to the rest of the trilogy, your magic talisman to get you safely into the most arcane reaches of dreamland, from which, in the opening words of *Straight:* "Paul Calvert wakes about an hour out of Auckland on a train journey back from dreamland."

From talk with Michael O'Leary I gather that the trilogy as a whole will be entitled *Dreamlander Express. – F W N Wright*

Dumber

Date of Publication: 2003
Publisher: ESAW
Category: Poetry

(See also the launch report for *Dumber* under *Toku Tinihanga*)

Review of Mark Pirie's *Dumber*

The back cover of Mark Pirie's book says the collection 'laments that our culture is getting "dumber"'. It certainly seems unarguable that imagination and logic are unfashionable, and even among the thousands of Kiwis who turn out poetry, one wonders how many actually read much or much variety of other people's poetry. So how can the poet respond to such circumstances? Pirie takes different approaches. One or two of the pieces simply aren't poetry at all, such as the opening dialogue. The rest is poetry which is straightforward in vocabulary and structure. Some pieces deal, with some irony, with preoccupations of a 'dumbed down' culture such as sexual activity, TV, putting the blame on the gender, and what might be called the stance of always being in two minds about everything and being unsure whether any action really matters or can just as readily be replaced with daydreams. Some poems are succinct. Some poems have real bite to them:

> ...how her legs flash apart,
> reminding him of Paris
> in the spring-time, of
>
> Baudelaire, of how his
> Death drum beckons
> beyond this town, beyond
> his land's narrow seas... ('Eying the Broader Perspective')

One of the best is an apparently artlessly simple lyric:

> But

how do you know or guess
until now
which way the ball will turn
and break
my bough?

sang the boy at cricket. ('A Boy's Song').

And all the time in the background is a sort of satirical religious motif:

Lord, hear my prayer, 'cause I'm

down here at the crossroads,
getting dumber.

('The Dumber Blues') – *Review by Bernard Gadd*

(From *Kokako,* Winter issue of *Spin,* 2003)

Dumber was included in the NZ Poetry Exhibition: *Main Trunk Lines*

Dunedin years

Dunedin memories

I met Michael in 1978 in the top house at Seacliff, where he flatted with Brian Hare. I had just left school and was on a working holiday around the South Island, and had visited an old friend Tim who lived in the village and I ended up living there.

Michael was one of the first writers I met. My teenage years growing up in Taupo were a cultural wilderness, it was a revelation to find someone I could discus literature with and who encouraged me. It was the beginning of a lifelong friendship and many great times, whether it was invites to Sunday night roast (with the inevitable phone call before, 'can you bring the food') or the wild nights of poetry readings at the Globe Hotel in Auckland with Iain Sharp, or the parties at France Street with John Pule.

The train stopped at Seacliff in those days, and on Friday night after the Captain Cook, we would all spill out and dash to the station, and sing all the way home. Michael always knew the conductor. A few times we caught the train to vague locations a few miles north of Seacliff, with Michael expounding the wonderful virtues of train travel, as the train crawled homewards through the mist.

When I returned from a sojourn overseas, Michael and I flatted together in Mt Albert, at the back of a house. Michael was always resplendent in his satin paisley dressing gown in which he spent a lot of time. Here occurred the famous incident of Michael returning after a night shift of building paths on Queen Street. They had all been to the pub at 8 in the morning on payday, and he was rather intoxicated. He was calling out to a toothless woman he had met in the pub.

"May, May," he called, sometimes tenderly and longingly, other times like a command. I was so relieved he hadn't brought her home!

Michael and my father became great friends. I think Michael also enjoyed seeing me - the ardent feminist at the time - being put in her place by her Dad! Michael often wrote long poems dedicated to his women friends or lovers, often starting either with a train going thru a tunnel or a view from his window in Seacliff.

I said to him once "Michael, you have never written me a poem, in all the years we have known each other!"

On the spot he composed what is, probably his shortest poem: "Sandra Bell, what a gal!" – *Sandra Bell*

Evidence of Life - O'Books and ESAW, 1990-1995

"Poetry is just the evidence of life" – Leonard Cohen[1]

There has only been one earl in my life and this could of course only mean Michael, as there will only ever be one Earl of Seacliff in the history of Niu Tireni[2]. It is a unique title and after so long we can claim justly that ours has been a unique friendship forged in the strife and the love of the period when ESAW and O'Books were both found in the Octagon, Dunedin, though our friendship had begun at least 15 years before.

This volume is about his publishing house - and it is of this house that he was the Earl. My contribution concerns where, in our lives, that earldom and our friendship overlapped most closely, where major tributaries and distributaries ran, from one to the other, through the sibling (O'Books) that did not survive those Dunedin years.

This period began at Seacliff where the bookshop that became O'Books was conceived when Michael lived there with Bryan Harold (and Peter Olds, in the background, working away, chipping into their dreams, then leaving them to it), and its eventual incarnation at 10 the Octagon, Dunedin, as O'Books in 1990.[3]

Begun in a landscape still dominated by the ghosts of the Seacliff Lunatic Asylum and its clockless clock tower, O'Books was a short-lived sibling to ESAW, also in a sense conceived at Seacliff. How else could an earl have arrived in Niu Tireni? What other womb could have nurtured ESAW and then O'Books? Then both of them lived for a while with the steady tolling of the Dunedin Town Hall's clock tower. How else could the measure of many lives, fictional and real, be summed up with the name O'Books?

I cannot do justice here to all of those who for a while entangled their living, briefly or more intensely, with the life of this shop. This is the shortest of memoirs and so many will be missed out and only those I knew well will be mentioned - I hope the others will not be too disappointed.

Some of these were customers down in their lives and regular sellers of one or two volumes that we could recycle and give them a little to spend on coffee or bus fare or alcohol. Some came with boxes of books, leftovers of lives no longer lived fully or expendable in the service of the life being lived now, booksellers who were often disappointed with the money offered for volumes that had little but some value in the trade. Some were those looking for a volume to help them pass the time while others were looking for out of print gems they already knew. Some were collectors looking for treasures to add to their other treasures.

Some were well known authors and authorities who had come looking for copies of their books no longer in print, like Professor Peter McKeller, former head of the University of Otago Psychology Department.

Of those that helped in the shop, apart from Bryan and Michael, I remember in particular Nigel Yates, who once had to deal with a famously infamous Dunedin dissolute disrobing completely in the shop in her alcohol addled state of the time and urinating on the floor, Pat O Day who combined with Nigel to look after the shop when Michael was sick, and Margaret Laube whose intuition proved correct with respect to the misfortune eventually suffered by O'Books - they often helped out there, paid and at times unpaid.

Amongst the regulars who called in to share conversation and tea or coffee, were Peter Olds, Hone Hawkins, Nigel the accordion player and busker, and Clive Hallows, who helped when the partnership be- tween Michael and Bryan imploded.

The years of O'Books were the brightest and darkest of an era for Michael and me. It was the cauldron of the love and pain of my marriage to Winsome and Michael's concurrent love for her which bound us as brothers in all of this - brothers in love and the compassion that flows from it rather than the brothers in love and hate bent on possession and control which we could have been had we made different decisions, had we been different types of men, had we not been reaching for truths that transcend all of that.

And so we put together a volume of poetry, half written by Michael and half written by myself, dedicated to Winsome. And we were able to help each other through these turbulent years despite an apparent conflict of interest

As well as founding O'Books with Bryan, Michael continued with his publishing and writing. He finished and published through ESAW, *The Irish Annals of New Zealand* (with Sean Tate-Manning's wonderful cover), and *Wrapper* (with Bryan Harold's wonderful cover), a collection of poetry in which my verse appeared with a great number of well-known and other unknown poets (including Hone Tuwhare, Kim Eggleston, Judith Laube) - great company for my first appearance in print. Peter Entwisle's *Elaine and other Stories* was also a first - Peter's first published venture into fictional writing. ESAW also published the second edition of the book of photographs, *Dunedin: An Essay* by Nigel Yates.

These were also the years of the band Blackthorn's performances at the Albert Arms, a regular feature of Michael's Monday nights, and I went along some times. He wrote the words of the song 'Potatoes, Fish and Children' and Paul and Patsy Ryan, of Blackthorn, wrote the music - a tribute to the elements that had helped both Irish peasants and Māori survive the injustices of their histories on their poles apart, far sides, of the earth.

These were also the years in which Michael began to embrace the technology of the 20th century after years of refusal - that is he bought his first car and obtained his driving licence (in that order) and he embraced reluctantly the utility of computers in the operation of the shop with the assistance of Martin Schanzel.

These were also the years of Michael's courtship of Aroha, a relation of my wife, and a courtship that swung between the great heights of pain and love that make and break many a relationship. Michael's son was conceived before it was broken and this life was the greatest miracle to come out of these turbulent years.

At the beginning of this time I was travelling up and down Te Wai Pounamu recording oral histories of poua and taua of Kai Tahu Whanui, finding a space between the 150th celebrations of the signing of the Treaty of Waitangi and the sickness and dying that characterised that year. Eventually I was given the opportunity to give to the wider community some of the knowledge gained then and through earlier work. I was commissioned to write a history of Kai Tahu Whanui in Otago by the Dunedin City Council in 1993 to mark the 150th anniversary of the purchase of the Otakou Block in 1844, which enabled the Scottish settlers of 1848 to come and establish the city of Dunedin and the province of Otago. I was given the Mayor's *robing* room, the only unoccupied space suitable for this work that I could occupy at all hours. That work was sustained by many visits to O'Books for coffee and rest and good conversation, at all hours, while my marriage also lurched to and from both poles of the title of the resulting volume, *Te Mamae me Te Aroha.*

Added to this over these years, was the concurrent failure of one of my goldmining ventures at Beaumont and the decision by ECNZ to develop the Tuapeka Hydro scheme as their next major power generating plant after completion of the Clyde Dam, a scheme that would destroy my family home at Beaumont. For a while O'Books became a centre for my meeting with Graeme Collins as we sought ways to challenge the wisdom of that scheme and obstruct its course.

Over this period there were interesting connections to other events. It is said that David Gray, whose madness took all those lives at Aramoana in 1990, visited O'Books. He had earlier that year been at Bill Brosnan's shop opposite the Law Courts looking for second-hand magazines and books about war and guns. Bill Brosnan told David Gray that another second-hand bookshop had opened nearby in the Octagon and that he was worried he might lose business to it. Gray said he would deal with them for him and Bryan can remember him coming into the shop. A story from that terrible tragedy that later became known, was that David Gray had shown a firearm in his bag to the attending employee of Bill Brosnan and this had alarmed him enough to contact the police. It was later seen by some as a lost opportunity to defuse the events before they exploded but further necessary evidence of his madness was not found.

Psychiatrist Julia Faed carried out a posthumous forensic study of the character of David Gray from available evidence and concluded that it was very likely David Gray was suffering from an untreated schizoid psychosis characterised by extreme paranoia. She later bought a portrait by the late artist Owen McLay of his wife Alison from the short lived gallery O'oops, downstairs from and part of O'Books operations. Possibly Owen's best work at that time, it was hung in her consulting rooms and is a testimony to the transforming effect of art and love on madness through the dedication of Owen McLay to his art and the transforming effect on his life of his love for Alison. He would later complete similarly substantial works focused on his children, the miracles that came out of a marriage that was itself eventually defeated by madness. In this case art and love combined to prevent the sort of cataclysm out of madness that overcame the people of Aramoana.

Toward the end of the era Michael attended a lecture by Alan Duff at the University of Otago after the phenomenal success of Duff's book *Once Were Warriors*. Duff spoke of the terrible poverty and alcoholism that characterised the reality that his book reflected. Michael posed a question to him in which he sought to draw attention to the love and mutual support that could also characterise state house suburbs and their poverty - a valued memory of his own life growing up in an Auckland state house suburb. But Duff mistook Michael's intent and appearance, responded aggressively and what could have been an interesting discussion deteriorated into a shouting match. Duff probably remains unaware that Michael had been living in the house Duff once stayed in at Seacliff when he was unknown and desperate, as a guest of our mutual friend, and one of ESAW's authors, Brian Hare.

The term 'Kia Ora Begorrah', created earlier by Michael, became a part of shop talk and was adopted as part of a shop letterhead. It was later used by Hone Tuwhare in his published story in the *Listener* (and then play), 'Don't go past me with your nose in the air'.

This era closed with financial disasters that ESAW survived because Michael survived but which resulted in the death of O'Books. These began with the divorce in business between Bryan Harold and Michael that resulted in Michael buying Bryan out of his share of the shop. Clive Hallows generously acted as guarantor, using his house as security, for the loan necessary for Michael to buy Bryan's share of the business.

They had been a very effective team, combining an awesome knowledge of books old and new, and bringing different but essential skills to the business. In particular Bryan's business acumen was an important break on Michael's flair with its sometimes mistaken (business-wise) flourishes of generosity.

Sometime later, financial disaster nearly destroyed ESAW. ESAW had been operating out of an office on the other side of the Octagon in the Regent Theatre building. Operation of ESAW was entrusted to a fellow poet who absconded leaving the bills unpaid - even though he had been given the money to pay them. Michael was woken to this fact by the management of the Regent Theatre sealing the doors to the office until one of its outstanding debts, the rent for several months, was paid. Margaret Laube had sensed that this man was untrustworthy. But Michael disregarded this, perhaps out of his generosity and desire to give a struggling fellow poet a break.

Indeed, over the lifetime of O'Books, Nigel and I can both remember occasions when people we did not know, people obviously down in life, asked us for some money, usually $5 or enough for bus fare home or a packet of cigarettes, and when we expressed doubt, they would say it was okay, Michael did this for them.

As the financial difficulties increased some of us began more and more to help Michael run the shop by being paid in books rather than wages. Some of the memories that Nigel Yates and I share of this time, are of Michael on occasion willy-nilly grabbing handfuls of cash from the till to enable him to continue in his courtship and in his generosity to others. But only a strict financial discipline could have saved the day. It was his way of thumbing his nose at fate - but eventually it caught up with him. The books of O'Books and his own substantial rare book collection had to be sold to pay the most pressing debts and enable him to leave town with honour. But even today you will meet people in Dunedin who will frown (at this distance in time, frown rather than growl) because of some debt Michael was unable to pay at this time. These have been subsequently forgotten as matters of urgency by all parties with the passage of time, and are balanced by his quietly forgetting monies many owed him. But the major debts he never forgot, maintaining for instance the minimum payments on and eventually paying off the loan from Credit Union Otago that had enabled him to buy Bryan out, thus freeing Clive Hallows from the threat to his house implicit in his acting as guarantor of that loan.

And so Michael loaded up his green Triumph 2000 with what was left of ESAW and left Dunedin. He took with him from Dunedin the unfinished text of *Unlevel Crossings* that we had started together, each writing consecutive chapters but I could not continue with this because of a number of pressing concerns in my life at that time.

At Wellington, then at Paekakariki - midway between the two cities he celebrated in his story 'Neither Here nor There', Dunedin and Auckland - he found more trustworthy and effective collaborators. He found a middle way, a point of balance with which his writing and ESAW could prosper between the extremities of his life in those two cities. He completed *Unlevel Crossings*. Though we could not join in that work we have continued to support each other when we can. And so I travelled to Wellington in 2003 to help him complete reports for the Waitangi Tribunal that he had been commissioned to carry out and in 2004 ESAW published my first book of poetry, *To..*.

That financial security and success beyond that necessary for sur- vival and continuance of the struggle, have eluded him is not surpris- ing. The struggle for greater prosperity goes on. – *Bill Dacker*

Notes

[1]From words by Leonard Cohen used on the cover of the DVD version of *Leonard Cohen, I'm Your Man*.

[2]New Zealand, a transliteration once used commonly in the south.

[3]Its first incarnation was briefly at Waikouaiti.

Tribute to Michael O'Leary on the 25th Anniversary of the Earl of Seacliff Art Workshop

Please allow me to polish up my best Michael O'Leary anecdote. I have many; the most dramatic of them arise from the drunkest evening I ever had and remained conscious: the occasion was a whiskey tasting at Chan's Garden Restaurant in South Dunedin, after which we ended up at the Mongrel Mob headquarters in Caversham, with Michael so off his tree he accidentally gave the Black Power salute. That was just one of a few memorable moments that night. I've also written two poems for Michael: 'Blood on the McCahon' which is based on a tale John Pule used to tell, and 'The Rake' about the first time I met Michael, when I was living under cover as a suburban housewife, and he invited me to "come away from all this", and I damn near did. But the jewel in the crown concerns the time in the early 1990s when we were both living in Seacliff Village and we used to flag the Dunedin-bound Southerner down at the Kilgour Street crossing and ride that last exhilarating section of seaside track into the city. One day I had a secret rendezvous planned; my aunt Janet Frame was travelling south from Christchurch and I had arranged to meet her on the train at Seacliff and travel through to Dunedin with her. It was my habit to protect Janet's privacy so I didn't tell Michael she'd be on the train, but I was delighted when he decided to join me on the journey, just for the hell of it, because it would give me an opportunity to introduce two of my good friends.

So here's the story: we got on the train, and when Michael met Janet, he shook her hand and said: "I'm the Earl of Seacliff." She smiled graciously, and said, "And I'm the *Queen* of Seacliff."

Blood on the McCahon

(for Michael O'Leary)

It was a wild night
nobody remembers except for the cry next morning,

There's blood on the McCahon!

The collateral damage
is not really that astonishing.

But what's the big picture?

A kind of art that's more than the art on the wall.

Almost as surprising
as self-knowledge.

The Rake

'You are a lady who has suffered,'
said the rake, his brown eyes sparking
for another conquest. (His life had marked him too
and this can be attractive.) She nodded gravely.

'It's true, but this is how I cope:
I find great sorrow not so hard to bear;
it brings me into contact with great truth,
which for me is consolation. There's peace in it.'

He stared at her. 'Does anything upset you?'
'Oh yes,' she said, 'a little itch...
A little itch can drive a person crazy.'

– Pamela Gordon

"Bob Dylan - a visitation"

Date of Composition: 1998
Collections: *Ka Atu I Kopua, Toku Tinihanga: Selected Poems 1982-2002*

Like most writers of O'Leary's generation, Bob Dylan had a big influence on his writing and his life. Dylan was the link between pop culture and the Beat poets. David Eggleton, O'Leary and several others, including Tony Fomison, Michael Brosnan and Herman Gladwin, who at various times lived at 8 Margaret Street, Ponsonby, in the early 1970s, lived out the 'Down and Out' fantasy and reality of Dylan's 'Desolation Row', with a bit of the Kinks' 'Dead End Street' thrown in. In O'Leary's 2003 selected poems, *Toku Tinihanga*, he eulogises this period in a poem he composed after seeing Dylan in concert in 1998 at Wellington, 'Bob Dylan - a visitation'. The cover of O'Leary's 2008 collection of poetry, *Paneta Street*, is an affectionate 'tip of the hat' to the master from his 1976 album, *Desire*.

The Earl

During the Margaret Street times O'Leary gained the nickname 'The Earl of Ponsonby.' O'Leary writes: 'I was at art school and was into DADA and surrealism and David Eggleton and I used to carry out art 'events', a practice we rejuvenated in the 1980s when I again returned to Auckland from the south. I left Margaret Street when I got fed up with drug squad raids and the fact that the dealer, 'the man', came around one night with a revolver, and I ain't talking about the Beatles' LP. I handed over my title Earl of Ponsonby at a special ceremony as I stepped down from the Ponsonby trolley bus and took up the more literary/rural title, The Earl of Seacliff, taken from the Otago coastal township I had moved to. An earl was an appropriate title for me as all the Irish earls had either been murdered or exiled by the English and I had come back to haunt the heirs of the perpetrators, proof that there is a political dimension to my 'art for art's' sake veneer.'

Elegy in Memory of Barry Mitcalfe

Date of Publication: 1987
Publisher: ESAW
Category: Poetry

Barry Mitcalfe died on the morning of March 17, 1986. He had gone to Wellington to take part in that city's Festival of the Arts and, more specifically, to launch his latest book of poems, *Look to the Land*, the same afternoon. Now, less than a year later, fellow poet Ron Riddell offers elegant tribute to the man he identifies as one of the country's 'most original, creative and catholic (not to mention prolific.) writers.' *Elegy in Memory of Barry Mitcalfe* is an extended verse sequence published by Earl of Seacliff Art Workshop. – *Michael Gifkins*

(From *New Zealand Listener*, 23/1/1987)

> ❝ ❞
>
> 'Riddell's clear, affectionate tribute to Barry Mitcalfe is homage to a writer who was also a supporter of other writers, and to the spirit of his life — "A death-defying/life-affirming man/who sang the common lot."' – David Hill, *Auckland Sunday Star*
>
> 'The death of Barry Mitcalfe in March of last year saddened many people in the world of the arts and in the peace movement. Mitcalfe was a robust, outgoing character, and at 55, he seemed to have more fields to conquer.' – *Otago Daily Times*

ESAW Mini Series

Let's Get Small: The ESAW Mini Series

In the beginning was the word and that word was ESAW. The Earl of Seacliff Art Workshop, since its establishment by Michael O'Leary in 1984, has always pushed innovative print culture concepts and is now a central locus of alternative publishing activity in this country. In his book-length survey *Alternative Small Press Publishing in New Zealand (1969-1999)*, published by Steele Roberts in 2007, Michael O'Leary lists many of the Earl of Seacliff Art Workshop's small press forerunners. They include Bill Manhire's Amphedesma Press, Trevor Reeves' Caveman Press, Warwick Sven Jordan's Hard Echo Press, Alan Loney's Hawk Press, Bob Gormack's Nag's Head Press, Christodoulos Moisa's One-Eyed Press and Sam Hunt's The Bottle Press. The ESAW imprint has proved itself one of the most long-lived, partly through its identification of gaps in the market, partly through its almost divine inspiration (beginning with the pamphlet of verse entitled 'Flip Side of the Ballad of John and Yoko'), and partly through its sheer cussedness - its devotion to the revolutionary cause with its clarion call of 'power to the people'.

The clamour of other voices to be heard via the prose tract and the poetry pamphlet has a long and honourable history in New Zealand, beginning with the evangelical zeal of the Pakeha missionaries in the nineteenth century and taking in the twentieth century the efflorescence of Denis Glover's Caxton Press and Bob Lowry's Pelorus Press, before the big bang of small press publishing that arrived in the 1960s. (In that era of alternative beginnings the word was, as Alan Brunton proclaimed it, FREED.)

A prodigious programme of new releases began early in 2006 with the ESAW poetry mini series, which in early 2009 is nudging two dozen separate publications, with some of them, including *Inside It* by Robin Fry, *Guild of Scavengers* by Ralph Proops, and *City Limit* by Tony Beyer, out of print.

In the downsizing era, when even time is commodified and precious, it was a stroke of brilliance to come up with very short poetry books for those in a hurry. True, some things nowadays have very much been scaled up, from the big box store to the supersize meal to the vacuous blockbusting bestseller. All the more need then for big little books, pocket books, miniature books, which offer the meditative reflections, select imagery or fervent whisperings of new New Zealand poems in enough bulk to establish a sense of personality, the creation of an atmosphere. These ultra-slim volumes in the ESAW mini series, in fact, have a careful specificity. As Gregory O'Brien writes in a response to a questionnaire in Michael O'Leary's *Alternative Small Press Publishing in New Zealand (1969-1999)*: 'A piece of work of 24pp is just as valid as one of, say, 172pp. It's important for works to be presented intact, as "works"'. And if you're travelling light, any one of these compressed power packs of poems is an accessory more weightless than an iPod, or a mobile phone, or a flash drive datastick, or a DVD. However that doesn't mean as small as possible, that means sensibly small with eye-friendly print. Slimmed-down, weight-watching and tiny for the planet - like, let's get small - each little white book is nevertheless crafted like a collector's item: made with simplicity, elegance and an economy of means.

The front cover is entirely given over to a black and white photograph of the poet, while the back cover carries assorted simple information: a big numeral establishing the mini-book's place in the release schedule; the title; the poet's name; an ISBN number; and of course the ESAW logo. Each boppy booklet may emerge to leap off on its own like a getaway frog, but they are all linked by that reduced drawing of an hirsute man in a hat. Appropriately, ESAW is a homonym for Esau, hairy man in the Book of Genesis. As depicted by artist Bryan Harold, the Earl himself has had his outline simplified to that of some nineteenth century French Impressionist painter - Renoir, Cezanne, Gauguin - or perhaps to that of some prophet of the Groucho Marxist tendency. He is the bearded radical in a bubble the shape of a paperweight.

Fan out that stack of ESAW poetry collectibles and begin to read them and you soon see that they are an eclectic bunch, a tribe of scribes celebrating the bardic impulse, their tonal qualities multiplying in the resonance of their ways of saying, the echo chambers of their words.

Some poets have themselves been small press operators, determined to set their own boundaries. Amongst them is Peter Olds with Montgomery Publications and The Broadsheet Company, and Sandra Bell with Apron

Press. Olds, who has contributed two collections of poems to the series in separate booklets, demonstrates an offhand yet spot-on mastery of the colloquial and the vernacular. But it's not a casual mastery. The last poem in *The Mad Elephant* (Number 8) tells of the never-ending daily struggle 'for a descriptive line' the poet can live with. Like a jazz musician, he is ever alert to improvisatory cadences, to the bargain bin imagery of the everyday.

Sandra Bell, in her *postcards from Friedrichshain, notes from Pomerania* (Number 12), is the curious traveller; a scene-shifter who, discovering decadence in Berlin, writes well about bad behaviour. Her dark vaudeville, her bohemian muse, the razzmatazz of her wanderlust have a kind of outlandish magnificence.

However, she is not the only visitor to foreign shores. Australian poet Ken Bolton in his *Three Poems* (Number 17) winds up 'sitting at an outdoor table / in a tiny square in Tastevere' in Rome communing with a pigeon from Perugia. Bolton's quicksilver reflections have a jazzy, bantering quality to them. His poems in fact remind you of the daily logbook, note-it-down-before-it-fades quality of Peter Olds' poems.

Another overseas poet to stray into the ESAW fold is Cambridge- based writer Richard Berengarten (aka Burns), whose *Manual (the first twenty)* (Number 10), a sequence which celebrates human hands, has an incantatory weight deriving from its formal patterns and rhythmic aplomb. The effect can be almost hypnotically repetitive and percussive, as if the poetry is about to strike up a tune and set off on a march. He has since added a further two collections in his *Manual* sequence to the series.

Jeanne C. Bernhardt, by contrast, in *The Deaf Man's Chorus* (Number 7) offers a musical minimalism, a distilled language that reminds you of raindrops dripping from fern fronds, with delicate phrases about mutability and fragility. Her poems, pared-down, spare to the point of elusiveness, seem like explorations of fragmented identity. Out of isolation they emerge as small gestures of communication: 'I dug a garden / gathered books to me like children.'

There is a different kind of lyricism to be found in Iraqi-born (now Laos-based) Basim Furat in his *The Moon That Excels in Nothing But Waiting* (Number 1). These poems in translation are about memory and witness and exile. Sometimes the imagery is poignant, as with the woman 'who lights the candles of her youth' on the grave of the poet's father. At other times the poems with their political anger and sense of displacement seem like a high-anxiety high-wire act with poet as funambulist performing dazzling pirouettes a hundred metres up in the air.

The cover of *Doppelganger* (Number 9) is a grainy group photograph taken at a University of Iowa Writing Workshop, while the poems inside (English and Polish versions) seem like a kind of duet between Vivienne Plumb and Polish poet Adam Wiedemann, who met at the Workshop. These poems are about the historical fate of Central Europe, where whole countries vanished into the maw of rampant communism only to reappear more or less intact after an absence of nearly half a century. The poems are parables about resemblances and differences, the tragi-comedies of loss and survival.

There is a different kind of comedy in *Wellington Fool* (Number 2) by Mark Pirie. He offers wry, deadpan lines based on sharp observations. He prods in an ironic way at the notion that smallness is a distinctive New Zealand virtue. His collection is thus self-referential, self-aware, self-questioning, turning smallness as a subject over and over like a pebble plucked from a Zen garden of stones.

Nelson Wattie's *Early Egypt and the Late Egyptians* (Number 11) has a droll, comic take on things too. He examines the long perspectives of ancient history the way Percy Bysshe Shelley did in his poem about Ozymandias. This is time doing its inexorable work: 'And the lake, enormous, that made my world / green - its floor is a dusty plain.'

Francis Cherry, in more contemporaneous fashion, mines the mundane for epiphanies in *Stories I've Told* (Number 15). Writing about family life using snap-shut lines, Cherry's poems are at once bitter and passionate. She might be the truth-telling everywoman, harbouring her thoughts amidst the dirty laundry generated by both domestic and public life.

Victor O'Leary, in *The Sensual Anchor* (Number 14), examines life as a matter of sin and syntax and relief hereafter, confessionally elevating the ordinary towards grace. His satirical poem 'The All Black' is a kind of high dirge that memorably commemorates an aspect of our communal psyche: the need to belong.

Karen Peterson Butterworth, too, in *fluid* (Number 6) explores the power of community through the power of her observations and with some gently precise imagery that derives its flavour from her almost culinary skill with the strict, taut form of the Japanese haiku: 'harvesting pears / all the street's children / arrive to help.'

And if the suspicion lurks with all these books that they are all in a way offering poetry as a dryly dadaist performance art - is the anorexic status of these publications also maybe evidence of poetry's existential crisis? - Gemma Claire (aka Rowsell)'s *Uncivil Servant* (Number 16) somehow seems to bring that prospect out into the open with her sweet and sour routines where premises and their complications are carried to logical extremes, with daily life in a media-saturated landscape just a branch of cheesy showbiz. Her candid observations are discoveries announced with comedic oomph. She crams big themes into small subjects, seemingly-trivial pursuits, and thereby reveals certain fixed truths:

> Employed at New World down on Willis Street
> is a handsome and strong-looking young man.
> He serves customers delicious baked treats
> and decorates cakes and muffins by hand.

> ...

> Each expression he paints on is unique,
> from timidity to crazed happiness.
> Some pupils are choc dots, some messy streaks:
> every face is beautiful nonetheless.

– David Eggleton

ESAW Poetry Prize

The ESAW Poetry Prize was created in 2007 as an annual award for New Zealand poets. Its inception was at the Poetrywall: Winter Readings 2007. A prize was awarded by the Earl of Seacliff to the winner of the Poetrywall competition. The winner and inaugural recipient of the award was Evelyn Conlon. Her poem featured on the cover of the *Poetrywall* anthology, edited by Mark Pirie and Gemma Claire. In 2008, the award was given for Will Leadbeater's manuscript *Jubal's Lyre* (published in the ESAW mini series) in recognition of his long standing involvement and achievement in New Zealand poetry.

> " "
>
> 'I am honoured to win the [ESAW Poetry Prize] and feel much gratitude towards Michael O'Leary. It has been an inspiration to keep reading and writing…' – Evelyn Conlon, personal letter

"ESAW Preservation Society"

Earl of Seacliff Preservation Society (a song)

We are the Earl of Seacliff Preservation Society
God save Helen Clark, Kim Hill and National Radio
We are the University Press Appreciation Society
God save New Zealand poetry in all its glorious varieties
Preserving the old ways from being abused !
Protecting the new ways for me and you !
What more can we do ?

We are the Liquor and Breweries Preservation Society
God save Fred Dagg, gumboots and Dick Seddon
We are the Kiwi blokes' speaking vernacular
Help save Pukeko, Kiwi, Wood Pigeon, and Kea

We are the Ivory Tower Persecution Affinity
God save all the little traders, vanity publishing and do-it-yourselfers
We are the Careerist Condemnation Affiliate
God save the sports bars, the Black Caps and the All Blacks
Preserving the old ways from being abused !
Protecting the new ways for me and you !
What more can we do ! Kia Kaha !

God save the Earl of Seacliff !!

Anon

The Estuary of Komo

Date of Publication: 2004
Publisher: ESAW
Category: Poetry

Review of Moshé Liba's *The Estuary of Komo*

Moshé Liba is a Wellington-based Israeli poet. He has published 49 books, including 25 books of poetry in several languages. *Over the Waters* (HeadworX) and *The Estuary of Komo* (ESAW) are his latest two works.

In both these books, Liba sticks closely to what he does best. He states the way he sees something quickly, quietly and then disappears. Liba's depth of feeling can be felt in his poems.

Over the Waters is a series of stripped-down poems that are simple to read.

The Estuary of Komo is a lament for the children of Gabon. This poem is a brief sequence to be absorbed over time. There is no doubting the heartbreak and violation that can be found over 31 short pages of this small book.

Liba really wants to talk to the reader following his 18 years of life and work in Africa. Komo is a commentary of quiet despair coloured by the whispered voices of those who have gone away. – *Hamesh Wyatt*

(From *Otago Daily Times*, 2004)

Andrew Fagan

Andrew Fagan (born 1962) is a prominent New Zealand writer, singer and songwriter. He was born in 1962 and grew up in Wellington. He gained fame in New Zealand in the 1980s as the lead singer of pop group The Mockers. Following the success of The Mockers' 1985 hit 'Forever Tuesday Morning,' Fagan won the RIANZ 1985 award for Top Male Vocalist of the Year. Since the Mockers broke up, he has recorded and performed as a solo artist under the name Fagan and with his band, Lig. He has authored a sailing-themed autobiography, Swirly *World*, the *Solo Voyages* (2002), and several collections of poetry. He has also been involved with the TVNZ *Intrepid Journeys* television series. Fagan has lived in London and now resides in Auckland. He is married to writer and television/radio broadcaster Karyn Hay. The couple currently host a talkback show on Radio Live from 7pm till 10pm weeknights. In 2006 Fagan appeared at *Poetrymath: Winter Readings* in Wellington to launch his new book *Overnight Downpour,* published by HeadworX and contributed the first poem to the Winter Readings' Poetrywall the following year in 2007.

"Farewell to the Hotel Paekakariki"

Date of Composition: 2001
Collection: *Paneta Street*
Anthologised in: *Mahones: Four Poets*

The old Paekakariki Hotel has a place in New Zealand literary folklore, alongside the Gluepot in Ponsonby and the Captain Cook or the Robbie Burns in Dunedin. It was particularly known as a drinking hole for the likes of Sam Hunt, Denis Glover and many others who lived on and around the Kapiti Coast during the 1960s and 1970s. O'Leary happened to be living in Paekakariki the year they decided to pull it down. An interesting coincidence was that in 2001 the play based on O'Leary's novel *The Irish Annals of New Zealand* was the last piece of work performed at the pub before it was demolished. O'Leary wrote the farewell poem based on the song 'Hotel California' by the Eagles 'in recognition of the many bands etc that had played there over the years.

Flesh and Blood

The case of the bearded man in Paekakariki

Review of *Flesh and Blood* by John Harvey (published by Heinemann)

About two years ago, following a publisher's promotional tour of New Zealand, John Harvey walked unannounced into Michael O'Leary's bookshop in Paekakariki. As you do, the pair got taking about books and established that they were writers. At some point Harvey graciously forked out for O'Leary's most recent novel, *Unlevel Crossings,* and presented him with a copy of one of his own works. The connection did not end there.

O'Leary has been given a cameo in *Flesh and Blood,* in which the mystery of a missing Yorkshire woman is solved at Paekakariki Beach. O'Leary is described in the book as a bearded man with long grey hair who was 'singing contentedly to himself, something slow and old by the Rolling Stones'. I asked O'Leary if this was true. He says, 'Yeah, could have been, and the song would have been "Wild Horses".'

O'Leary admits that he had never heard of Harvey or his books until their chance meeting, but the Englishman is a distinguished all-rounder from way back. He is the author, under various names, of more than 70 books, including cheap westerns, has written and published others' poetry, done radio and television plays, and lectured in American literature. He is best known for his series on Charlie Resnick, the down- beat Nottingham detective, who like O'Leary gets a sentimental walk- on part in *Flesh and Blood.* After all these years, the 65-year-old Harvey is so in tune with himself and his craft he probably knocked the book out over an August Bank Holiday with one million behind his back. This is not meant to do him a disservice, but he does make writing look easy. I wish.

His hero is Frank Elder, a retired detective inspector who lives by himself in a cottage in a remote part of Cornwall. Sudden events stir Elder into revisiting an unresolved missing persons case. A young woman disappeared from Whitby 14 years before, around the time Elder put away a teenage boy for murder and rape. He is out of prison and has broken his parole.

The plot rumbles around the north of England and the Midlands like a reliable long distance lorry. Elder is back in his old stamping grounds. There are truck stops along the way where he refuels on sugary cups of tea and fresh information from names in the old case file. One of the names takes him to her bed. We are happy for Frank that he has not lost his knack. He has an independently minded daughter. Is she in danger? Harvey pulls it together with masterly skill - and neatly wraps it up in Paekakariki, Well done that man. – *Hedley Mortlock*

(From *New Zealand Listener*, 8 May 2004)

Flip Side of the Ballad of John and Yoko

Date of Publication: 1980, 1999 (2nd ed.)

Publisher: Privately printed; ESAW (2nd ed.)

Category: Poetry broadsheet

Collection: *Surrogate Children, Ka Atu I Kopua, Toku Tinihanga: Selected Poems 1982-2002*

The two books by Lennon, *In His Own Write* and *A Spaniard in the Works,* plus the lyrics to Beatles' songs were O'Leary's introduction and early inspiration to words. The title of this poem reflects the 'other side' of the positive, life-affirming aspect which the people known as the Beatles (and Yoko Ono) brought to his generation. The poem was written the night Lennon was shot and states the deep emotional hurt that he felt when confronted with the evil that also exists in the world, to wit - the 'flip side.' O'Leary writes: 'After writing it I made my way to the Captain Cook Hotel in Dunedin where Peter Olds and I held a roaring wake for the man who had given us so much. I first published the poem as a broadsheet in 1980, four years before ESAW was born, but in some respects it could be considered the first ESAW publication because it showed me that I could write and publish my own work without the wrath of God descending upon me.'

"For My Father in Prison, 1965"

Date of Composition: 1986

Collection: *Toku Tinihanga: Selected Poems 1982-2002, Before and After*

Anthologised in: Whetu Moana: Contemporary Polynesian Poems in English, Te Ao Marama 3

O'Leary's father had been in the air force during WW2 and never settled into life in the state house with a wife and children existence. He was a clever man and a good artist, but worked at a series of factory jobs and spent a lot of time at the pub and the TAB. During O'Leary's first college year his father was in Mt Eden Prison in Auckland in 1965. O'Leary remembers 'going to visit him with mum, and while they talked [he] had a great discussion with a young prisoner about the Beatles and music in general. After [they] left [his] mum told [him] the boy [he] had been talking to was in prison for murder but [he] should not think badly of him.' When O'Leary's father was released from prison he went to meet him off the train and the first thing he said to Michael was 'get a haircut', which didn't do much for their father/son relationship. Both O'Leary's parents died in 1968, and Michael wrote this poem to reflect upon the fact that his father had been so humiliated over his time in prison. O'Leary comments: 'The line about the table being our only family heirloom is pretty exact, the only thing they left us when they died was lots of aroha and five hundred dollars worth of bills at the local grocery store.'

Giving Poetry a Bad Name

Date of Publication: 2005
Publisher: ESAW
Category: Poetry

Review of Mark Pirie's *Giving Poetry a Bad Name*

Mark Pirie is perhaps best known as founding editor of the journal *JAAM,* editor of the anthology *The NeXt Wave* and the publisher of a number of New Zealand poets with his publishing house HeadworX. He is also known for his own poetry that has been widely published.

Giving Poetry a Bad Name is a collection of his work from 1992 to 2004. The book divides into four sections representing his develop- ment as a writer. There is also a biographical introduction and several pages of photographs showing the author with an assortment of his colleagues.

The first section, 'The Young Writer', contains poems that experiment with rhyme, shape, politics, love and desire. There is social comment, 'Going to the Naked Show'; humour 'The Myth Killer' and a number of poems such as the section's title poem, about being a writer.

> ... And, as
> he slowly raised his pen
> and began his descent,
> he watched his words spitting across
> the page, knowing the strings
> were all but cut

The second section, 'Letters Home to Heartbreak Hotel', shows the development of observation. Here the poems are more honest and sceptical. There is even the hint of a mean streak in poems such as 'The Spelling Problem', and some insight into his own pretensions as in 'The Bible Problem':

> and the Bible just seemed to be the right size,

and besides, it had that gutsy Bukowski
look about it

In this section, as throughout the book, Pirie continues to experiment with style:

... and with your legs inching
out of frame
there's the sound
of a whisper...

...it tells you
about the short cuts
and the spaces
in between

This section also points to many of the writer's influences. Pirie has many points to make; he sometimes makes these directly as in 'Note for a Particular Lady', sometimes with a bludgeon as in 'Making a Point', or with a degree of subtlety and good Kiwi colour as in 'Rant for Creeley'. Here we find sublime delights like 'Hyacinth' and some good shots at the establishment in poems like 'So You Want to be Respected Like Curnow':

... and you'll stand there,
tall and proud,
watching them digest you
as easily as a Tuwhare poem.

The poems in the third section, *No Joke*, are more lyrical as in 'The Discussion', and there are some interesting prose poems. There are more poems on the art of writing and indeed some poems that come from darker places.

The last section comprises poems written in the last two years. Things happen as you grow older. From 'The Day A.B. Died':

And I'm driving along The Quay

where he bought me a drink the day
before Xmas, toasting our lasting
success as 'publishers', He gave me some
good advice about punching
at fog...

All told this is a collection that is as cynical as it is honest. Here is a poet in love with the world yet disgusted with its values. It is a huge book but among the juggernaut of words the reader is bound to find a number of poignant gems:

...After you've left
I wait outside

until the jingle of milk bottles
fades in the distance.

Now,
nothing stirs

except the peaceful mutiny
in the rose garden...

– *Linzy Forbes*

(From the *New Zealand Poetry Society Newsletter,* August 2005)

66 99

'...a generous sampling of the Wellington poet's torrential output ... The pace of his composition must be Baxteresque, but Pirie avoids lyric excess at all costs. Urban irony is his stock in trade, across clipped short verse as well as long, Whitmanesque rants. The energy of his rhyming poems suggests an inspired Pakeha rapper.' - Mark Houlahan, *Dominion Post*

'*Giving Poetry a Bad Name* is a book that those who like to be acquainted with the shakers and makers of literature should see as essential reading.' - Alistair Paterson, *Poetry NZ*

The Globe

A Quick Word

Dedicated to David Mitchell (either you get it or you don't)

Poetry readings were quite common in Auckland when I was growing up there in the late '60s and early '70s. It was possible to take in performances by both old troupers like Allen Curnow and James K Baxter and young tyros like Alan Brunton and Ian Wedde. The desire to strut some stuff of my own kicked in early, but it wasn't until Dave Mitchell set up regular readings at the Globe Hotel in 1981 that I summoned up the nerve. Some of the routines gathered here date back to Globe days. Others were performed at the Shakespeare Tavern in the early '90s. A couple come from 2002: I knocked out 'Amnesty Day' for an event organised by Riemke Ensing and 'Two Minute Poem' for a gala evening arranged by Auckland University Press involving 28 bards limited to 120 seconds apiece. Anyone who's been to a few poetry readings will be aware of the distinction between what works on the page and what works on the stage.

Energetic crap delivered with a friendly smile and an attempt at soft shoe shuffle often pleases a crowd better than ingenious stanzas. I know 'The Splog' isn't *Paradise Lost*. The words of 'The Ponsonby Strut' changed every time I did it. So did the dance steps. I once persuaded a gaggle of cronies to storm the stage of the Globe and play a kazoo version of the 'Strut' with me. I still think this was the definitive rendition.

It was Dave's habit at the Globe to open proceedings with a recital from an elderly lady of dubious sanity who read straight from her diary. Her 10 minute mumble gave him some breathing space to order drinks from the bar, greet friends as they arrived and plan the rest of the programme. This sad, lonely woman was usually a bit tedious, recount- ing indifferent meals fed to her cat and humdrum conversations with her neigbours, But one night she reached the point in her journal when the men in the white coats carried her off to a mental hospital. I guess the diary was either several years old or else she somehow escaped from her confines to read at the Globe. 'I might not be back here for a while,' she told us. Then in a faltering voice, which began as a whisper but soon grew to a potent crescendo, she sang the old Engelbert Humperdinck hit 'There Goes My Everything'. It was simultaneously horrible and terrific - the best performance poem I've ever heard.

In a similar vein, there was another evening at the Globe when Michael O'Leary put paper bags over our heads, we played air guitars and sang more or less together - the John Lennon number 'I'm a Loser' from the *Beatles For Sale* album. People present told me it was my most convincing performance. The trouble with the Beatles' original is that their obvious musical talent undercut their credibility as losers. O'Leary and I, on the other hand, nailed down loserdom magnificently. You had to be there, though. A lyric sheet won't give you the full story. – *Iain Sharp, Harp of Erin, 2004*

(Author's Foreword to *The Singing Harp* (ESAW, 2004))

Gorilla/Guerrilla

Date of Publication: 1986
Publisher: ESAW Category: Poetry
Illustrations: Gregory O'Brien

Gorilla/Guerilla

I'm riding on the back of Greg O'Brien's motorbike, a carton of *Gorilla/ Guerilla* pressed between us. We go into a cafe, clear the salt shakers and sauce bottle away, and start signing. 250 copies later our signatures are illegible but the copies are back in the box.

Such a small book (15cms x 10cm) it slides behind other books in the bookcase. I used to feel uncertain whether I should count it when I wrote a CV: I can easily cover my copy (no 8, signatures still intact) with my palm. Then I look at Greg's in-between gorilla-guerilla on the cover, with its soft gentle paws, small eyes, raised nostrils (as if scenting which way the language is going) and wide lips, not unlike Homer Simpson, the fringe of leaves under which it shelters. The damage language can do to the wrong body, rendering it defenceless. How would a BBC announcer differentiate between gorilla (peaceful) and guerrilla (guns)? The Shining Path guerrillas versus the gorillas in Zaire building their nightly nests.

It began with larking around in the library, with a librarian called Viv Bone. 'I always picture gorillas when I hear guerrillas,' I told her. A few verses began to form themselves. Besides I was quite familiar with gorillas in 1986. My daughter was finishing a degree in anthropology and art history and that year I had been literary fellow and Sarah had had the use of my office in the English Department. I had typed several long essays about gorilla patriarchal structures. I knew how they constructed their nests like a maid in a hotel putting on fresh sheets every morning. When the essays were typed (for my daughter and a fellow student) I was presented with a large bouquet of flowers which I felt were from the gorillas themselves.

And I had met Michael O'Leary, the most hospitable and endearing of publishers. Or met him through Greg. A publisher who would accost writers on the street and invite them in for a drink and a chat. Shades of City Lights and Sylvia Beach. The beard of Ginsberg.

Michael O' Leary made it feel good to be an author. A little (sometimes rhyming) book about gorilla/guerrilla confusion - why not? Why aren't there more publishers like that today? Literature and fun first, let the profits fall like chips.

Greg's drawings, from the first little poem,

> Why do we have it
> This awful confusion
> Gorilla and Guerilla
> The result is not funny

to the last excessive wish-fulfilment

> The gorillas are coming
> There's only one kind
> The other guerrillas
> Have become obsolete.

create a creature as endearing as Tintin's dog Snowy. A gorilla that lies in a nest or hurls a soldier-guerilla, separated from his gun, into a pile of fronds and flowers; a gorilla with its paws cupped protectively in front of a blazing town; a gorilla that has grown broad-shouldered and wise, like Martin Luther King; a gorilla that confronts a guerrilla with vacant-looking eyes and silly pith helmet. GUER and GOR read the half-pages of a book that illustrates the damage that can be done by a dictionary.

I don't remember whether we rode off on the motorbike with the signed copies - I think we did. We ordered coffees because the café owner was looking bemused and his table was covered with piles of small books. We were certainly smiling.

You've got to be at a distance to see faith and genius, and that's what is obvious now about Michael O'Leary and the Earl of Seacliff Art Workshop productions. Publishing is not what it was but Michael represents what it should be, what it is in every writer's heart of hearts. Books produced without fuss or flourish; not a meddling accountant in sight. Just good friends, word of mouth, faith in literature, motorbikes. And the presiding generous spirit of an alpha gorilla. – *Elizabeth Smither*

"

'A gem of a publication ... a whimsical polemic in verse by Elizabeth Smither, written while she held the literary fellowship at Auckland University, and illustrated in inimitable style by Gregory O'Brien ... a true collector's piece...' – Michael Gifkins, *New Zealand Listener*

"Greatest Hits"

Date of Publication: 2004
Publisher: JAAM Publishing Collective in association with HeadworX and ESAW
Category: Poetry/Fiction

Review of *JAAM 21: "Greatest Hits": An Anthology of Writing 1984-2004*, edited by Michael O'Leary and Mark Pirie

This twenty-first issue of *JAAM*, edited by Michael O'Leary and Mark Pirie, is not just a retrospective of hits from the literary magazine. The editors note that it is "a smorgasbord of the best writing from 100 publications by our productive small presses [*JAAM*, O'Leary's Earl of Seacliff Art Workshop, and Pirie's HeadworX] in the last 20 years." The order of the poems and prose is alphabetical according to an author's last name with an indication of the publication date. *JAAM 21* proves to be a rich collection with much to appeal to various tastes despite a handful of pieces that seem either trite or pointlessly esoteric.

In the past, these editors have sometimes prompted debate by claiming that their authors represent a unique, young literary vanguard. *JAAM 21*, quite rightly, makes no claims in this regard. Some forty percent of its authors were included among the current poets in Bill Manhire's *100 New Zealand Poems*, which was published more than a decade ago in 1993 and covers the better part of two centuries. Manhire's collection features many established writers such as Hone Tuwhare and Sam Hunt who are also in the *JAAM* retrospective.

Pirie and O'Leary do claim that their presses have been unique in connecting popular music and literature. They note that the issue has been arranged as a kind of musical and literary jam session, that they have included a number of musicians, and 'have emphasized the crossover between popular music and literary culture in New Zealand that neatly influences the title "Greatest Hits"'. This focus enhanced my anticipation of poems by the various singers, musicians, and also performance poets. In some cases, I felt able to discern a fairly specific relationship between the words and sound. Tony Chad's 'A Possum's Tail', the tale of an ongoing hangover, reverberates for me as a cross between Country and Celtic rhythms. Hip-Hop, with its minimal instrumentation and emphasis on lyrics is relatively easy to imagine; so Dean Hapeta's incisive 'Why I Don't Cry' (written about *9/11*) hopped off the page. However, many others did not. Since a poem and music or performance can interact in various ways, it would have been helpful to have some specific elucidation in the author blurbs. One welcome exception is Mike Eager, where the inclusion of such an introductory sentence does much to set the mind humming: 'Eager often links poems as narrative sequences, including chant and song for variation of rhythm and emotion.' His poem, 'When', follows:

> When it comes it comes like rain
> We can dance, oh, we can dance
> We can slam our feet on clay
> Or we can pray.

The variety of *JAAM 21* yields a particular pleasure: in a number of instances the collection presents a variety of 'takes' on a single topic. Regarding love, for example, Alistair Te Ariki Campbell's 'Love Song for Meg', is exquisitely lyrical and suggestively sexual:

> It was the way
> the sun came sidling
> through the branches –
> points of light
>
> exploding into stars
> as the wind,
> eddying overhead,
> delicately sprung
> the leaves apart.

In 'The Hook', writer/musician Jordan Reyne ironically mocks traditional expressions of love in both poetry and Blues lyrics:

> SHE (a princess):
> Baby I miss you
> Without you I am nothing (oh yeah)
> My life is meaningless
> without your love (oo baby come back)

However, poems focusing on society are primarily and dauntingly negative. Bill Sewell, a writer and legal researcher, effectively uses the language and spirit of legal jargon to briefly convey a society that has surpassed Orwell's vision in *1984*. 'The Regulations' are so all- encompassing of people and their actions that simply living becomes an offence:

> Every person who
> discontinues their employment;
> makes any payment or contribution;
> prints or publishes any statement;
> encourages, procures, incites, aids or abets...
> commits an offence

In 'Off-Motorway Notes', a prose piece, writer-performer David Eggleton effectively depicts a vacuous human landscape where men whiz 'along the road inside little metal and glass cages with rubber wheels. Or just sitting in the little wooden cubes (houses if you like) ... they sip hot liquid. Squabble. They listen to noises. Organized static.' Blame or change are not issues here: 'Their eyes blink in time with the screen's changing pictures. They go on doing these things because they must.' Even the musician can only whistle 'Please Release Me', consider speeding in his car and getting drunk. 'In his perversity he shouts, "Here's piss in your eye." Nothing answers.' Lyrics about 'little ticky tackys that all look just the same', pale in comparison.

Ten prose pieces are scattered throughout the collection and include dialogue and description as well as the traditional short story form. Some of the strongest, most evocative of these pieces have been written by authors with music affiliations.

Dedicated to James Baldwin, 'Fingerprints' is a powerful piece that manages to evoke Baldwin's tone. By L E Scott, who describes his work as 'Jazz blues'. 'Fingerprints' opens with a circuitous conversation between mother and child. 'The child has his father's hands. / Long dark fingers. And what will his last words in life be?' the mother wonders. Images of fingers, fingerprints, hands, flicker through- out, bestowing a rhythmic sense to the piece and uniting the generations of this family, the black community and, ultimately, all of humanity. Images of eyes and blindness also resonate. Brief depictions of life in Harlem are presented then epitomized in the more detailed, tragic life of the ironically named 'girl next door':

Had three children, one died and two got killed. One by a policeman who didn't like uppity niggers ... She still plays the piano that the rent man never brought back. The blind would say she's mad. But they don't see that she's got red eyes.

In closing, the piece returns to the mother and child at a later time with haunting effect:

The voice of mother

Child, get up out of that bed I know you sick and mad, but you ain't tired. I know you feeling old but you ain't.

You my son and now you got a son...

The fire next time

It is the blind of the world who will burn in the fire unless they learn to see what their fingers have shaped.

'Can I Play with your Janet Frame?' by Grayson Cooke provides a welcome and scintillating comic relief along with some apt comments. A drummer in two Wellington rock bands, Cooke has created savagely funny dialogue between two writers considering cliches and the state of their craft:

> **James** - Yeah, the troubled artist, the rural upbringing, '30s working class New Zealand. The emergence of literature with a capital L from humble beginnings ... God and god damn, writers have a lot to answer for.
>
> **Bee** - Shoot the whole fuckin' lot of them. Line them up and give' 'em one in the belly for maximum pain and one straight through the forehead to end the torment.
>
> **James** - Burroughs, I feel, has been here before us. Burn the books. Kill the priests. Smash the control machine.

The repartee proceeds to mock cliches a la B movie villains 'with facial eczema and huge, awe-inspiring vendettas to play out.' and the portrayal of dictators, 'Hitler spitting in guttural German at legions of aspiring fascists.' James concludes with an ambitious variation on the image of poets as unacknowledged legislators:

> We're recycling. We are the mouths of the world. Without us the world would stay silent; some empty-faced mute stuck halfway between vomiting and swallowing...
>
> – So, we are God then?
>
> – Yep.
>
> – Wow, that's pretty cool.
>
> – *Andrea Mudry*

(From *Takahe* 54 (2004))

Come together

Come together was the catch cry for Mark Pirie and Michael O'Leary as they put together the 21st issue of *JAAM (Just* Another *Art Movement)*.

'There is a lot of powerful writing throughout the book but the individual works do gel,' says Pirie. 'It's a lot of different writing that comes together like a jam session.' The issue is a 'greatest hits' collection of works from previous publication.

It's not just different styles that blend in JAAM 21 - there are different disciplines too. The 200 page anthology is dedicated to the memory of John Lennon and George Harrison and includes poems and song lyrics from many well known musicians.

'Charlotte Yates' lyrics are in the anthology but she has also published a book of her lyrics and Bill Direen writes prose as well as songs,' says Pirie.

Both Pirie and O'Leary have a deep love of music and JAAM 21 highlights the connection between literature and music. As well as musicians that write prose, poets and writers such as Alan Brunton, Ron Riddell, Sam Hunt, Richard von Sturmer and David Eggleton have all worked closely with musicians.

'Michael used to do readings in The Globe in Auckland,' says Pirie. 'That major venue for bands created a real mix of musical and literary personalities.'

Choosing highlights from 21 publications was time-consuming but not as arduous as it sounds says Pirie. As well as writings from the previous editions the anthology includes samplings from books published by O'Leary's Earl of Seacliff Art Workshop and Pirie's HeadworX publishing companies. 'The issues vary in size from quite large to quite small,' he says. Some of the early issues were not much bigger than pamphlets.

'We tried to pick a mix of major talent and up-and-comers. Michael chose his and I chose mine. We didn't ask each other's opinion.'

That approach is reminiscent of the Beatles' song 'Day in the Life' from Sergeant Pepper's in which half-a-Lennon song was attached to half-a-McCartney song.

The anthology's cover is a recreation of the cover of Abbey Road, the album that 'Come Together' appears on.

'That cover has been imitated many times,' says Pirie. 'But never in the context of New Zealand literature. It also shows the dichotomy of the street and rock'n'roll (which is public) and the university which represents higher learning and literature.' – *Capital Times reporter*

JAAM 21: "Greatest Hits" launch, Unity Books, February 4, 6pm (From *Capital Times*, February, 2004)

Brian Hare

Brian Hare was a close friend of Michael O'Leary who lived with him in Seacliff days. The two published their first collection together, *Surrogate Children*, with Sandra Bell in 1981. The following poem (for Michael O'Leary) is from the collection:

The Final Rebirth

For my brother of words, Michael

Let us climb the winding path
Tonight to the peak above the stream
Before the dusk doth blanket
The pleasure of my senses
To that place of revelationary consultation
Where possibility of perfection gained
A yielding, renewed heart poured out
A kiss upon that domain of prayer
In recognition of abundance and Glory
The Living Lord Christ Jesus.

So wander I shall henceforth
Retracing the importance and footsteps
Past the Rosehip that harkens
Earlier confused penitence
And stay I shall the way to gather you up
That the Tokanui phone shall absolve
As our immensity in struggle, striving
Our shared goal initiated Irish soil.

That the Jew piteously rebuilds the Temple
A third time, we show our respects
Endeavouring fervently in the memory
Of the maiden aunt; for God

To bypass the Epicurean of type
And compile an adjunct of the Holy Land
And ridicule of the Bear and damned
Shall sow where folly through solace
Is replaced by rejoicing of Soul.

Amen.

"He Waiatanui kia Aroha"

Date of Composition: 1992

Collection: *He Waiatanui kia Aroha, Toku Tinihanga: Selected Poems 1982-2002, Con Art: Selected Poems,TAB Ula Rasa: New and Selected Poems*

Anthologised in: *JAAM 15*

This sequence of poems addressed to O'Leary's friend Winsome Aroha is loosely modeled on Baxter's poem 'He Waiata mo te Kare' in *Autumn Testament*. The thoughts behind this poem sequence are expressed in the novel *The Irish Annals of New Zealand*: 'He tried to compose the most beautiful poem in the world to her, which was something he had always wanted to do for her, he thought, and random lines from past poems he had written to her sauntered through as someone stood looking at the starlit sky dreaming, titiro ki te tonga, saw the pot and heard the scorpion's tale .' An edition of 55 signed copies, published by ESAW in collaboration with Fernbank Studio in 2001, was handset and printed by Brendan O'Brien when he was living at the Rita Angus Cottage in Wellington. Earlier Brendan had produced a book in a similar fashion of poems written by Colin McCahon to fellow artist Rita Angus.

Helen Clark Exhibition

Tongue-in-cheek art exhibition a real scream

A selection of artwork and paintings - including such classics as 'The Scream' - have been popular at a Paekakariki art gallery, but only because of a tiny signature on each one. The 10 works featured in One Eye Gallery have all been signed 'Helen Clark' as part of a tongue- in-cheek exhibition by Paekakariki writer and poet Michael O'Leary. Mr O'Leary said it was his response to the controversy over the Prime Minister signing artworks which had in fact been done by other artists. 'The reason I did it was to have a bit of fun really. The art world is so serious and Helen Clark is the Minister of Arts and Culture, so the irony is too good to miss.'

Mr O'Leary has also written an explanation about each work, in part a send-up of the 'overblown intellectualism' of descriptions of artworks in galleries and museums, he said.

One artwork is an old Coleman's Mustard advertisement showing a young woman who could pass as a teenage Clark. 'An early self- portrait in which Helen Clark, the younger, sees herself as a fresh virginal maiden reaping the harvest of political idealism and artistic freedom, circa 1973,' the description says.

Gallery owner Gary Freemantle said he was at first reluctant to have a show about the controversy because it could reek of 'cheap opportunism', but he was impressed with Mr O'Leary's work. Mr O'Leary, who owns Pukapuka Books, said he chose artworks, including a Constable painting, as much because of their titles so they could be sent up. As for copying Miss Clark's signature ... 'I studied it for five minutes - a full five minutes.' The exhibition will re-open this Saturday and Sunday, 11am-5pm. – *Evening Post reporter*

(From *The Evening Post,* April 2002)

"Hone Tuwhare: A Personal Memoir"

Date of Composition: 2008
Collection: Paneta Street
Anthologised in: *Ka Mate Ka Ora* 6 (online journal)

O'Leary writes: 'As I state in my poem to Hone written after his death: "we were different kinds of poets / Railway Workers first, comrades, drinkers." In the early 1980s Hone and I gave a poetry reading in the maximum security unit of Paremoremo Prison and I'll always remember his aroha towards these tough and dangerous men who had committed very serious crimes. When he collapsed after receiving one of the inaugural Prime Minister's Literary Awards in 2003 he "escaped" from Wellington Hospital and checked into a motel at a secret location where my sister Clare, my friend Moana and I kept him clandestinely supplied with kai moana and other food and drink. It was here that he gave me his hat with his writing all around the inside brim. I was meant to wear it for the Dylan photo on the cover of my 2008 collection *Paneta Street* but I unfortunately left it on the train. So someone is walking around Wellington with a head full of Tuwhare ideas, which could prove fatal.'

Robert Sullivan included the poem for Hone in the special tribute issue to Tuwhare, of *Ka Mate Ka Ora* 6. Michael felt 'it was honour to be included just as it was an honour to have locked horns with Hone when he was alive.'

In Janet Hunt's biography of Hone Tuwhare, O'Leary is given a mention concerning Tuwhare's story 'Don't walk past me with your nose in the air'. It was dedicated to O'Leary using Michael's phrase 'Kia Ora Begorrah!'. The Listener editor Andrew Mason who published the story in 1990 wanted to delete Hone's dedication to Michael from the story for unknown reasons.

Incantations for Warriors

Date of Publication: 1987
Publisher: ESAW
Category: Poetry

Review of Alistair Paterson's *Incantations for Warriors*

This major work completes a quartet of highly innovative writing. *The Toledo Room* in '78, *Qu'appelle* in '82, *Odysseus Rex* in '86 preceded *Incantations for Warriors*.

These four poems form one long poem; a journey through a galaxy of experiences, and 'journey' is the operative word.

The title suggests a battle - in this case it is a metaphorical war in which ironies burst with a shimmer of jostling innuendos.

I don't believe it is too much of an exaggeration to suggest that Paterson is a romantic in spite of himself, for in 'Complaint 4' the negative imagery of

> Everything falls apart:

> and

> the things you 'own' will outlast you

is an oblique reminder of Keats' 'Ode on a Grecian Urn'. 'Complaint 22' contains an even more direct allusion to Keats:

> the worst and best of wild surmise ...

for even though Keats got his historical facts wrong in 'On First Looking into Chapman's Homer':

> Stout Cortez, and all his men
> looked at each other with a wild surmise

both Balboa and Cortez were explorers - and *Incantations* is an exploration.

Proving the measure of the poem's expansiveness, the reader could approach the complexity of these statements and responses from a less romantic and optimistic angle to tie in with the final 'Incantation'*:*

> [you] can't negotiate a peace
> you have no choice ...

So one can pick up clues from the Carlos Castaneda quotation:

> The thing to do... is turn to your left and ask advice from your death.

or from the repetitious use of *Mescalito.*

Above all this poem is a cerebal experience with a high voltage emotional input quivering just below the surface.

The whole poem comprises 12 'incantations' and 11 'complaints' and perhaps eventually the whole quartet might be printed under a single title like T.S. Eliot's *Four Quartets.*

If so it would certainly be a powerfully impressive work. – *Will Leadbeater*

(From *New Zealand Herald,* 28 November 1987)

Irish Annals of Aotearoa

Irish Annals comes home to roost in Paekakariki Pub

Review of Irish Annals of Aotearoa: A Psycle Drama (*adapted for the stage by Simon O'Connor from Michael O'Leary's novel,* Irish Annals of New Zealand*), Paekakariki Pub, Saturday, 3 February 2001*

The wandering Irish Māori Pakeha Michael O'Leary has been settled, an unsettling presence, in Paekakariki for a year or two now. Last Saturday a packed hall at the local pub greeted with delighted applause a boisterous presentation of his short novel, *The Irish Annals of New Zealand*, freely and brilliantly adapted for the stage by Simon O'Connor. After a successful try-out at BATS theatre in Wellington, the play came home to roost.

Bookseller, trainlover, publisher, erstwhile navvy and latterly painter, O'Leary, also known as the Earl of Seacliff (don't ask, it's another story) has long enjoyed the respect of a smallish band of friends and admirers for his novels and collections of poetry. As he acknowledged in a gracious, and graciously brief, speech after the performance, O'Connor and the company have made *The Irish Annals* accessible to a wider audience. They did him proud, playing out with great skill and energy a tale that weaves slapstick and knockabout comedy around the poignant memories of colonial devastation: "Land took and dear ones lost."

'Himself', a young Irish Pakeha, hopelessly drunk on a train journey through the central North Island and desperate for a leak, stumbles through the wrong door altogether and is hurled out into the snow, smashing his head on a rock. As he lies bleeding, half-dead, he is visited by his ancestors, Irish and Māori, two histories of grief and rage intertwined in a common whakapapa. This is not a solemn narrative of the grand cycles of history, but rather scraps of history as seen from bicycle seats, as the cast wheel and pirouette on mini-bikes, mountain bikes and boneshakers. Remarkably, the physical shenani- gans in no way diminish the emotional power of episodes such as the murder of a Samoan member of the Mau "rebellion" - a tale from the diary of Himself's demented Da - or the poignancy of an Irish ballad, hauntingly sung by Peter Daube.

The ending is a wee bit of a cheat, frankly: our hero, it transpires, has not taken a fatal tumble at all, but at the last moment has seized the right door handle and taken refuge back in the warm carriage. Rather than a near-death experience, we've shared a nearly- near-death experience, and who's to quibble at a happy ending?

The venue was quite the right place to enjoy such a good night out, even though the actual hall is not ideal for theatrical performances. The flat floor and lack of a raised stage make sight lines tricky for people at the back, and although the effects the lighting designer achieved were both simple and clever, no doubt she would have liked a few more circuits to play with. The acrobatic cast did wonderfully well at making the space work for them. The music was witty, inventive, altogether of a piece with the other elements of a production crammed with physical and verbal jokes, wordplay in several languages, pratfalls and profundities, and passages of real pathos. Well done indeed. – *Martyn Sanderson*

(From *Kapiti Observer*, 12 February 2001)

The Irish Annals of New Zealand

Date of Publication: 1991
Publisher: ESAW
Category: Fiction

Rebel writer with a cause

When Michael O'Leary - aka the Earl of Seacliff - moved from Auckland to Seacliff near Dunedin to work on his third novel, he brought with him 12 boxes of books and a stuffed hawk.

Books he regards as a vital companion, and the hawk was perched on one of his big shoulders to provoke a reaction from his fellow train passengers. He enjoys recounting the response he got from the American tourists ... "would you look at that guy with the bird Martha!" The bird now hangs in a perpetual pose of attack from the ceiling of the Seacliff cottage where he's been working on the novel for several months. The book, called *The Irish Annals of New Zealand*, is a sort of late-coming 1990 project from the other side of the fence, mixing the stories of what O'Leary regards as two of the rebel cultures in this country - the Irish and the Māori.

You couldn't call it history, he says; it's more of a melding of the personal, the real and unreal, though it does draw on actual happenings, such as the fact that a nun who was the sister of James Joyce lived on the West Coast for 40 years. Stylistically, he laughs through his black beard, it's Milligan meets Beckett.

"It begins in 1990 in the North Island when a drunk falls off a train in the middle of the night. He breaks every bone in his body and he's left lying there in the snow, "His Irish and Māori ancestors will come up to meet him ... they're all on bikes. The book travels back through the previous 150 years and it's all about him trying to understand his life." O'Leary himself is a confluence of Irish and Māori blood, and he says it's given him an outsider's perspective on this country - "the Irish came here to escape the English and the potato famine, not like the Anglo-Saxons who came to conquer. The Irish were dispossessed of their land just like the Māori."

His bloodline, coupled with a Catholic upbringing - "being brought up a Catholic is like being brought up in Disneyland, except everything is painted black" led him to write. "I haven't come from a background of being surrounded by books - we hardly had any in our house - but I've always had this thing with words. I used to make up pop songs as a kid and I'd always be telling stories to other kids on the way home from school.

"But I didn't start reading books till my mid-twenties when I went to night school to do School Cert and University Entrance. By reading books I could better understand what's happened to me and where I've come, that's the main contribution writers make - you come across something you recognise and you learn more about yourself." O'Leary, however, doesn't see writing as being a po-faced, serious, cerebral activity, regarding it as no more important than the labouring jobs he's had. New Zealand literature, he maintains, has been hi-jacked by the academics, and lacks humour.

He's kicked against that and writes satire: his second novel, *Out of It*, focuses on the ruminations of Patrick Malone, and is set at a cricket match between New Zealand and the 'Out of It' 11, captained by Te Rauparaha, and featuring dead sixties rock heroes, Nazis, and writers, including a seminal influence, James K. Baxter.

"On one labouring job I left a copy of *Out of It* in the smoko shed. I worked with some pretty hard characters and they recognised the title and had a laugh at that and one or two of them read it. They really liked it which means more to me than what some university-type might say."

He expects his new book to be out later this year. Like his others, it'll be self-published through his company, Earl of Seacliff Art Workshop, which has promoted an alternative roster of writers, including poet David Eggleton; the country's first gay novel, *Passion*, and a book on the Rainbow Warrior affair by Colin Amery.

O'Leary's labouring stints, including a nightshift job grinding concrete on Auckland's Queen Street, have kept the venture solvent. He's returned to Seacliff to free himself of the hassle of being a business director, and write the book which has been brewing in his head for three or four years.

He loves the small coastal settlement so much he named himself the Earl of it, partly in jest and partly in defiance of the English having "exterminated" the Irish Earls back in the 18th century. Having grown up among the state houses of Ōrākei in Auckland, he values Seacliff for its solitude, its rolling greenness, its open summer skies contrasting with brooding coastal mists, and its infamous mental hospital. "A lot of people won't come out here because of that," he says, pointing across the road to the old brick building of the hospital, "but to me it just adds to the whole atmosphere".

"From the first moment I ever saw Seacliff from the window of the train I felt an empathy with it. My rationale now is that because it's so physically beautiful yet has a tormented past it brings out something in me which gives an expression of my view of life. The fact it's half beautiful and half terrifying." – *Richard Langston*

(From *Dominion Sunday Times*, 10 March 1991)

Irish Laurels

The Irish Annals of New Zealand (ESAW) by Dunedin author, Michael O'Leary is a short novel with many twists and turns. It's about a drunk man who opens the wrong door and falls from a train, cracking his skull and slowly bleeding to death. He dies and then reappears throughout the novel as a series of reincarnations who may be descendants, or ancestors, or alter egos, until at the end of the book he reverts to his former drunk self, opens the right door and resumes his seat on the train. A happy ending.

The subtext of this tall tale is the history of the "Paddy Irishman" in New Zealand: the historical determinism that brought him here to work on the railways (eviction from Ireland by English landowners, the potato famine), the Anglo-Saxon racist attitudes that persisted through- out the nineteenth century (examples of which included the trial of a Catholic bishop for treason, the arrests of known Fenians, and the eviction of Irish "squatters" from Dunedin.) The persecution of those who fell short by the old British Imperial standard of measurement was succeeded by New Zealand's own repressive double standards applied both at home and in the Pacific.

This book is an angry attack on artificial class-consciousness and the hierarchical impositions of the coloniser, a revisionist rereading of some of the shaping forces in New Zealand society, siding with the dispossessed, the deliberately disadvantaged.

At the same time the book is very entertaining, the historical digest is presented as a black comedy. Bits of local legends and lore, fragments of Celtic kitsch, and cloves of wild Gaelic wit are flung together and seasoned with outlandish puns to produce a bubbling Irish stew of fact and fiction.

Written in a kind of stream of consciousness dream language that openly acknowledges the influence of James Joyce's multilingual Finnegans Wake, this oblique essay about cultural relevance and value systems is, once you get past the initial feeling of dyslexia provoked by the ruptured sentence patterns, slurred syntax and the sound of broken English, a work of polyphonic brilliance. It has the hectic pace of wild Irish music, and often seems to be driven by the proverbial anger of the Fenians, directed as much against themselves and their own destructiveness, as against outsiders and the force of history.

Like a rackety time machine it hurtles backwards and forwards between the 1840s and the present day, taking in the story of an abashed narrator's love for a dusky Samoan maiden, Protestant folk devils, an IRA Spud missile attack that covers London in mashed potato, and garbled Catholic confession box tabloid sensationalism with a nun named Sister Mary Himself that ends in a wierd dipsomaniacal mixture of Hail Marys and Bloody Marys.

Bicycles, trams, buses, trains and a Zephyr Mark II are the transport of the people, the salt of the earth, while Northern Ireland UDR men on the run switch identities, Nazi-hunters question German-Samoans and religious ecstatics speak in tongues.

The whole book is a quick-fire word raffle, showing how language can eradicate, displace or distort history. No cliche, term or place name is free from deconstruction and reinvention, guided by fuzzy logic. The sounds of words and their throwaway comic possibilities turns into a kind of oral fixation. Both a long cry of social maladjustment and a virtuoso manipulation of word associations, this novel makes a tuneful medley out of ordinary everyday speech. – *David Eggleton*

(From *Otago Daily Times,* c.1992)

"Irony and Impressionism in the 21st Century"

Date of Composition: 2006
Collection: *Paneta Street*
Anthologised in: *Sounds of Sonnets*

On one of O'Leary's visits to Dunedin during the 1980s a group of his friends went to dinner at Chan's Garden Restaurant in South Dunedin.

They had several bottles of the best whiskey and probably some food and then Harry Tan invited them all to a party at the Mongrel Mob Headquarters in Caversham. By this time the friends were all pretty out of it and they turned up to a darkened hall with all these Mob members playing pool and drinking beer. The thing that struck O'Leary was how much like an ordinary Kiwi 'down the hall on Saturday night' the scene was, with a row of women along one wall and a row of men along the other side and 'ne'er the twain shall meet.' O'Leary comments further that he 'wanted to laugh but quickly learned that a Mongi party is no laughing matter and if you're kissing the woman you are with you "gotta share, bro."' Anyway, O'Leary was so out of it that he also felt tempted to give the Black Power salute, just checking himself in the manner of Peter Sellers trying not to give the Nazi salute in Doctor Strangelove. Fortunately a mobster called Harvey with a full facial moko took him under his wing and he and O'Leary played pool. This elegy O'Leary wrote for Harvey after meeting him again recently was a way of thanking him, and acknowledging mortality is part of our human experience no matter how tough an impression you may have once given. As O'Leary says: 'The real toughness is how you deal with that.'

"It's Not the Leaving of Wellington"

Date of Composition: 1997
Collection: *Ka Atu I Kopua, Toku Tinihanga: Selected Poems 1982-2002*

The title 'It's Not the Leaving of Wellington' echoes an old Irish song 'The Leaving of Liverpool', which was about the Irish having to leave Ireland and go to America and the rest of the world in order to survive, often via Liverpool. This poem is about not leaving Wellington, but making it a home after O'Leary arrived from Dunedin destitute and on the run in the mid-1990s. It is a *tour de force* around the Wellington region and how it is a city connected by wires, literally with its trolley buses and electric trains. It is a celebration of the human and natural elements that make it what it is, how everything spreads out from its centre, the veins and synapses from the head of the fish. It is dedicated to O'Leary's friend Moana who has shared so much of O'Leary's Wellington experience. Part of the poem became a public piece of art when the Wellington City Council used a stanza from it for a mural on the Brooklyn Bus shelter outside the library in Brooklyn.

Jubal's Lyre

Date of Publication: 2008
Publisher: ESAW
Category: Poetry mini-series

Will Leadbeater's *Jubal's Lyre* was the first collection of his distinctive minimalist, light verse for a number of years. It was awarded the ESAW Poetry Prize for 2008, and Leadbeater attended the Winter Readings in Wellington that same year to receive his award. Leadbeater was the poetry reviewer for the *New Zealand Herald* from 1980-88. He had published several previous collections of poetry. He wrote in his author's note to the collection: 'I have had poetry published in the past but nothing recently. Over the past few years I have judged competitions for I.W.W. and in 1975 I won an American Poetry Competition judged by Donald Hall. For several years in a row, I was invited to three schools by the "Writer's in Schools" programme.'

Ka Atu I Kopua

Date of Publication: 1999
Publisher: Original Books
Category: Poetry

Review of Michael O'Leary's *Ka Atu I Kopua*

This is a major collection of Michael O'Leary's poetry. 51 poems reflecting the many changes in O'Leary's life over the years. Residing in many places including Auckland, Seacliff, Dunedin and now Wellington. 'Ready for anything that comes my way / words are beginning to make themselves heard / as they trivialise and enhance reality / destroy to create / degenerate into life' from 'Moving Again - Overnight Train'. O'Leary's unique mixture of Māori and Irish themes and references are heady, to say the least and he breaks into rhyme here and there: 'Then if you put one and one together / Stargazing and drinking the jars / Your immortal soul will fall through a black hole / You'll end up on Orion or Mars / after being at O'Ryan's & Mahers'.

There's a strength and a kind of sinuous honesty running through O'Leary's work. A bluntness, yet a levity that brooks no intellectually obscure allusions. I found this selection of O'Leary's work thoroughly rewarding, very even and above all definitely entertaining. Those who control literature in New Zealand just hate people coming in through the 'wrong door' to poetic excellence and acceptance. All power to Michael O'Leary and all the best for his continued success. Buy this book, check out a poem called 'Speculation'. It will reward you. – *Trevor Reeves*

(From *Southern Ocean Review* 14, 12 January 2000)

King Kapisi

King Kapisi (aka Bill Urale) was the first Polynesian hip-hop artist to receive the prestigious APRA Silver Scroll Award for Songwriter of the Year for his single 'Reverse Resistance' in 1999. Both King Kapisi's albums, *Savage Thoughts* (released 2000) and *2nd Round Testament* (released 2003) were released in Australia with local sales hitting the gold status mark. King Kapisi has performed alongside Janet Jackson, Moby, Black Eyed Peas, Beastie Boys, Michael Franti & Spearhead and the Red Hot Chili Peppers and many more. In 2002, Kapisi started his own clothing label, Overstayer Clothing. Overstayer Clothing was the first local urban street label to be made available in Farmers Trading Stores nationwide. His sister, playwright Makerita Urale, is a long-time friend of the Earl, who when she first met him thought he was called the Eel of Seacliff. Recently he presented Michael with one of his Kapisi T shirts, with an inscription to Michael from King Kapisi.

Signed Overstayer T shirt for Michael O'Leary from King Kapisi

Chris Knox

Chris Knox is something of a living legend in New Zealand. Since the Invercargill born misfit started Dunedin's first punk band The Enemy in 1977, Chris has always been centre-stage, and always been his own man. His CV is full of wonderful artistic endeavours, much of them, excluding his time leading Toy Love, one of New Zealand's most popular bands of the early '80s, created in the front room of a rambling Grey Lynn villa where Chris lives with his partner Barbara and kids John and Leisha. Michael O'Leary often ran into Knox on Queen Street, Auckland, in the 1980s, trying to distribute records and O'Leary trying to distribute books, and the two had a laugh together about the business of small press and small record company distribution and its similarities, and how they were each struggling in their own ways.

Livin' ina Aucklan'

Date of Publication: 1988
Publisher: ESAW
Category: Poetry

This is a funky little collection designed to capture the good things about Auckland in the 1980s to offset against the feeling of loss and emptiness felt at the end of an intense love affair. The idea of 'Mount Albert being just as important as Montmatre if you live there' pervades the whole collection. At the time O'Leary's friend John Pule was beginning to explore his artwork, having been known as a poet up to this point. He had done a Pacific Island version of a totem pole in O'Leary's Parimoana Bookshop in Kingsland so O'Leary asked him if he would be interested in illustrating his latest collection of poetry. The title *Livin' ina Aucklan'* reflects the language of the streets and the whole project was a coming together of the way they lived in those days. O'Leary, Pule and David Eggleton were out busking, and David and Michael were making artworks under the Earl of Seacliff label and selling them on the streets downtown during the weekend and on Friday nights. Forthcoming from ESAW will be a new edition of *Livin' ina Aucklan'* which will include a new sequence called 'Auckland Revisited' (from O'Leary's 2005 collection *Make Love and War*). In 2008 the poem 'Livin' ina Aucklan'' appeared in Stu Bagby's anthology of Auckland poetry, *JAFA (Just Another Fantastic Anthology)*.

London Notebook

Date of Publication: 2005
Publisher: ESAW
Category: Poetry

Mark Pirie's *London Notebook* presents a witty artist's sketchbook written whilst staying in Acton, London, and later revised in Wellington, New Zealand. It comprises anecdotes, images, photos and jottings of his travels around London, Paris and Cambridge, England. Poet Michael Harlow wrote of it:

> Meant as an artist's sketchbook, it provides a brief traveller's album of chance experiences and events', is aptly accurate to practice in this latest collection by poet and editor Mark Pirie. Briefs and letter- poems and post-card snaps, and the occasional *apercu* - like a passing messenger-bird snatched from the air - comprise an album of observations and reflections that remind us how it is travel can sometimes return you to yourself. And in ways that keep the reader alert to more than just field-notes and diary jottings. Pirie, at the top of his form, can be sharp-witted, tender, sometimes even loitering with the best kind of intent at the very edge of the ordinary. When he's on his 'mark', as it were, he can open up and extend the everyday in ways that matter beyond the brief encounter and the passing glance.

Review of Mark Pirie's *London Notebook*

Presenting Pirie's new collection as 'a witty artist's sketchbook', the publisher's press release expands: 'Hundreds of New Zealanders travel to London each year for a holiday or for their big "OE". Written in the spirit of this social 'pilgrimage' is [Pirie's] new collection.' 'OE' is in speech marks: it's the authentic voice. Overseas Experience is real, valuable. 'Pilgrimage', however; is in scare quotes. We're not to take it seriously. Instead, we should realise Pirie is aware of the term's misuse in a secular, postcolonial context. He's *not* on a spiritual journey to the land of his literary/cultural origins; the overseas voyage won't yield the final maturation of the artistic self. If we accept the publicity puff, the notebook is a more consciously bathetic enterprise than it might seem. Describing the collection as a sketchbook highlights incompletion, immediacy. A sketch is a rough, unpretentious outline, especially one intended as the basis for something else. The collection does have a dashed-off, diary style: it reads like a series of notes-to-self along the trip. As Terry Locke has said elsewhere, Pirie celebrates inconsequence. He catches the downbeat moments, the typical post-modern failure to achieve epiphany. See 'First Glimpse' on seeing England from a plane:

> have you been here before?
> no, this is my first time
> well, then, welcome to our country
> we hope you enjoy your stay!

The language consciously avoids difficulty; it's public and democratic in that sense. The effect is often of overhearing phatic chatter between people on a bus. These are poems of thinking aloud, of first undigested impressions, where irony isn't so much the internal stance as the general spirit of the age, and so the tone in which we're meant to read the works. It's poetry about how little people have to say, when finally confronted with sites of cultural/artistic pilgrimage, as in these lines from 'Visiting Graves':

> *5 Apollinaire*
>
> well, Guillaume, this is nice!
> most beautiful, well-kept
>
> I think I like yours best
> it's no telephone box-tardis
>
> but it's nicely done

a quote from the poetry too,

always a nice touch!

One angle on the banalities: they deliberately mock the varieties of 'nothing' tourists produce when racing through a checklist of must-sees. A pitfall of this conversational, un-emphatic style, however, is that the poems might seem as off-the-cuff as the mutterings of their personae. (Pirie reworked the notebook in Wellington: the style aimed for, then, is artfully tousled/designer ripped.) There is humour in understatement, yes, or in undercutting grand gestures and impulses towards rhetorical flourishes. But if we always go seeking the bathetic, if every moment is underplayed what are we building, separately or together? 'Traffic jams - big ones! / Crowds - *big ones!*' ('Discoveries'). Perhaps that's Pirie's point. The collection might be another warning - like *Dumber* (2003) - against the idiocy of mass culture. For some poems do burn through the conscious numbness of the rest of the book. One example: 'The Photographer' (from 'Framing') is intensely visual, and works as an intra-genre rhyme for its accompanying photograph. Another, 'The Deadwatch', shows a stronger sense of technique, using assonance, occasional rhyme. Its couplets step carefully down the page, much as the speaker navigates deliberately past the homeless. It bears the effects of witnessing misery's erosions, despite the speaker's attempts to avoid them:

You pass; you don't look; it's that simple
I mean, if you look, you might catch their faces,

you might catch their sores, around their beards,
their shabby clothes. Usually they don't look up.

Instead they sit for hours with their head in hands,
a note on the ground: PLEASE SPARE SOME CHANGE.

Pirie is astonishingly prolific, an enthusiastic performer, and a generous, inclusive editor. His best poems make me wonder whether he could be more generous to himself: allow more time to mull, and drive himself less furiously to publish. – *Emma Neale*

(From *New Zealand Books*, Volume 16, Number 3, August 2006)

Magic Alex's Revenge

Date of Publication: 2009
Publisher: ESAW
Category: Fiction

Magic Alex's Revenge is the final instalment of Michael O'Leary's trilogy, *The Dreamlander Express*. Following on from the first two parts, *Unlevel Crossings* and *Straight*, *Magic Alex's Revenge* is a complex and often beguiling look at the 'Sixties' generation of peace and love and anti- materialism degenerated into the 'I, me, mine' selfishness sparked by the mid-eighties Rogernomics which continues into the 21st Century Schizoid Person, fuelled by technology and greed.

Last Ride on the Dreamlander Express
(Launch speech for Magic Alex's Revenge)

i

Having launched the first two volumes in this trilogy of publications I take great pleasure in launching the third and final volume, *Magic Alex's Revenge.*

I did not write the blurb on the back cover. I don't know who did. But it is a good one.

I say of C K Stead that he has written some excellent examples of the C K Stead novel. And I say something similar, that in *Magic Alex's Revenge* Michael O'Leary has in fact written the finest example of the Michael O'Leary novel. Take on board what it is you are dealing with and you will appreciate that it is done superlatively, every word of it. My commendation of this book is full on, as you see.

Many people of Michael O'Leary's generation and later have tried to write a novel in what might be called a post-modernist way. I have not looked at such novels from James Joyce down, but it seems to me that Michael O'Leary has made a success of this mode of fiction simply by working harder and longer than most people, 30 years at least on this book. I recognise that there are many significant resemblances in Michael O'Leary's work to my own work. So Michael O'Leary is in good company.

ii

You have to come to this book understanding what you are dealing with.

The pattern is simple. A man thinks he is working in London. A man returns to his roots and Auckland and learns about or remembers goings on in his lifetime back to childhood. At least the focus is on such a run of episodes however real they are or whoever they apply to.

Magic Alex's Revenge i.e. the character's revenge is the situation in which we live and which we all face in future, for which he takes responsibility and perhaps we should too. Michael O'Leary informs me this is made clear in the last sentence on page 11.

Much of this book is written at the point where history and fantasy collide, so the question is whose history and whose fantasy.

The simplest answer is given at pages 57-72 where there are repeated references to Bishop Liston who was tried for sedition in New Zealand in 1922.

Throughout this passage sentences from the legal defence of Bishop Liston are interwoven with more recent events in Auckland. I don't know whether the legal defence is taken from historical documents, or is a reconstruction or is a parody or satire, whatever.

iii

I have pointed out that every work of art needs signposting to direct the attention of the reader/observer wherever so that they can keep their bearings.

Michael O'Leary does signpost Magic Alex's Revenge by the devise of email headings, which for instance signpost a cricket match across pages 72-127 and an episode of geographical confusion across pages 148-183.

When the signs change you can say the subject matter changes.

I have said that to those who know Michael O'Leary's writings they all hang together and cross-illuminate one another. So here much of this novel draws together material previously published separately, as in the page references I have just given you as well as elsewhere. Included is some of Michael O'Leary's finest prose and verse writing, material that has been widely and highly acclaimed.

On page 49 a prose passage begins. The last train is about to leave etc. On page 171 you will find the same text as a poem. This is an extreme example of how everything hangs together in Michael O'Leary's writings. It is a good example that you sense you have been here before is justified. Both times however this is an impressive piece of writing.

But there is also considerable new material in the book.

There are a few misprints in the book, but most of what you have got there is what Michael O'Leary intends.

iv

What I have given you are some hints on how to find your way through Michael O'Leary's new book, *Magic Alex's Revenge*. All you have to do now is buy a copy and get thoroughly lost in it. It is worth the money and the effort to do so. [You will find you are dealing with a brilliant piece of literature according to the Earl of Seacliff].

Now I have told you all you need to cope with the book as I also was able to do with understanding and pleasure page by page all through. Michael O'Leary doubts whether he will add any more prose fiction to his corpus. But what he presents in the Dreamlander Express is a significant achievement for those who can to match. – *F W N Wright*

Mahones

Date of Publication: 2005
Publisher: ESAW Category: Poetry
Contributors: Bill Dacker, Michael O'Leary, Mark Pirie and Iain Sharp

Review of *Mahones: Four Poets*

Writing about Joni Mitchell's 'Woodstock' in her 2005 book *Break Blow Burn,* Camille Paglia states: 'In the 1960s, young people who might once have become poets took up the guitar and turned troubadour.' Today it is the rock star that cultivates the bad boy persona that, borne out of the era of romanticism, poets once had. Rock stars rather than poets are now likely to be 'mad, bad and dangerous to know'; I like to think the equivalent of Lord Byron and Lady Caroline Lamb these days might be Tommy Lee and Pamela Anderson.

This anthology gives a nod towards this idea. It is another in the series of 'album cover' book covers by Michael O'Leary and Mark Pirie - this time a take-off of the Ramones' album Anthology. On the cover, instead of the four Ramones, it's the four poets, Bill Dacker, Michael O'Leary, Mark Pirie and Iain Sharp, in Ramones dress and stance. Lined up in exaggerated imitation of the original cover, the poets aren't taking themselves too seriously; it's a humorous take on the original.

Each of the four parts of the book is named from a song from the album. However, in content, only Pirie's poetry really seems to suit the concept, both in style and in the youthfulness and urban disaffectedness he writes about. The other poets reach further back in the past such as with Dacker's 'Didactic Goldmining' and O'Leary's 'Farewell to the Hotel Paekakariki'.

Dacker seems to write in a generalised style that keeps the reader at a distance. The 'The Three Brothers' opens 'They avoided the throng to approved / slaughter (so avoiding that trauma) / by age or some blemish that never / turned a bullet fired true by any / .....'; there are few specifics that make the individuality of these lives come into focus. And although

O'Leary and Sharp are more specific and Sharp more entertaining, I often found myself wondering why they had divided their lines and stanzas just where they did. To my mind, there were often surprisingly prosy rhythms for an anthology where the reader is inevitably going to make the association between poetry and music, whether of songwriters being the poets of today or the poetic forms that have come from the troubadours and minstrels of the past.

The Earl of Seacliff website describes the publication as follows: 'Functioning as a type of side project to the poet's more traditional individual collections, this collaborative project allows the poets to test the water with experimental and rare works just like the form of the music EP where bands often release unusual rarities or B-sides along with their hit singles.'

The album cover idea lets poetry bask a little in the reflected glamour of its more exciting rock songwriting relatives. It's a good way to do an anthology, with each poet seemingly 'representing' a band member, and it's attractive and witty presentation.

However, perhaps because the album conceit wasn't sustained throughout the content or perhaps because the quality did seem variable, I ended up feeling a bit disappointed. – *Anne Tucker*

(From the *New Zealand Poetry Society Newsletter*, August 2006)

Mahones cover, photo by John Girdlestone

"Make Love and War"

Date of Composition: 2004
Collection: *Make Love and War*

The title 'Make Love and War' is an abandonment by O'Leary of his generation's simplistic slogan 'Make Love Not War'. It is about the Iraq war and contrasts the war going on at the moment with a love affair O'Leary had been involved in. O'Leary writes: 'The references to the Viet Nam war come from a friend of mine who fought there and is totally critical of the US and New Zealand governments' hypocritical stance on the war in the first place and then of the treatment of the Viet Nam veterans subsequently. He says at least the Nazis were more up-front and honest about their aims. Jesus said "there will always be wars and rumours of wars" and it is true in personal relationships as well as international relations between countries and cultures.'

Make Love and War

Date of Publication: 2005
Publisher: HeadworX Category: Poetry

The cover design of O'Leary's collection *Make Love and War* by Mark Pirie was an emulation of the Price Milburn edition of Baxter's *Jerusalem Sonnets.* It was an acknowledgement of Baxter's influence on O'Leary becoming a writer through his encouragement of O'Leary as a young man.

Make Love and War was a collection that was particularly pleasing to O'Leary as it covered many aspects of his writing housed in a very aesthetically stylish manner and incorporates several of his drawings.

Mark Houlahan, in the *Dominion Post,* wrote that: 'Michael O'Leary's *Make Love and War* (HeadworX) mixes ballad and elegies with notebook poems, observing local disasters, such as the Paekakariki floods and the sad demise of long-distance passenger trains. The final section here, 'Re-appearing and Disappearing Railroad Blues', takes us up the main trunk, with snapshots (like the old folk song) of each stop on the line. The last poem of all takes the last journey of the night train from Auckland to Wellington, denouncing the death of the Northerner as a "piece of corporate vandalism".'

Another great event around this volume is the fact that fellow poet L E Scott read the title poem 'Make Love and War' on the State Television Arts programme when he visited Cuba for an international poetry festival a couple of years ago, the equivalent of having it read on TV1's *Artsville* show.

The Manuka Tree

Date of Publication: 2005

Publisher: ESAW

Category: Poetry

Contributors: Alistair Te Ariki Campbell, Meg Campbell, Bill Dacker, Robin Fry, Tim Jones, Scott Kendrick, Therese Lloyd, Joy MacKenzie, Harvey McQueen, Amelia Nurse, Michael O'Leary, Mark Pirie, Vivienne Plumb, Helen Rickerby, Harry Ricketts, L E Scott, Iain Sharp, Yilma Tafare Tasew, Richard von Sturmer, Moira Wairama and F W N Wright.

The Manuka Tree is a collection of poems celebrating the Winter Readings at St John's Church Community Room, Wellington, presented by HeadworX, ESAW, and Kwanzaa - The Afrikan Shop, in conjunction with Writers International (the first multi-ethnic writers group in Wellington), 4 August-24 August 2005. Edited and compiled by Mark Pirie, the anthology is dedicated to the Irish band U2. The book's front cover photo is by John Girdlestone and is after the U2 album cover *The Joshua Tree*.

"Meeting with Te Rauparaha"

'Meeting with Te Rauparaha' is a poem from Michael O'Leary's collection *Make Love and War* (HeadworX). It was written in 2005, and was illustrated by John Pule on one of his Wellington visits. The photograph was taken by Martin Schanzel. The text of the poem is below:

Meeting with Te Rauparaha

The early evening finds me
Emerging from the water
At Paekakariki Beach
After swimming long and deep

The late summer colours
Cover the sky and the hills
I am alternately looking from
Land to the seaward visage

Towards and beyond Kapiti
My eyes straight to the horizon:
He stands suddenly beside me
He has heard I am with

A Raukawa girl, and he gives me
A distant, yet easy blessing
The beach towel over my shoulder
Becomes his korowai as a koha

So, the great man who haunts
This coast has visited me
In friendship and aroha, and
When I look away, he is gone

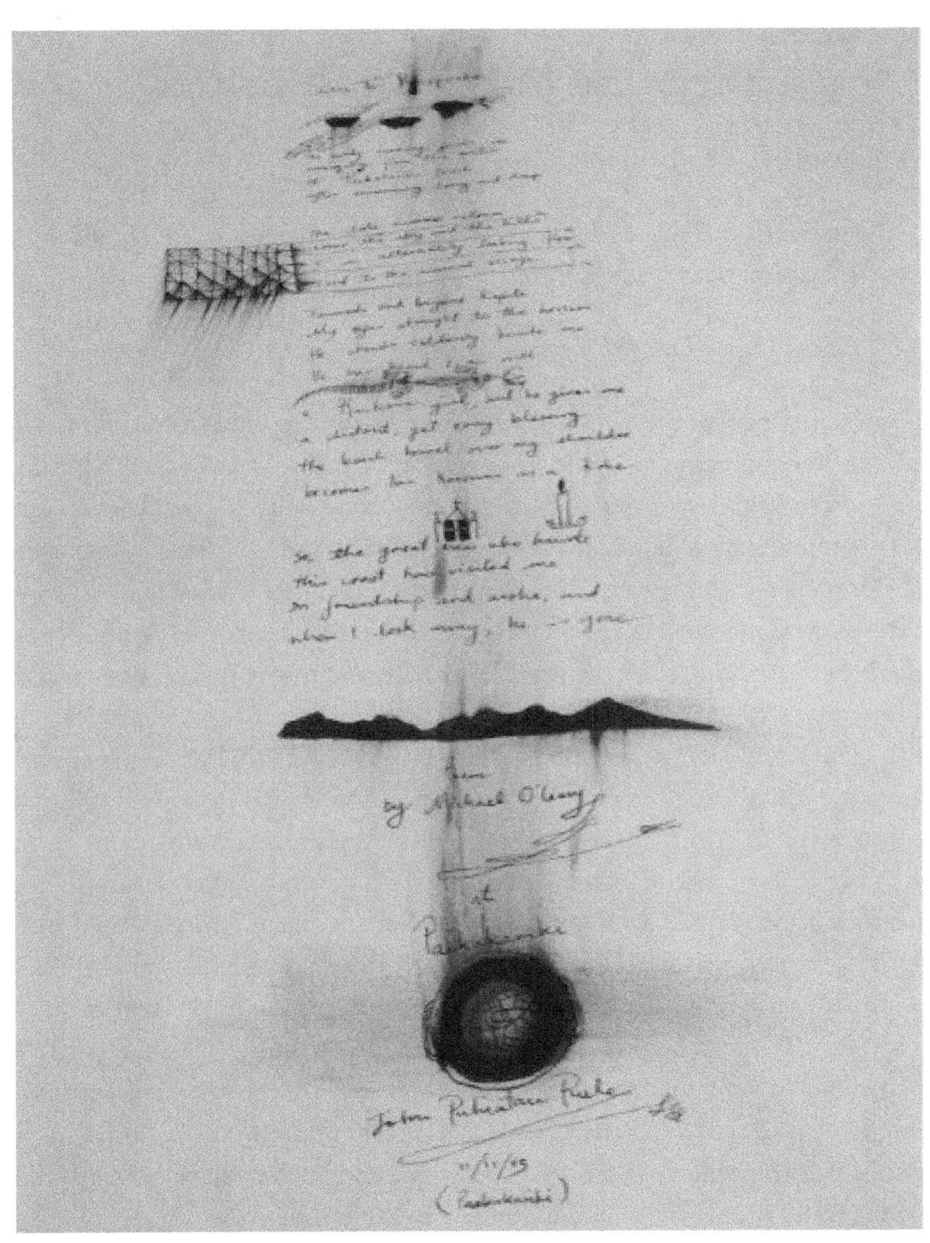

John Pule's artwork incorporating the poem 'Meeting with Te Rauparaha'

"The Mind of My Lai Revisited"

Date of Composition: 2001

Collection: *Toku Tinihanga: Selected Poems 1982-2002, TAB Ula Rasa: New and Selected Poems*

Anthologised in: *Wellington Sonnets*

For the first part of the 1980s in Auckland the poetry scene was dominated by the weekly readings at the Globe Hotel run by David Mitchell. They were often raucous affairs full of fun, *bonhomie*, with a crowd who were very supportive, if somewhat drunk. O'Leary and his friends cut their performance teeth at these Rabelaisian gatherings and David Mitchell always played *mein host* with fairness and flair. Mitchell had made a big impact on the New Zealand literary scene with his first, and only, book, *Pipedreams in Ponsonby* in 1972 which was published by Stephen Chan with artwork by Pat Hanly, and later reprinted by Trevor Reeves' Caveman Press. The Earl wrote a sonnet for David Mitchell, 'The Mind of My Lai Revisited'. O'Leary comments: 'The poem 'The Mind of My Lai Revisited' was written not long ago when I saw David Mitchell in Oriental Parade in Wellington. I had heard that he was not well but I got a real shock when I encountered him, so deteriorated in mind and body. I always felt that he had been treated with neglect by the New Zealand literary elite and this is the sentiment of the poem. It also has a bit of a dig at the 'radicals' of the 1960s and 1970s becoming part of the system they so despised.' The poem was awarded a 'Highly Commended' in the recent Wellington Sonnet competition. ESAW published, through their poetry mini-series, the booklet showcasing the 13 winners and highly commended sonnets in the competition.

Music Therapy

Date of Publication: 2001
Publisher: ESAW
Category: Poetry

Review of Peter Olds' *Music Therapy*

Music Therapy by Peter Olds is from Michael O'Leary's Seacliff stable of impressive small-run limited editions. This is a well-produced and sensitive collection, written after a 'long illness'. Olds has been around for a number of years, but was most prominent in the '70s as a recipient of Baxter's verse epistles ('Have a wank for me, on the grass, beside the varsity', *Letter to Peter Olds, Verse 7*) and also with his V8 and Beat poems that roared their way through the country, dosed up heavy on mandrax. I still have a copy of his *Freeway* collection (Caveman Press, 1974): a very cool, nicely produced journey of lines. This book is perhaps mellower than his early collections; the beast has been nullified. These are thoughts of a different and much older man.

Divided into three sections, the book opens with a convincing series of reflections on life, outside of the 'mad city'. The poet here is living in a hut in Seacliff (next door to a closed-down mental hospital) overrun with mice. The opening poem 'Letter from Seacliff' echoes Louis Johnson's 'The Mouse' in its descriptions of mice removal, and indeed the first section captures something of the demeanour of Stephen Oliver's evocative *& Interviews* poems (1978), similarly set in the Dunedin coastal area.

The poems are rich in their descriptions: 'No patient's names / are carved on these trees / old man's beard / where the names should be' - a kind of hip New Zealand version of Henry David Thoreau's famous cabin-in-the-woods prose:

> For tea tonight I think I'll have
> stuffed marrow
> baked over a pinecone fire
> in the new fireplace made with bricks

from cow gully swamp -

washed down
with ragwort wine.
('Uncovering the Hospital')

These poems are picking over old bones, 'the ghosts of mental patients', and are written from personal experience and historical knowledge of our asylums.

Section Two, in contrast, focuses on group therapy in the city, Dunedin, and it's a kind of blues written with empathy for those who have undergone and survived that therapy. This is something done powerfully elsewhere in the writings of Janet Frame for instance or more recently in the poetry of Jenny Powell (*Sweet Banana Wax Peppers,* 1998) and Simon Williamson (*Storyteller,* 2002). Olds's take in *Music Therapy* is, like these books, a significant addition to our writing on mental illness:

'How was therapy?'

I don't stay long
I never do –
I'm like a child
running across your lawn
chasing unidentified lights.
('The Broken Houses')

The third and final section opens with a rhythmically charged poem, 'Night Fishing':

Full moon off
pipi point
writing this
with coat hood up

sound of train
in the dark

slippery mud
pontoon blood

on the jetty
night fishing
sound of men
laughing

plastic bucket
brighter eyes
crabs' fingers
climbing lines

wet black wood
yellow light
over there
a wading bird

shrill calls
above light
up there
beyond night

sudden yell
in the dark
something there
something caught

ghostly laughter
colder wind
sound of water
going home.

Note the use of shorter, non-punctuated lines. There is the use of rhyme
here to carry the force of the rhythm: 'mud/blood', 'fishing/laughing', 'light/
night'. It is a technically impressive piece, and serves as a warning to those

critics who might view Olds as a mere Beat poet of the '70s, with little technical trickery. There is clear evidence here in this simple but effective poem of Olds's staying power, of a dedicated craftsman at work. It is a poem comparable to those of the much-loved Brian Turner and his successful brand of Deep South writing.

The final poems, like the first section that observes from a hut window, are evocative, dealing often with deaths, and the book ends fittingly with the 'arrival of the annual carwrecker's get together'.

Visions of Bruno Lawrence in *Smash Palace* perhaps, but no, just 'Hairless men & toothpick women / in skin & leathers / erect[ing] their tent between beach flags - / We fuck anything that moves'. Here the 'sea is a mass of vibrating radiators / & dismembered elderly.' This *is* a satisfying read. Nice to see Olds back in book form. There is much to celebrate here for serious readers of New Zealand poetry. – *Mark Pirie*

(From *JAAM* 18, October 2002)

"The National Anthem of Ocussi-Ambeno"

Date of Composition: 1984
Collection: *Toku Tinihanga: Selected Poems 1982-2002, Ka Atu I Kopua*
Anthologized in: *JAAM 21 "Greatest Hits"*

In the 1970s and 1980s anarchist Bruce Grenville and his followers were the masterminds behind an extraordinary hoax involving the creation of an imaginary state: Occussi-Ambeno. The anarchist group behind the hoax chose the island of Timor as the location for their fictional country. There was actually an area called Occussi-Ambeno on the north-west coast of the island. Originally a Portuguese enclave in the Dutch-held western half of the island, Occussi-Ambeno disappeared officially from our maps when the Indonesians invaded East Timor in 1975. With little more than this as a starting point, Grenville and his comrades proceeded to create a state with its own unique history and bureaucracy. They invented a succession of rulers going back to 1848, when seven tribes united for protection from the interloping Portuguese. Independence was achieved in 1968 and from then the seven provinces had full internal autonomy. The scam took off in earnest when its creators began to print stamps, letterheads and other material. In the early 1970s articles began to appear in British and American philatelic magazines about Occussi-Ambeno and its stamps, and some income was generated through the mail-order sale of stamps. Diplomatic relations were established with a number of other tiny states, including Monaco and Liechtenstein. In the 1980s Michael O'Leary, as Poet Laureate, was invited to write the National Anthem for Occussi-Ambeno which was then recorded by the Massed Choir of the Sultanate of Occussi-Ambeno.

Nice Nazis

This was a Punk/Reggae band that the Earl was lead 'shouter' for in the Auckland of the 1980s. They had a drummer, a bass guitarist, and Jeremy Dart was their lead guitarist and wrote the music for the words. They made one tape, the lyrics of which were taken from the Earl's 1987 poetry collection *Livin' ina Aucklan'*, such as the iconic 'Russian Roulette'. Unfortunately, due to the often-dissolute lifestyle of the Earl and his Seacliff Mafia comrades, this gem of recorded archive is no longer with us. O'Leary writes: 'The name comes from the internal conflict within the band and within myself over what to call a band which was meant to represent the anarchic spirit of 'punk' mixed with the mellow good vibes of reggae, not to mention the philosophical and spiritual struggle between good and evil. So it's "Nice Nazis", already!!!'

Notes from Underground

Date of Publication: 2007
Publisher: ESAW
Category: Art Book

Notes from Underground is a photography book by Nigel Yates. It includes a few photographs of Michael O'Leary, including a photo of Michael with his friend Winsome Aroha. Gemma Claire wrote a poem- response to one of Yates' photos. The poem was written on the Poetrywall at Winter Readings in 2007. Later it was published in the ESAW *Poetrywall* anthology:

Photo on p. 22 of Nigel Yates' *Notes from Underground*

He's firmly belted into a wheelchair,
a strap cutting into his skinny thighs.
He disconcerts the viewer with his stare;
mixed feelings are apparent in his eyes.

He seems to know he has Yates' attention
for reasons beyond gratuitousness.
Stirring pity is not Yates' intention -
he strives to capture subjects' humanness.

He'll savour this decency while it's there -
most people either gawk or patronise.
But, he must know that such insight is rare,
hence, both delight and sadness in his eyes.

Due to Yates eschewing smug sympathy,
this photo exemplifies empathy.

Gemma Claire

O'Books

O'Books was Michael O'Leary's bookshop in the Octagon, Dunedin. (See under 'Dunedin years' for Bill Dacker's essay on the O'Books period.) It is also memorialised in Bill Dacker's poem:

O'Books

'O'Leary of O'Books, gathered survivors
of the new book gloss, to another reading'

The poet proprietor of O'Books knew
the truth the Irish poet sang, that no
better could be had than what old books told
and in his prime, at 10 the Octagon, set
himself as a trader in their tellings at a junction
of unlevel crossings where hazards of the soul

and himself contended with commerce
for right of way. Love entangled and trust
betrayed, Arohanui and trysts of a jokestar
could not balance and prices came down;

with the hustle and bustle of autumnal leaves
the old books sold for a song and he left town
with only sheafs of his own songs from all
those runarounds at a place of unlevel crossings
saving him from the madness of old men.

Bill Dacker

"Ōkāhu Bay"

Date of Composition: 1985

Collection: *Toku Tinihanga: Selected Poems 1982-2002, TAB Ula Rasa: New and Selected Poems, Con Art: Selected Poems, Livin' ina Aucklan'*

Ōkāhu Bay is a small bay on Auckland's inner harbour in the eastern suburb of Ōrākei where O'Leary grew up. O'Leary and his brother and sisters spent a lot of time at this beach, swimming and exploring and trying not to stand on stingrays. Ōrākei was an interesting suburb as there was the state housing areas where they lived interspersed with some of the richest people and real estate in the country. They had a two bedroomed house which housed seven of them, including their bed-ridden grandmother, so a lot of our time was spent outside, roaming the streets and at the playground just over the road from Ōkāhu Bay. This poem was written in 1985, years after O'Leary had left Ōrākei after his parents both died in 1968. O'Leary returned there one evening to show an old girlfriend where he had grown up. It is a meditation on life and love and their impermanence, alongside the aspects of life that give us hope and a sense of belonging, both to people and places, and ultimately to eternity.

Peter Olds

Peter Olds was a close friend of Michael O'Leary during his Dunedin years. After Michael moved to Wellington, he requested a manuscript from Olds (*Music Therapy*) to kick-start his ESAW publishing operation after a break of a few years. Olds has published three further mini series collections through ESAW and has remained a strong supporter of Michael's work. Two poems that feature O'Leary are included below:

Adolf the Spider

(for Michael O'Leary)

My name is Adolf,
I live outside Peter's back door
high in the corner of the porch.
I pay no rent -
each morning I raise my leg in a Hitler salute.

No one bothers me -
I catch only the odd unsuspecting fly
in my intricate swastika-shaped web.
I sleep all day
high in the corner of the dark porch.

I love the fat, juicy moths.
Moths have no brains -
the mob instinct drives them -
they stick to my swastika-shaped web blinking
night after cold night.

My name is Adolf the spider -
I live in a cruel, tangled
web of deceit -
no one bothers me.

Each morning I raise my leg in a Hitler salute.

The life of an outsider is a lonely life.

Watching a Friend on the 'Southerner' Speed Through Seacliff Heading North

And there was Michael standing
on the observation platform at the end
of the carriage, happy as a sandboy,
waving and whooping like a Red Indian
(or a smiling Duke after a successful tour
of the provinces): a dark bearded train-buddha
speeding through Seacliff crossing connected
all the way by wires (over Cook Strait)
to magical Auckland where he was headed.
And I yelled Hurrah! involuntarily like a kid
bursting with love, anxiety and hot lungs –
like when the young Queen in 1953 on tour
around the country swished by (at Milton)
in her black open-top car and my brother
nearly fainting from madness and adoration.
And afterwards (no cows to drive home) –
dawdling up the gravel road carrying my
penny flag - quiet because school
and the town were closed for the day
and life was suddenly empty
with so much happening
and not understanding
what it was all about.

Clare O'Leary

Clare O'Leary is Michael O'Leary's younger sister. She is a film-maker and artist herself, having produced the documentary film on Michael King. The film was premiered at the 2007 Wellington International Film Festival and was shown on Māori TV in April 2009. She is currently making a documentary film about her brother, Michael. She wrote the following biographical piece especially for this book:

My Brother Michael

In 1968 my father died of a cerebral haemorrhage. My mother died of a heart-attack six months later. My two brothers (Michael and Gerrard) and my sister Tricia and I were orphaned overnight.

We were taken in by our father's oldest brother and his wife - they already had six kids so it was not an easy move. We lost contact with our mother's family and never heard from them again. Michael was 17, the oldest, and I was 8, the youngest.

Michael left home in his early twenties, feeling the pressure of our uncle's conservative Catholicism and he got into the uni scene in Ponsonby then, soon after, went to live in Dunedin. We lost touch for several years until 1977 when I decided to find him.

I was accepted into nursing in 1977 and had a month between leaving school to have a holiday - so my best mate Stella and I planned a South Island trip. I was determined to track down my brother Michael who I hadn't seen for several years - he moved to Dunedin - and it was like he fell off the face of the earth!

After catching buses, trains and hitch-hiking we cruised into Dunedin – found a uoth hostel, dumped our heavy packs and went exploring.

I headed for the biggest music shop I could find and walked up to the girl behind the counter... 'I don't suppose you know Michael O'Leary do you?...' 'Yes, everyone kmows Michael,' she said... 'he'll be in the Cook...' - it's dole day, they all come in on Thursdays.'

So, the famous Captain Cook Hotel ... I couldn't believe it was so easy ... after all this time - I knew it would be a shock to him, the last time he saw me I was really a little girl ... of 12 maybe ... now, at 17 I was launching into a new career, life, everything... I wondered if he'd even recognise me!

As the evening closed in, Stella and I found the Captain Cook Hotel and went in ... we asked a few people and they pointed towards the back of the bar. There were a lot of people sitting around jugs of beer and whiskeys ... long hair, big black coats and there, in the centre of it all was my brother.

In those days he looked like Rasputin, long black hair, long black beard, his dark black eyes and crazy look in his eye ... I walked up to him and said 'Hi, long time no see!' ... he just about fell out of his chair - then it was all on ... 'Hey bro, I didn't even know you had a sister' ...

Everyone welcomed us in then and it was a wild night of drinking, storytelling, student parties with loud music and all the time, I couldn't believe I was in the same place as my big brother ... he had found a new life that spoke to him and welcomed him in.

Stella and I spent the rest of the time out at Seacliff where he lived with Brian Hare - we met up with Winsome and Bill and the kids, Bryan Harold and Juanita Ketchell and Jules, Robin Swanney-McPherson and all the poets and writers and artists that surrounded them all.

Since that time, he has walked alongside me my whole life and introduced me to the wide variety of artists and writers who have surrounded him, the Earl of Seacliff Art Workshop.

Gerrard 0'Leary

Gerrard O'Leary is the Earl's younger brother. He was born in 1955 and grew up in Ōrākei. He has lived in Australia for most of his adult life and has a wife and four children. Gerrard has worked as a geologist and as a dancer in an Eastern European folk ensemble, where he met Tracy, his wife of many years now. He has taught in a Steiner School for several years in Northern New South Wales. Gerrard is also a talented singer and musician, and an artist. He recently did the art work for the Earl's latest novel, *Magic Alex's Revenge,* and has also contributed the cover painting and the title for the ESAW 25th Anniversary book *The Earl is in...*

Only a Bullet Will Stop Me Now

Date of Publication: 2004
Publisher: ESAW
Category: Poetry

Review of F W N Wright's *Only a Bullet Will Stop Me Now*

Niel Wright's *Only a Bullet Will Stop Me Now* is a re-issue of a work originally published in 1970. As a collection it's somewhat unusual since the bulk of the book consists of two large and very different epic works, with a few unrelated short poems and fragments of verse. The first of the long poems, *A Hero's Welcome,* appears to be the initial part of what in subsequent years has grown to become *The Alexandrians,* a vast epic re-telling of classical Greek legend. The book's somewhat bizarre jacket blurb praises Wright's prolific output, and states that *The Alexandrians* presently stands at 30,300 lines. Confronted with this kind of 'never-mind-the-quality-feel-the-width' endorsement, one is inclined to wonder about the possible literary merits of, say, Windows source code.

Fortunately, *A Hero's Welcome* (which tells the story of Theseus's reunion with his estranged father Aegeus) is highly readable. Wright's plain and economical style is a model of clarity. While there's little dramatic tension, and the somewhat flat verse ensures that this work will not engage the reader in the manner of an epic such as the *Kalevala,* the division of the work into short, tersely-titled sections: 'The Surprise', 'The Upshot', and 'The Welcome' provides a generous accessibility.

The second long poem, *The Sun Wheel,* subtitled 'a verse novella', is less straightforward. A huge sprawling poem, occupying more than half of the book, it centres on the death of a Canterbury top-dressing pilot, and its effect on his associates. The tone is reminiscent of Denis Glover's 'The Magpies', and certainly evokes the Cantabrian atmosphere giving a convincing sense of the lives of the doughty plainspeople. Divided into chapters with numbered verses, with a short epilogue and prologue, the verse-form changes to suit the writer's purpose. Like *The Alexandrians,* the language is straightforward.

The tone is largely cool and cerebral although on occasion disappointingly flat. For the most part the characters' actions and motivations are described by a detached narrator, but when they do speak directly Wright employs an interesting variety of techniques. Sometimes they converse in conventional dialogue. Sometimes they address the reader directly. On one occasion a conversation is presented as a form of stylized play script. This gives the poem an impressive texture and variety, and prevents it being overwhelmed by its sheer scale. These days you can get a good cappuccino in Darfield, and the world of *The Sun Wheel* can seem very distant. Nevertheless, the work has a timeless quality, and it's good to have the opportunity to read it all these years after its initial publication.

The few short poems which complete this collection reinforce the sense of Wright as a disciplined and plain-spoken poet, able to evoke images and ideas with an impressive economy of words. The one element not present in the longer poems is the occasional flash of playful wit. Whether this is in evidence in any of his later poetry I have no idea. As to the meaning of the collection's title, *Only a Bullet Will Stop Me Now*, and the significance of the truly awful cover illustration, the poet appears to provide no obvious clues. – *Joe Wylie*

(From *Takahe* 53 (2004), reprinted *Takahe* 54 (2005))

> " "
>
> '... an interesting museum piece ... The stultifying conformity of Kiwi culture appears to be [Wright's] principal theme (in this instalment of his work, at any rate), and one can't help agreeing with him there!' – Jack Ross, *brief*

O'oops Gallery

O'oops Gallery was the gallery run by Michael O'Leary and Bryan Harold downstairs in their O'Books bookshop in the Octagon, Dunedin. It was so named as the stairwell was reasonably hazardous to walk down. The gallery features in Jenny Powell's poem below:

The Earl of Seacliff Travels from the Octagon to Tokyo

i
Eight sides of the city
converging in his book shop
basement.

Exhibition of Seacliff,
Lionel Terry and the yellow
peril.

Evidence of captured
insanity in tender plots of
vegetables.

Extended lines of lunacy
squinting from barred
windows.

Each time now, this wild
eyed memory climbs the
stairs.

ii
Tokyo central and yakisoba
cooked with greengrocer
vegetables.

Trailing fat noodles damp

on his chin, the taste bitter
sweet.

Trees weary with tourists
lean over his avenue, their
palette

troubled by pale pinks
and grey from a wood block
print.

Tumbling wisteria drapes
over subdued blossom on his
wall.

– Jenny Powell

Author's Note: A long time ago now I went to a wonderful art exhibition of paintings by Ivan Hill (one of New Zealand's few naive-style artists). It was held downstairs in Michael's O'Books bookshop at O'oops Gallery in the lower Octagon of Dunedin. The poem begins with this exhibition, which was the first time I met Michael.

After hearing my Vietnamese poems in Wellington, Michael told me about his Tokyo poem, 'Songs of a Tokio Greengrocer', and how he too was imagining being in another place. I wanted to take him back to Tokyo in the second part of the poem.

Crosses christen new gallery

When Dunedin artist Hardwicke Knight saw the space destined to become a new gallery downstairs from O'Books in the Octagon, he knew he wanted to exhibit there.

As a result, Knight's exhibition 'Vita, Vita, Vita' is the first show to open in the new O'oops Gallery.

The images are of wayside crosses in Cornwall, England, which the artist photographed in the 1930s.

'They're symbols of life more abandoned - some of them originated as fertility symbols in an earlier religious era,' Mr Knight says.

Mr Knight searched for these symbols - some were on the wayside, others had been taken into churchyards, 'where, unlike the gravestones which commemorate death, these crosses are redolent with life,' he says.

'I cannot bring away with me the grave stones, but in photographing them I bring away the quintessence which I can share, and in which I find an inspiration for life.'

The term 'vita' refers to life. 'The reason why I've called it that is photography is a refining, a distilling. Photography which is expressive is looking for a meaning, an essence, or quintessence.'

The exposed stone wall in the O'oops Gallery provides a great setting for Knight's images.

'As soon as I saw this place and I knew it was going to be open as a gallery, it clicked. I felt it could be most expressive for my work.'

Although the 80-year-old showed two exhibitions of his current and past works at the Otago Early Settlers Museum over the last couple of years, he has not had an exhibition of photographs from his extensive collection for some time.

The images in 'Vita, Vita, Vita' were taken on a Fothderby camera with an astigmate lens, using VP size films.

'I want to emphasise that they are symbols, that a photographer, by photographing these crosses they become emphasised as symbols - or icons.

'Because they are symbols of life, they inspire me and I would be happy if they inspired others.'

'I'm sure people will enjoy coming down here to see them, it's a bit of an adventure coming down here anyway.'

Mr Knight's comment refers to the steep staircase, from which the gallery gets its name.

The bookshop owners, Michael O'Leary and Bryan Harold saw the potential in the area as a gallery space, although it required a lot of work.

'It was always going to be part of our concept and it's good having this space in the Octagon,' Mr O'Leary says.

'We were going to call it the Dunedin Central Art Gallery, for a joke, to beat the Dunedin City Council to the Octagon.'

The owners are interested in developing the Octagon into more than just banks or commercial buildings.

'It's an extra revenue thing as well. The bookshop's doing all right, although it's taken a lot of time and money to get the gallery to this stage.'

Messrs O'Leary and Harold have been approached by several artists keen to use the space, and it is now booked up until Christmas.

'It's really good starting off with an exhibition by Hardwicke - it sets a standard we're going to keep, but we want to be flexible with the concept of art,' O'Leary says.

The next users are a group of women putting on the 'Mothers of Invention' exhibition and performance, starting on November 1 to November 8.

And appropriately to O'Leary's heritage, the Irish Gaelic-speaking language classes will be held in the space. It is not surprising either that the Irish music group, Blackthorn, played at the 'Vita' opening.

Hardwicke Knight's exhibition remains on show to the end of October.
– Lee Harris

(From *Otago Daily Times,* 22 October 1991)

"Oscar Wilde Park"

Date of Composition: 2000

Collection: *Toku Tinihanga: Selected Poems 1982-2002, TAB Ula Rasa: New and Selected Poems*

The occasion of this poem was the placing of a plaque renaming the old law court's park 'Oscar Wilde Park'. This was the brainchild of bookseller and bibliophile John Quilter, whose antiquarian and second hand bookshop is at the lower end of Lambton Quay not far from Wellington Railway Station, and who has among his personal collection a book signed by Oscar Wilde which he bought in London. This establishes him as a genuine devotee of the much maligned Irish playwright, poet and scholar. O'Leary and his friends in the literary and book fraternity cheered as the plaque was fastened to the concrete wall, before heading across the road to drink to Oscar's memory, some of them having very little memory the following day of what happened on that day. In the poem O'Leary evokes a little of Wilde's tragic twists and turns and his ultimate triumph as a writer and as a human being. This in the face of an adversary who had no compunction about hitting below the belt despite the basic gentlemanly rules of boxing forbidding such practice being named after him: to wit, Queensbury. Ten years ago O'Leary and his friends celebrated John Quilter's twentieth anniversary as a Wellington bookseller. Now they are able to confirm his thirtieth year, 2009.

"Oscar Wilde Place"

Park Plaque too Wilde for WCC

It would have made Oscar Wilde's day. A mysterious, well-crafted plaque appearing on an inner-city Wellington wall announcing 'Oscar Wilde Place' - but no-one seeming to know where it came from.

Wilde, the Irish wit and writer who died a century ago this year, would have enjoyed the fuss. As he said: 'There is only one thing in the world worse than being talked about, and that is not being talked about.'

The plaque, on a wall outside Justice Park - on the corner of Lambton Quay and Ballance Street, has been passed unnoticed by hundreds of pedestrians in the past few months. Now, though, it's caused a bit of a stir for Wellington City Council and the Department for Courts, which owns the Park.

Behind the mysterious monument is Lambton Quay bookshop owner, John Quilter, of Quilter's Books.

'A group of us just wanted to have a memorial to Oscar Wilde as a seminal 20th century figure,' he said. 'The park has no name, no icons, no legends ... we created one.'

Mr Quilter said the choice of the park had nothing to do with its reputation as a gay haunt - it was simply an 'unnamed place ... It has a pleasant ambience and it seem a good place to give the name to.'

And it certainly wasn't done in the dead of night. A champagne unveiling ceremony was held on a Saturday afternoon about three months ago, with local poet Michael O'Leary providing suitable verse, but Mr Quilter concedes it hasn't generated much public attention.

But alas, no approval was sought for erecting the plaque. Courts spokesman, Barry Ebert, said the courts would not be acting to remove the plaque.

'Whether it stays or goes is a matter for Wellington City Council.'

It has reportedly already been dubbed, 'the park which dares not speak its name' by Cr Alick Shaw, but council spokesman Richard MacLean said the sign would indeed probably have to go. 'It's all about the importance of avoiding confusion on the issue of street names,' he said.

Wilde, of course, would have had an appropriate comment on hand: 'Arguments are to be avoided; they are always vulgar and often convincing.' Mr MacLean was sympathetic.

'We desperately want to avoid a vulgar conclusion to this issue. But the short and sad answer is that the sign may have to come down unless there are some very good reasons for it to stay up.' – *Steve Rendle*

Oscar Wilde Park
We come here at three o'clock, when saviours die
A portentous time of day, neither
With the light full of midday sun
Nor the blackness of night either
But it seems fitting to celebrate the plaque
At the juncture between light and dark

For it is at such a point
Where Oscar lived his wild life
At once the proud father to a son
And constant husband to a loving wife
Then a darker, more dangerous side embarks
On 'a love which dares not speak its name,' but hark

The truth lies somewhere in between
The degenerate and uplifting aspect
Of this great and fallen man's compassion
And his very neglect gains our respect
For showing us the two poles of light and dark
For his killing of what he loved we use this plaque
To commemorate his humanity, who heard the lark
Sing, when others only saw mud - I give you
Oscar Wilde Park

Out of It

Date of Publication: 1987
Publisher: ESAW
Category: Fiction

A view from across the page

'Tennyson's dead, and Browning's dead and Dickens is dead, and I'm not feeling any too well myself.'

(Anonymous)

I used to like to think that the Stock Market crash of 1987 had been engineered by Michael O'Leary, the purpose being to knock some of those Herne Bay high rollers off their very impressive perches and divert 'the responsible dollar' back where it belongs - in the realm of independent publishing. '87 was the year O'Leary's cricketing novel, *Out of It,* appeared from the Earl of Seacliff Art Workshop. He had enlisted me to illustrate the book - which I happily agreed to, adopting the pseudonym Thomas Hickey, lest people think the Great Earl's creative gene pool was growing lamentably small. I had just illustrated Elizabeth Smither's *Gorilla/Guerilla*, published by O'Leary in an edition of 250 copies, which sold out almost immediately. Overnight, we had become as rich and infamous as those Herne Bay futures traders. If only.

~

There was a lot of coming and going. Transportation nestles very close to the heart of O'Leary's existence, as it does his books. Back in the 1980s I had my motorcycle; O'Leary had the Main Trunk Line and a crumpling remnant of an urban rail system in Auckland. There must have been people out there in the world who owned cars, but we weren't among them.

My Suzuki A100 made a guest appearance on the title page of my literary journal *Rambling Jack 3,* surrounded by Franciscan monks, and with my one year old son Rambling Jack(-Marcel) astride the beast. But it was Michael who was the real maestro of transportation in recent New Zealand literature. Count the modes of travel in this paragraph from *Unlevel Crossings* (Huia Publishers, 2002, p. 131):

> The toy trainsets and slotcar motorway entered the heart of the Meccano Set buildings of the downtown area; the overhead wires of the buses and railway hung like strands of spaghetti in the sky. As the *Aratere* sailed past Soames Island towards the Pencarrow heads, Fitz saw the small Tiger Lily Two ferry beginning its journey from Days Bay into Wellington City with a load of late-morning shoppers. The sky was dark and drizzly, and as the aeroplane flew overhead following its trajectory towards Wellington Airport, he understood the intrigue and interest that this city held for him despite the little time he had been resident in it.

Around the time O'Leary was writing his earlier rail-bound spectacular, *The Irish Annals of New Zealand* (ESAW, 1992), I was having a crack at a road-based travel-book, *Diesel Mystic*. My novel is, I guess, a near/distant relative of O'Leary's productions - a book which, I am happy to say, in libraries around the country, still keeps O'Leary's books close company wherever books are filed alphabetically by author. In the present climate, I imagine our novels ducking and diving the scythe of the de-accessioning librarian.

~

With our extravagantly qualified friend, Dr Iain Sharp, we were readers of a lot of the same books: Joyce, Beckett, my great uncle Flann, B. S. Johnson, Graham Greene, James K. Baxter and Peter Olds. (It was pretty boysy, I'd have to say.) With a few sideways glances towards Raymond Queneau and Rene Daumal's classic *A Night of Serious Drinking*.

~

A few years earlier I'd had cooked up some ink and charcoal drawings for Michael O'Leary's first novel, *Straight*, which appeared in an A4-

xeroxed-ringbound edition thanks to the stewardship and departmental guile of Professor Terry Sturm, who arranged for the English Department photocopier to spend some long evenings getting acquainted with O'Leary's prose and my illustrations (the drawings O'Leary also published as a series of postcards which were, I'm sure, very popular with shoplifters in the Parimoana Bookshop on New North Road, where O'Leary conducted business for a good year or two).

~

For *Out of It*, I concocted a suite of eight collages. Iain Sharp provided two further collages for the front and back covers. The book didn't garner as much praise as we all thought it deserved. In the media-at- large it was probably overshadowed by The Crash.

Around this time, O'Leary was heading for his own personal version of The Crash. Up the top of Pitt Street in their lesbian-purple printery, the firm who produced his books weren't as cheap as he was led to believe and, within a few months, O'Leary was to be found late on weekday nights manning a jackhammer in downtown Queen Street, working a cruel nightshift to stave off the debt-collector.

~

I snipped a photo of Richard Hadlee in full flight as an element in the first collage in *Out of It*. For another image, I hoisted Jimi Hendrix up onto the roof of the southbound train. In the end, the book was about the heavenly transportation of rock music as much as it was concerned with the delivery of cricket balls and pints of Guinness.

There hasn't been that much great cricketing art in this country. In recent decades, Harry Ricketts has lately contributed a deft volume of prose, *how to catch a cricket match*. Hamilton printmaker Campbell Smith has, over the years, made a number of spirited wood engravings of players and umpires. Somehow, O'Leary has always, in my mind, had the demeanour of a cricket umpire - when he says it's out then it's out. He can also lob an impressive ball down a pitch, as he can play a riff a la Hendrix on any available instrument.

~

While O'Leary was busy preparing the pitch for *Out of It*, I was flat out publishing the aforementioned journal *Rambling Jack*, initially from the living room of my friend Jane Coombs's Grey Lynn flat then later at my bed-sitter in Epsom. Five issues rambled out into the world - between June 1986 and July 1987. The second issue featured O'Leary's *Noa/ Nothing I (an irony)* - high existential utterance in a journal noted more for its mischievous spirit and Mark 'Leaving the Highway' Williams's parodic detective yarn, 'On the Trail of Tracy Dick'. Looking back on those journals now, they are a bit of a shambles, a casualty of the hot- wax-and-paste design technology of the time and my own over-enthusiasm to cram as much of everything as possible into the journal's 32 pages.

After five issues, the publishing company responsible for *Rambling Jack*, 'Miracle Mart Receiving', was sold to Michael O'Leary for one million and three dollars, the deal sealed with a handshake and a signed cheque (which - in 2008 - has still yet to be banked).

~

The design of *Out of It* bears the imprint of its times and its shady cast of helpers, illustrators and hangers-on. Apart from the type on the front cover, the entire book is set in sans serif, giving it the appearance of a technical manual or religious tract. Such was the youthful, if at times inelegant, industry we were all engaged in. The last collage I made for that book bore the melancholy caption: 'With the tear in the eye he boarded the southbound train.' That was about it from me. I moved to Wellington, bundling my Suzuki A100 and record player onto the overnight train. I have lived in the capital ever since.

A year or maybe two later, O'Leary moved even further south than me - to Dunedin. Based in the Octagon, O'Leary clicked his fingers and, lo and behold, an anthology of New Zealand writing appeared - *Wrapper* - this time with collage maestro Bryan Harold providing the eye-candy up front. A maverick crew of writers kept company inside the volume, among them John Pule, Bob Orr, Pamela Gordon, and three poet-laureates-in-waiting Hone Tuwhare, Elizabeth Smither and Jenny Bornholdt. On the final page, Nigel Brown provided a crackerjack woodcut of O'Leary reading under a ponga - part Hemi Baxter, part Māori Jesus and part Krapp. A bunch of my ink drawings was scattered through the publication and I contributed an extract from an early version of *News of the Swimmer Reaches Shore*, which bears no resemblance whatsoever to the book of that title that appeared from Carcanet and then VUP in 2008.

~

About O'Leary's writing itself, much could be written, but I like to think of it as a collision in a crowded bar room between a straight-talking, korero-enriched Hone Tuwhare and an unabashed Irish avant-gardist, Jimmy Jazz, both of them carrying trays of drinks. That's the kind of Irish-Māori nexus O'Leary has single-handedly pioneered-another kind of 'crash' entirely, with drinks flying and a healthy mixture of singing and cursing. Raymond Queneau had that kind of linguistic collision in mind when he wrote:

> They were speaking two different languages, agglutinative languages with bitter roots, and at first that didn't bother them. Moreover, the rolled words in their rocky inlets spread mauve reflections but little information. They tried various categories, faux nemes, pure verbs, clicks, moos: every time some eggs of sumethin' else hatched under their words.

It is not a question of the Māori Renaissance or, for that matter, the Irish Renaissance. It boils down to the fact, as O'Leary's work asserts belligerently as often as it does eloquently, that great writing should place both writer and reader in a perpetual state of renaissance.

~

The trains kept roaring off into the night. And, in 2002, Huia Publishers in Wellington produced O'Leary's *Unlevel Crossings*, this time with seven of my drawings. The publishers wouldn't let me near the cover design. Maybe they had been scared off by the *Straight* cover of two decades earlier. It all amounts, as O'Leary would say, to 'a long dazed journey into night'. History

167

never repeats. History never does anything. All aboard. This train is bound for glory. You've got to be on it to be out of it. – *Gregory O'Brien,* May 2008

O'Leary Out and After

(Review of Michael O'Leary's Out of It and Before and After)

On the cover of *Out of It* what looks like a levitating commentary box with occupants, is hovering over the Out of It Cricket Eleven team as their photograph is being taken. In the foreground stand the 'new' Patrick Sean Michael Malone (P.S.M.) and his distraught and abandoned wife. In this novella, P.S.M. will revert to his youthful, wicked ways and begone, begorrah!

He does so under cover of a cricket match at Eden Park between his 'out of it' heroes of the past, and the current New Zealand Eleven. He absconds from wife and work to do so (how many of us have tried, but wilted?). There were many champions in the Out of It Eleven. Hemi Baxter slipped in his bare feet while acting as a runner for Jim Morrison of the Doors. The fearless captain Te Rauparaha scored six sixes off a rampant R. J. Hadlee before he was bowled. Rather than ending as a precious taonga for his tribe, Te Rauparaha's unfortunate bat was most probably heaved into the nearest hangi woodpile.

At the end of the book did P.S.M. fall or was he pushed? Or will he ride the City of New Orleans forever? If you are a collector of Bohemian cricket memorabilia, this book is for your shelf. It is certainly a boon to te kirikiti o Aotearoa in the Spike Milligan mode. One small point: in my copy of the book, pages 37, 38, 43 and 44 were printed twice and out of sequence. They were definitely out of it!

Before and After follows a different route. There are few sparks and fewer flames in either the poetry or the prose. The nine poems of 'After' are uneven. Some have strong moments. In 'For My Father in Prison, 1965' the poet says: 'And when he emerged / he had a matchstick table and was very quiet.'

There is no denying that 'Rubesahl' is a sober and thoughtful poem. The tone is dark and the message is darker. It stands out in stark contrast to the other poems.

'Noa' illustrates the condition of nothingness imposed by the state of tapu. It is almost indescribable on paper - 'not even like the invisibility of salt in a pot of cooking potatoes.' 'Neither Here Nor There' is a light hearted short story about two friends who shut themselves away from reality - so much so that they refuse to recognise their place in the world. Their city has no name. The signposts are nameless and pointing in the wrong directions. It is a puzzling story with rewards for those keen to dig deeper. – *Rangi Faith*

(From *The Press* (Christchurch), 30 July 1988)

Paekakariki

Home of the Earl

Paekakariki is the current home of the Earl. From Paekakariki he has run two bookshops, Pukapuka and Kakariki, and continued his extensive publishing operation, organised readings and been involved with local community efforts including the Rail Museum and caretaking of St Peter's Hall. Two poems that include O'Leary and the area are below:

Bards of Paekakariki

(for Michael O'Leary)

Behold Paekakariki where late sun trawls,
throwing nets of light across strong seas
to the afternoon anchorstone of Kapiti.
Surf bawls out its test-match cheers
that seem to echo on from yesteryear,
like the engine rush of departing trains,
or dance-band songs in the local hall.
Froth subsides with a shush on shingle,
while from dense bush a swaggie roves.
He out of swamp forests of the brain,
trudging across the sand, strives
to knot with twine his coat of green.
From his swag tumble bays and coves;
heep like brooches from pockets fall.
Scarves of scrub he pegs on hillsides;
he gathers armfuls of flowering lilies;
glides slopes plunged giddy to the flat,
as sunset flees from pink rambler roses
swathed in the dust of roadside verges.
Days are an indigestible richness,
that sneak off and leave us in the dark,

just here where clifftops slide away.
Days end in boil-ups of puha and mutton flaps,
in storms hurling land back to stone and bone.
Dwellers here choose a poem without words,
discovering words are unsure of the truth.
They scrape fat from their plates in silence,
content at last with the marrow of existence.

David Eggleton

Poets at Paekakariki

One thing is certain:
The waves will weep on,
Wave after whisper,
Wherever they come.

One thing is certain:
No wave like another,
No wave unlike wave,
They beat us and soothe us
Batter our sea-shells
And scatter our pebbles,
Bring nothing, or seaweed,
Or twisted branches,
Or heavy trunks,
Unnaturally smooth –
No splinter splits skin
When we stroke them to soothe them
And soothe perhaps us.

One thing is certain:
Wave follows wave.
All else may surprise us.
Campbell and Glover
Pulled up at the pub,

Tosspots and watchers,
Filling, like smoke, with words
(Swirling and wafting, dispersible
Words) the comforting fug.
Wave after wind
And word upon wave
And - gone: silent,
Even the pub.

One thing is certain:
Wave after wave will lift
Beach-burnt bodies
And bring them down. Gently?
Word upon word
Will lift and will fall.
O'Leary and Pirie
Earnestly midwiving
Word-flows and verses
Out of foam closets
And onto the page.
And the beach still beaten
By wave after wave.

Nothing is certain
But generation, and see:
They come and they rise
And they foam and they fall,
Wave upon wave
Upon poet and poem.
And driftwood is lifted
And carried again
To distance and swells,
Squalls and horizons,
Unnaturally smooth.

"Paneta Street"

Date of Composition: 2004
Collection: Paneta Street
Anthologised in: *Mahones: Four Poets*

O'Leary and his friend Moana Cleverley called it their 'Hacienda by the Sea', this little stucco, art-deco house with the Spanish-style wooden shutters on the windows which Moana and Michael shared for a couple of years at 11 Paneta Street in Paekakariki. As the poem suggests they healed each other's wounds, swimming in the sea and looking after each other, and protecting each other from the storms that had beleaguered their separate lives in the past. One photograph that Moana took of Michael on the verandah during their brief stay there must have let some light into the lens as she was taking it so it looked like he was on fire inside the house. Tragically, several years after they had left, someone died in the house when it caught fire in the middle of the night. His nickname was 'Kip' and he was the grand nephew of the New Zealand World War II war hero Kippenberger. The house itself was beyond repair and there are two photos of O'Leary and Moana in his latest book of poems *Paneta Street* standing in the wreckage before it was demolished.

Paneta Street

Date of Publication: 2008
Publisher: HeadworX
Category: Poetry

Review of Michael O'Leary's *Paneta Street*

Paneta googles as one of our local 21 streets, as bread and butter pudding, and now as a new book of poems by our poet laureate Michael O'Leary, published 3 September next. Michael partakes as mysteriously of the other two as 'The Third Policeman' did of his bicycle seat in that grand Irish whimsy of a story by Flann O'Brien.

Michael's book splits into three life cycles. The last gives the book its title 'Paneta Street', and will be most familiar to us as the third cross street off the north end of The Parade. The subject matter is as familiar, such as Lyndy McIntyre's social commitment, stepping off the train at Paekakariki, returning to the eponymous street's burned-down house where he lived. These are strong goodbyes, but there are unexpected hellos for the Mercedes car and Te Rauparaha whilst out swimming. The delightful pastiche of the Eagles' 'Hotel California' song is a grand hello/goodbye for Hotel Paekakariki.

It is hail and farewell too for his last poem in the Dunedin section, a eulogy for fellow railway worker, poet and drinking buddy Hone Tuwhare. Dunedin was where Michael fled and spread his winged words. These poems are Michael Agonistes pondering the lives and deaths of Seacliff mental patients, the man beneath the Mongrel Mob skin tats, junkie and rock 'n' roll victims, even Dunedin and Seacliff itself.

Hometown Auckland is the first section, with O'Leary Agonistic in a love/hate relationship with the city. He loves Morningside Station graffiti, the Avondale incline, another O'Leary stabbed in a pub, the Manukau tides and the banana bus at K-Road. He hates the alienation of Torbay, sacrificing the lemon tree in Pakuranga for a swimming pool, Takapuna yachtie yuppiedom. He travels the motorway bifurcating the dead of Grafton Gully.

Michael, of Māori/Irish extraction, straddles all sides with Rabelaisian gusto to rival the googled 116 bread and butter pudding recipes. He has poems as satisfying as traditional bread and butter pud with caramel sauce, like his Hotel Paekakariki, others as unusual as the savoury lobster bread and butter pud with vanilla chive sauce, such as the Mercedes. All are served up as precisely as the grid map of our streets. 'Still their voices are calling from far away,' in Michael's welcome 'Farewell to the Hotel Paekakariki'. – *David McGill*

(From *Paekakariki Xpressed*, 22 August 2008)

Paneta Street cover,
Photo by John Girdlestone

Passion

Date of Publication: 1990
Publisher: ESAW
Category: Fiction

Who he?

The first full-length novel about male homosexuality to be published in this country will come from the Earl of Seacliff Art Workshop early in the new year. Entitled *Passion,* it is the work of "Glynn Parker ... an Auckland educationalist, who has been writing for many years but to date has only published non-fiction in his specialised field".

The material of *Passion* is, the author; says, sufficiently close to his own experiences "for him to have chosen a *nom de plume* for this occasion". What this means for the book's launch remains to be seen - it is now endemic in the publishing community that books printed overseas arrive too late for the launch itself, but seldom, if ever, does a book get launched without the presence of its author. A masked ball, perhaps?

The Earl of Seacliff Art Workshop is one of the more interesting (and among the very few successful) small publishers in this country. Founded five years ago by the self-styled Earl, Michael O'Leary, and recently incorporated as a limited liability company with a further three directors, it has been responsible to date for some 16 titles, ranging from attractively produced slender volumes of poetry through a handful of novels to Colin Amery's book about the aftermath of the *Rainbow Warrior* affair. The Earl sees his venture, which has its offices in Auckland's Queen Street, as "perhaps the only example of Stalinist economics left operating outside of Romania and Albania".

"As the rest of the world drifts into *laissez-falre* capitalism," he says, "we intend to remain loyal to our 10-year plan." – *Michael Gifkins*

(From "Bookmarks", *New Zealand Listener,* 25 December 1989)

Comment on Glynn Parker's *Passion*

Here is a plot summary from the days before novelists had to worry about role models for Young Adult Fiction: A nineteen- year-old Samoan man rapes a girl in the car park of the Auckland Domain. Years later, as his young son dies of leukaemia, he discovers that he has an older son, the child of his crime. Resolving to atone for his past, the rapist - now a born again Christian - summons his lost son, aged sixteen, from his home in Christchurch. But rather than staying with his natural father, Tommy spends most of his time in Auckland at the home of Phil, an old friend of his step-father, forty seven years old, a university lecturer and gay. Tommy's natural father thinks God has sent Tommy to replace his dying son. But the Divine Plan unravels as Tommy falls in love with Phil and embarks on an Easter weekend of steamy sex.

In the heady days after gay sex was legalised, the Earl of Seacliff Art Workshop published this novel which turns on its head the notion - promoted in some sections of the media - that a consenting age of sixteen would mean no schoolboy was safe. (The publication date makes *Passion* the pioneer of the local gay novel. Witi Ihimaera's *Nights in the Gardens of Spain* was published in 1995.)

Tearaway Tommy - the author's prose has infected mine - is very much the driving force, a disrupter of the peace who unpicks Phil's long-standing accommodation to social injustice. Wearing sand shoes and an Afro haircut, Tommy represents the future of gaydom as it looked back then. Fusty Phil, meanwhile, comes from a past that feels much older than the late eighties - this is an Auckland in which a comfortable bachelor contemplates joining the Film Society then decides to take an overdose of sleeping pills instead. Even in 1990, the author Robert Leek - a university lecturer himself - felt it prudent to write under an assumed name (Glynn Parker).

For all we learn about real teenagers, the garrulous Tommy might be as mute as the adolescent love object of *Death in Venice,* yet *Passion* has a tenacity that makes it dated in a good way. Step by step, we are taken through a perennial debate - not for nothing has this sort of relationship been called Greek Love; we are talking *ancient* Greek.

Passion is a gay novel from before the gay novel settled into its mature form as a commodity. Shreds of old religion hang around it like graveyard vapours - the Catholic college orgies of mildewed paperbacks unearthed in basement book exchanges. In a dark night of the soul Phil even encounters Jesus in a sleazy sauna: 'There is much love in you.' Jesus tells him 'This is not the place to find it and waste it.' (Anyone who has sought repose on a red-lit black vinyl squab at three in the morning may wonder whether to snigger or weep). The book does not set out to present the best face of gaydom to a welcoming world, and there's an odd freshness in that. It is steeped in leper-humour and the assumption that to be homosexual is to be cursed - albeit with a good job, a home on the park and an exquisite record collection. Phil's oft-stated wish is that the best he can hope for his young lover is to grow up straight.

On the back cover of the first edition, Iain Sharp comments: '*Passion* is the first New Zealand novel to examine a homosexual love affair openly and directly.' Yet even where it is most out there, rampant and glorying in its lustfulness, careful checks are laid in the texture of the plot - consenting man/boy sex looks better against the backdrop of the man/girl rape that sets the story rolling. And Tommy's step-father turns out to have had an unconsummated youthful affair with Phil, so we are invited to see Tommy and Phil's lovemaking as a completion of unfinished business. This Tommy is not really sixteen at all, but forty-something plus sixteen.

The author has not gone to these lengths out of concern for an abolished law but for a continuing issue of appropriateness. Phil has many and lengthy scruples before taking the plunge. But plunge he does.

How have things gone in the years since the Earl of Seacliff gave us *Passion*? Set aside the surprising fact that boys in their late teens have proved capable of saying no to sex with older men - or at least that they are not saying yes in greater numbers than they did when it was against the law. (Who in the world of *Passion* could have imagined the age of metrosexuality - straight males posing as gay to make themselves more attractive to women?)

With The Bad Sex Award to guide us (who thought up that award anyway? A conservative British journalist) we can roll our eyes at *Passion's* cliches without stopping to think about the guts required to write them. We know we are safe from accusations of hostility; homophobia is finished, it is a crime against the economy. After the reform of '86 the gay community with its untapped resources of disposable income - was swept up into the arms of the consumer society.

This was the breakout from the hair salons, onto the boards of directors and the benches of parliament. But the clandestine culture underwent some cutting and trimming, some makeovers, some straight eyeing for the queer guys, in order to get its place at the big table.

Flapping your wrist and making self-deprecating jokes in a loud voice is no longer an acceptable lifestyle choice for a gay man, nor is hanging around in public toilets, or cathedrals, or worshipping Judy Garland. Nor is indulging in spring/autumn romps like the one described in *Passion,* even if it is legal.

The impossibility of Greek Love then, is finally an impossibility of marketing it. Men of 16 and men of 47 don't use the same cosmetics, they don't like the same music or wear the same clothes or go to the same bars and they don't earn the same money. Together, they are an advertising copywriter's nightmare, so naturally they can't be together. (It's obvious really, you'd think the Greeks could have figured it out for themselves and saved us the bother).

It would be hard to make the case that *Passion* is a great lost novel. But as a home-grown examination of the friendships that used to be called 'special' it deserves a special mention. And for reminding us that, in the days when everything was forbidden, some things were discussable that have since become taboo. – *Geoff Cush*

Mark Pirie

Mark Pirie, a prolific Wellington poet and publisher, has been a close friend of Michael O'Leary's since replying to a questionnaire about small press publishing in late 2000. The response he wrote for HeadworX was included in the book, *Alternative Small Press Publishing in New Zealand* (Steele Roberts). The two publisher/poets had many common areas of interest and formed an alliance of sorts to promote and publish authors of their publishing houses (usually ones not often recognized by the mainstream literary world). Their collaborations included the Winter Readings series of events in Wellington, their cover photo series with John Girdlestone, the 'Greatest Hits' anthology and a joint volume of their sonnets. Two poems by Pirie that feature O'Leary are 'Labouring' and 'With or without', one written in respect of O'Leary's hard labouring jobs; the other concerning a relationship of O'Leary's:

Labouring

For Michael

Hart Crane, the poet, dropped out of
college to find work as a labourer.

His father never wanted a poet.
It was the sheer hard grind

of the labouring jobs that gave
him a comfortable compromise, where

in a factory job he worked for his father.
Sea was his main symbol, in much

the same way as rail and trains
dominate your thinking. Like Crane

you liked the sweat of labouring:

your beloved old job for NZ Rail.

Like Crane you moved between
the twin worlds of the academy

and the earthiness of the street.
Like Crane you gave your generous

compassion to the world, as if
your writing too was your journey;

his by sea, and where he would meet
his inevitable end; yours by rail, and

always travelling on, stopping only to
connect people to places, ideas to dreams,

and to love - just as in a way Crane sought
to connect his country by The Bridge.

With or without

For Bill and Michael

When I think of you both,
I often think of various scenes from a film.
It's by Truffaut*, a dark French tale
of a *menage a trois* that goes
horribly wrong.

It's about two best friends, and
their enigmatic and elusive lover.
In the film, the last act is when
the woman played by the darkly
sensuous Jeanne Moreau
tries to end one of their lives.

She fails, and then later returns for
a final plunge, successfully driving
her car with her lover into a river.
That way, neither man can have her.
She triumphs, controls and subdues
all masculine compulsion. I don't know
why I think of this film each time I see you.

But I do.

Maybe it's because,
unlike that famous tale you both survived.
You came out of it as friends, strong friends
with compassion and aroha between you.
Love worked its 'mysterious ways'
and brought you closer together
with or without this woman.

Mark Pirie

**Jules and Jim (Jules et Jim),* France, 1962

Poems for Poets

Date of Publication: 2004
Publisher: ESAW
Category: Poetry

Poems for Poets is a collection of dedications and elegies for poets published in a limited edition of 50 copies for the poet Mark Pirie's 30th birthday in 2004. Its format was modelled on A E Housman's *Shropshire Lad* as a number sequence in Roman Numerals. Its cover and presentation playfully mimicked the old 'Faber & Faber paperback editions' series. Poems in the book were dedicated to poets as diverse as William Warner (Second World War Kiwi poet), Alistair Te Ariki Campbell, Bill Manhire, Allen Curnow, Katherine Mansfield, William Shakespeare, Kevin Hart, Daryl McLaren, Tony Beyer, Alistair Paterson, Brian Gregory, John Kinsella and T S Eliot.

Poet Laureate

The Poet Laureate of Paekakariki

Michael John O'Leary transmogrifies his dishevelled charm into the laid-back layout of Kakariki Books. He co-founded the second-hand bookshop with Irving Lipshaw and Peter Mounsey in Wellington Road in 1999, in the latest stop in a lifelong journey up and down the country as penman, publisher and purveyor of books about us.

Paekakariki caught his eye long before he settled here. It was not just that it was a magnet for poets and painters like himself; it is a railway settlement. Above almost everything, Michael loves railways. The only job he regrets leaving was tracklayer for NZR. He misses the camaraderie of men at work, cooking mussels on a shovel. He has travelled up and down the Main Trunk Line many times, from his hometown Auckland to his twice-adopted Dunedin.

'Paekakariki was the first place you'd see,' he says fondly. 'You'd wake up bleary-eyed and there it was.' In his 2002 novel *Unlevel Crossings*, about a real and mythical train journey between Auckland and Dunedin, he writes about reaching Paekakariki. His character has a sense of well-being and peace and he 'luxuriated in the mellow, fulfilled world of beauty from within and without, looking down on the top sawyer's rocks where the waves pounded'.

Perhaps this is why he has stayed put longer than anywhere else. Perhaps this is why he has put so much into the community. I first saw him the following year directing traffic on the corner of Beach Road and Ames Street during the aftermath of the terrible flood. He has been active in almost every local committee and community effort, recently stepping down as first Community Trust Chair, still serving on his beloved Railway Museum Trust. I have spent many happy hours at the museum exchanging another of his encyclopaedic enthusiasms, pop music memories.

His mother was a Fitzgerald and his character in his novel is Patrick Mika Fitzgerald, not unlike his author in his taste for word play and multi-lingual puns. Michael was born the same place I was, Ōrākei, in 1950. He accepted he was not going to be a rock star and went to art school in

Ponsonby, was waylaid by the pubs and drugs, becoming known as the Earl of Ponsonby.

He ended that by performing a final surreal art effort, burning his last ten dollar note in the Kiwi Hotel and entraining to Dunedin. There he called himself after his Dada hero, enjoying the barman shouting 'Marcel Duchamp!' when it was his turn at the pool table. He transferred his title to his suburban residence, the Earl of Seacliff Art Workshop bookshop established to create a cash flow for publishing. Instead it became a debt flow, but the habits were in place, his first published short story is about two people who don't know if they live in Auckland or Dunedin. He has had bookshops in both towns, but he has had two bookshops in Paekakariki, Pukapuka and now Kakariki.

Here he launches and sells books like my recent pop music memoirs, *The Treadmill Tapes*, sells and acquires rare books such as his beloved James Cowan Māori railway station names, performs, and publishes other poets and himself. Notable are his 'Farewell to the Hotel Paekakariki' fond parody of the Eagles' song 'Hotel California' and his 'After the Flood', when his brother 'wades through waste-high water / Bringing back wine from the semisubmerged pub' and 'The people rally to help each other / Paekakariki becomes sister and brother'. – *David McGill*

(From *Paekakariki Xpressed*, Friday, 21 September 2007)

Poetrymath

Date of Publication: 2006

Publisher: ESAW

Category: Poetry

Contributors: Sandra Bell, Jeanne Bernhardt, Alistair Te Ariki Campbell, Meg Campbell, Tony Chad, Bill Dacker, Chris Else, Andrew Fagan, Bernadette Hall, Siobhan Harvey, Joy MacKenzie, Harvey McQueen, Michael O'Leary, Peter Olds, Mark Pirie, Ralph Proops, Harry Ricketts, Iain Sharp, Richard von Sturmer and F W N Wright.

Poetrymath is the anthology of readers participating in Wellington's Winter Readings 2006. The cover features Michael O'Leary and Mark Pirie's latest album cover take off in their continuing series of photographs all taken by Kapiti Coast photographer John Girdlestone. This time they have 'covered' the Rolling Stones' cover *Aftermath*.

Poetrywall

Date of Publication: 2007

Publisher: ESAW

Category: Poetry

Contributors: Alistair Te Ariki Campbell, Glenn Colquhoun, Dinah Hawken, Tim Jones, Wanjiku Kiarie, Richard Langston, Michael O'Leary, Mark Pirie, Jenny Powell, Martyn Sanderson, L E Scott, Nelson Wattie, and F W N Wright.

Poetrywall is the anthology of readers participating in Wellington's Winter Readings 2007. The cover features Michael O'Leary and Mark Pirie's latest album cover take off in their continuing series of photographs all taken by Kapiti Coast photographer John Girdlestone. This time it was after the song 'Wonderwall' from the album *What's the Story, Morning Glory?* by Oasis, with the pair appearing as the Gallagher brothers in Cuba Street.

Poetrywall: Anthology of the Poetrywall

Date of Publication: 2007
Publisher: ESAW
Category: Poetry

Poetrywall, edited by Mark Pirie and Gemma Claire, is the anthology of the poems written on the Poetrywall at Winter Readings 2007. The event was dedicated to the British rock band Oasis and held at the City Gallery in Wellington. Michael O'Leary and Mark Pirie, the organisers asked the audience to participate that year by writing on their Poetrywall, a large paper wall pinned to the gallery's own wall. At the end of the readings, Michael O'Leary awarded the inaugural Earl of Seacliff Poetry Prize for 2007 to the best poem on the wall. The winning poem was 'Listening For The Ocean' by Evelyn Conlon. Other poems collected from the wall show a surprising and diverse mix of poetry styles from the more well-known names like Marilyn Duckworth, Stephen Oliver, Richard Langston and L.E. Scott, to new and younger writers. The first poem on the wall was Andrew Fagan's 'Then'.

Publishing

'The Earl of Wisdom' / 'A pearl of an earl' / …?

Anyone can be a publisher. In New Zealand a manuscript lurks in every bottom drawer and several more crouch in each computer, bursting to go forth and multiply. Anyone these days can typeset such a text, tweak it, affix their name and print it. Spread the books and *voila*, you're a publisher.

Not happy with the manuscripts on offer? If Disraeli wanted to read a good book he wrote one, he said, and many publishers in New Zealand quite properly continue this tradition too.

If it's so easy, how come there aren't more publishers? Well, there are. A recent survey identified 600-plus in New Zealand, churning out more than 3000 books each year. That's about ten a day, so yes, you could theoretically get all you need to eat and drink at book launches up and down the town. (In Wellington a few people do indeed give that a crack, and good on them, the more so if they buy a book every now and then.)

And yes, every week a new publisher starts out … but few last. The economics and the hours are daunting, and passion pales for these and other reasons. A survey on Beattie's Book Blog identified the high attrition and change among New Zealand's mainstream publishers, and Michael O'Leary's own recently published Masters thesis on small presses in New Zealand painted no different picture of alternative avenues into print.

With his long and distinguished history of publishing the work of others, the Earl of Seacliff has disproved these laws of the marketplace and confounded his own analysis. Through his travails, countless new writers' works have seen the light of the reading lamp, and he continues to offer innovative, alternative platforms to old-hand authors as well.

As an oft-published author himself, the Earl brings an unusual and welcome compassion to the dog-bite-dog world of publishing. Ever supportive and sympathetic, he often also reminds us of the funny side of it all. Asked the other day what books he had been reading lately, he replied, 'Hell, I write them, edit them, publish them, you don't expect me to read them as well, do you!' But of course he does read them, and has a finely-tuned ear for authentic voices of Aotearoa and all the cultural notes that make up the chords of our literature.

So what was Cyril Connolly thinking when he said that 'As repressed sadists are supposed to become policemen or butchers, so those with irrational fear of life become publishers'? The Earl is fearless. He is a stalwart in the tradition of publishers who against all odds do their bit to support Goethe's advice that we should all hear a little music, read a little poetry, and see a fine picture every day of our lives, 'in order that worldly cares may not obliterate the sense of the beautiful which God has implanted in the human soul.' Thus such publishers will not rest until there is a shelf of poetry by every bedside and in every parlour, until poetry is performed on television and infiltrated onto the political podium, and until story is woven into every fabric of our lives.

In the run-up to another United States election we remember President Kennedy and his comment that when power narrows the areas of our concern, poetry reminds us of the richness and diversity of our existence. 'When power corrupts, poetry cleanses,' he said.

All who know the Earl of Seacliff are aware that he is ageless, but it is less widely known that he has in fact been around since the time of the Old Testament. On reflection this should come as no surprise to us, looking for all the world as he does like a Biblical prophet. Here he is, millennia ago, announcing his passion for truth, social justice, and spreading the word, in Psalm 26:

> Judge me, O Lord; for I have walked in mine integrity ... I have not sat with vain persons, neither will I go in with dissemblers ... I have hated the congregation of evil doers; and will not sit with the wicked. ... I will wash mine hands in innocency ... That I may publish with the voice of thanksgiving, and tell of all thy wondrous works.

His psalm continueth with a reference to the Earl's principled practice of not holding out a begging bowl to the government to support his work, but forging ahead alone or with his own brave band in blithe self-sufficiency:

Gather not my soul with sinners, nor my life with bloody men: In whose hands is mischief, and their right hand is full of bribes.

And it endeth with what we can now see is an obvious reference to Paekakariki (26:12):

My foot standeth in an even place: in the congregations will I bless the Lord.

So there you have it: he has been around a while indeed, and (praise the Lord) for the benefit he brings to the literature of Aotearoa, he is clearly here to stay. For it is written. - *Roger Steele,* June 2008

The Earl of Publishers

to Michael O'Leary

In Hebrew
the language of the Bible
to bring something
to the light
is: *Lehotsi La'Or,*
he who brings
to the light.

The books of poetry
bunches of creativity
are like the cliffs
brought to light
as Seacliffs
of the Earl.

He is
the Earl of Seacliff,
a poet, friend

of the poets
and editor, friend
of the editors,
a publisher, friend
of the publishers,
he is the Earl
of the poetry.

You just
give him
a bunch of poems
and he makes
from it
a full-fledged
wonderful book,
another cliff
to the crown
of the Earl.

And he is
Everywhere
at ESAW,
with HeadworX,
at the Winter Readings,
by the 'Greatest Hits',
even with
the CD sounds,
you name it:
the Earl.

To ESAW
on its 25th anniversary,
to the Earl
who does it all,
we wish

in the best Jewish tradition:
until 120!

as the years of Moses,
120 books to ESAW
120 years to the Earl
who brings them
to the light!

The Hague, 25/5/2008

M. Liba

(From *My Country, the World, - and Me,* Cyberwit.net, India, 2009)

My story with the Earl

At the age of 58, I fell from a roof. Although the head damage limited my ability to concentrate for extended periods, it qualified me for a writer's grant from the Accident Compensation Commission. Having time on my hands, I decided to write a novel that had been rattling around in my head for a number of years. This novel had a history. It was accepted by two overseas agents and two overseas internet publishers. They all went out of business. My friend, Frances Cherry, liked the book and decided to invite myself and a publisher-friend to a dinner party. This was where I met Michael O'Leary for the first time. After an excellent meal, some bottles of wine and literary conversation Michael took Frances' word that it was a good book and agreed to publish. Eventually, he did actually read it, though his stated policy was - 'we write books, we publish books, we shouldn't have to read them.' The published book did reasonably well, partly because of a remarkable review by someone who thought I was someone else. (It appears I am a pretty good writer if I am someone with a reputation but not so good if I'm not.)

A couple of years later Michael asked me if I wanted to become publicist for ESAW. The distribution agency that Michael had been using had been sold and the new owner decided to abandon him. This seemed to be quite an interesting retirement occupation so I found a free newsletter email program and collected email addresses of bookshops and libraries from the internet. I also thought that a website might be a help. Initially I considered utilising free space provided by my ISP, however, it turned out that commercial space is pretty cheap so we bought some and registered our domain name - 'earlofseacliff'. Being a self-taught web designer, I developed a rough and ready site that seems to do the trick. There are over 350 files on the site. It gets hits from all over the world and has actually brought business from American universities. Nevertheless the email newsletter and website do not enable us to penetrate as far into the market as we would like.

The next step was to distribute the books. Over time the most efficient methods of using the postal system were developed. Also, having spent my life programming computers, I was able to develop a system for invoicing and recording of data in the Microsoft Access programming language. It's a rare system but it does the trick, although I'm probably the only person able to use it.

About this time it came to my attention that ESAW was not doing too well. Michael had had a sudden rush to the head and published half a dozen (or more) books of poetry at great expense. Very few books sold and he owed the printer $10,000. Michael, to his credit, eventually paid this money back but the funds did not come from book sales. The problem was that the books had been passed to a local printer in raw form and printed using the offset process. Not only did this entail a large one-off charge there was also an extra cost for typesetting. Such a process was surely uneconomical for short run books of poetry. This led me into an enquiry into the methods of digital printing. The local print shop was very helpful in this and we started publishing chapbooks (including the Christmas Surprise mini book). I utilised Microsoft Publisher as the typesetting tool, and eventually graduated to Adobe Pagemaker (which Mark Pirie, of HeadworX, had also been using to help typeset and design a number of works for us).

Still pretty ignorant as to the methods of publishing I decided to embark on the publication of two larger works of fiction, books by Frances and myself. Without going into details, this process was semi-traumatic and almost disastrous. Nevertheless the learning curve is complete, we do not lose money and I feel that I can call myself a publisher. We are still not selling books in large quantities; however, the press is financial. What we really need is an agent that will approach libraries and bookshops direct but as yet have not been able to find one.

So I am now publicist, distributor, webmaster, accountant and publisher. No it's not a take-over, it's just a retirement hobby. – *Brian E. Turner*

Resistance

Date of Publication: 2005
Publisher: ESAW
Category: Poetry

Meg and her Poems

(Launch speech for *Resistance* by Meg Campbell)

Many years ago, I asked Louis Johnson, a leading poet and friend to launch, I think, Meg's collection *A Durable Fire*. Lou agreed, but on the night, spent most of his speech praising the work of an Australian woman poet. Well, to prevent that sort of thing happening this afternoon, I thought I would say a few words. After all I know her poems better than anyone apart from Meg herself.

Meg began to write poems at a later stage in her life than do most poets. I can't give you the exact time. She was writing poems quietly without letting me know what she was up to. Then she began showing me poems, and I would help her a little by pointing out what I thought didn't work, or needed tightening. It wasn't long before she got into her stride and was writing poems good enough to get into *Landfall* and the *New Zealand Listener*.

When her first book, *The Way Back,* was published in 1981, the *Otago Daily Times* book reviewer wrote that Meg Campbell wasn't in my shadow, but had her own unique voice. This was the point that needed to be stressed now as it was then. I think there were people who thought I had a greater hand in her poems than I actually did.

Meg's poems are her own, and show a sureness of language that she arrives at after a lot of hard work. She is a thoughtful poet and though she doesn't ignore the wider scene, the world at large, she is happiest and most successful writing about the home, family and friends.

I remember when her first book came out, it was quite a hit. I heard of women mainly, anxious to buy a copy, and ringing round the bookshops in their eagerness. Meg says it's women who admire her work and buy her books. But I know that a lot of men also admire them. There are critics who have taken her to task for writing what they describe as confessional poetry. I think what they had in mind were the poems about her hospital experiences she had to write.

But I disagree that they are confessional, because that suggests that Meg had done something wrong, and had to atone for her sins. Meg's poems are personal in a good sense. Meg has suffered, but anyone who takes the trouble to look into her poems will find a brave woman trying to make sense of her life - and I may add, of her husband too.

To understand Meg you have to understand that in her poetry and personality she throws out a challenge. Her attitude is, 'Here I am. What are going to do about it?' But once you get past that facade, you find a very friendly, loving person - and that's the person you find in her poems. Ask her grandchildren, the joy of her life. Ask Abel.

I haven't commented on *Resistance*, Meg's new collection beyond saying it's beautifully printed and has her design on the cover. All I'll say is buy the book and read the poems, and you'll find they bear out what I've been trying to say. – *Alistair Te Ariki Campbell*

Review of Meg Campbell's *Resistance*

This is Meg Campbell's fifth volume of poems. Her striking, characteristic is the candour of her poems. They are honest in their feeling and expression, polished nuggets in a world where words are used so often sloppily and thoughtlessly. Maybe a better word would be essential - the commonplace seen elementally.

The title poem is worth giving in full. It is very typical - a wry wrestling through of thoughts, sparked by an event, to some form of resolution.

> A lone hibiscus flower
> drops to the floor. I am
> unfurling its petals
> pinning them open
> to resist its dying.
> I'll pin my colours open
> to resist love's dying,
> resist to the last breath
> the dying of love. Press

my flower in a page
of his book, where he
writes only of me,
and on that page -
one line - where my spirit
rests, I'll tell myself that
I'm unique, at the eleventh
month, eleventh hour
with midnight pending.
No, love is not ending.

Her themes are elemental - aged love, the garden, nature, depression, friendship, death, family and grandchildren, mothers, little acts of kindness, dogs and budgies and bumblebees.

Thank you, Meg I finished this volume feeling pleased to be human. Your poems contain that gift. – *Harvey McQueen*

(From *Bravado*, No. 5, 2005)

The Road Goes On

Date of Publication: 2003
Publisher: ESAW
Category: Fiction

Review of Brian E. Turner's *The Road Goes On*

From a New Zealand author known mainly for his plays, comes a novel about a man who arrives in a new country as a child. The story follows him through his complex family life; its tragedies and joys, that continually shape his social relations. But his development as a person has a spiritual side that is not limited by his predominantly Christian upbringing. The disappointments of his life are shot through with insights into the connections that we all experience with something larger than the personal. The characters are finely and deeply drawn, with enough diversity to rivet the readers attention. Authentically New Zealand in flavour it is likely to have even more appeal to readers from other countries, because the characters all include a distinctively New Zealand touch. John Johns meets a wide variety of people and encounters bigotry and prejudice without any apparent feeling that it is something against which he needs to crusade. He absorbs the artistic ideas of the time (mainly the '30s). He tramps through many parts of New Zealand trying to keep to places that do not interrupt the visions of his mind. Riots and business failures during the depression are seen largely from the limited understanding of the workers. The ghosts that inhabit the mind of John Johns include that of his wife and unborn child. The author seems to be intent on showing a world that was once described in folk tales in terms of spirits, but which he translates into a modern mythology. I enjoyed the book immensely. Turner uses the complexity of flash- back as a way of depicting inner life. Memory comes to us without any linear temporal sequence. Though, in novels, this technique generates its own difficulties for the reader, Turner manages his material well. The death of John's parents in the early part of the book seems like a literary device, but subsequently Turner never falters. He maintains the pace so that it is not easy to put aside.

'The Road Goes On' is highly entertaining reading and some may find it transforming. – *Ron Ward*

"Rubesahl"

Date of Composition: 1985

Collections: *Before and After, Con Art: Selected Poems, Toku Tinihanga: Selected Poems 1982-2002, TAB Ula Rasa: New and Selected Poems*

Anthologised in: *JAAM* 19, *Te Ao Marama* 3

In legends Rubezahl is a capricious giant, gnome or mountain spirit. With good people he is friendly, he teaches medicine and gives presents. If someone derides him, however, his revenge is severe. He sometimes plays the role of a trickster in folk tales. The origin of the stories is from pagan times. Rubezahl is the fantastic Lord of Weather of the mountains and is similar to the Wild Hunt. Unexpectedly or playfully he sends lightning and thunder, fog, rain and snow from the mountain below, even while the sun is shining. He took the appearance of a monk in a gray frock (like Wotan in his mantel of clouds) and holds a string instrument in his hand (the stormharp), and walks so heavily that the earth trembles around him. There are numerous similarities between Rubezahl and Wotan. This description of the German mythological character Rubezahl is suggestive of why O'Leary undertook to take the name on as a metaphor for his own life and character. An old woman friend of his, Hilda Burstein, called O'Leary this once when she saw him get off a train at Mt Albert station in the 1980s. She explained that the Rubezahl stories had been part of her childhood in Germany and that O'Leary reminded her of him. She was the only one of her family who survived the Holocaust, and was helped by a Nazi friend to escape, despite her Jewish background. O'Leary changed the z to an s in the name Rubesahl to give it his own stamp and has used it in many of his literary works, including the long poem *Shake Speer's Faith* and the novel *Magic Alex's Revenge.*

"Saturday Night"

Date of Composition: 1976
Collections: *Surrogate Children, Toku Tinihanga: Selected Poems 1982-2002*
Anthologised in: *papertiger* CD-ROM journal, Australia

O'Leary comments: 'This poem was written after one night being 'written off'. It was a Saturday night and my friend Paddy Rainsford and I had been drinking in the Captain Cook pub in Dunedin. At the time Paddy owned an old 1943 Chev truck and we drove from Dunedin to Port Chalmers where we lived. During the journey along that long and winding road, which has the Otago Harbour on both sides of the road throughout the route, we drank a bottle of whiskey and sang rebel songs. Neither of us has much memory of the night before as suggested in the poem.' The poem is also based, in the literary sense, on a poem by the French poet Baudelaire, who wrote in the 19th Century a poem which translates as 'Get Drunk'. In his poem he extols the idea of human beings having to be drunk, 'on wine, poetry, virtue, whatever you will', to escape the tyranny of our mortality. So the poem 'Saturday Night' is one of those happy marriages between reality and literature. It has been recorded with Trevor Bycroft on electric guitar as a talking blues number on the CD *Toku Tinihanga* (and later anthologised in Mark Pirie's '50 Poems by 50 Poets' selection of recent New Zealand poetry for *papertiger*, Brisbane - a CD-ROM journal).

L E Scott

L E Scott is an African American jazz poet and performer who has been involved with a number of readings/events and publications with O'Leary. Scott's *Poems for Gwen* (dedicated to Gwendolyn Brooks) was published by ESAW in 2004. O'Leary has given readings at Scott's African shop Kwanzaa in Manners Street, Wellington. Scott wrote the following tribute to Michael especially for this book:

The Man at the Sea
(for Michael - Row your boat ashore)

You are one of those rare lights
a human hand touching voices in the wind
you live by the sea
and dance in the forest of human seeds
a carver, a shaper, a shaker of words
dream maker

You are one of those rare lights
dancing in human nights
holding our dread until morning light
you kiss our lips with printer's ink
placing our covered bones on the washing line
we dance with life's winds
pages turning faster sometimes
than the music

You are one of those rare lights
knowing us as if you seeded us
we travel to you - dressed in our words
you bathe us in cold or warm water
baptising our words with today or the promise
of tomorrow
midnight is the writer's door

You are one of those rare lights
where the heart and mouth speak
in the same tongue
as you gather our footprints
near the sea-cliff

Seacliff Mafia

The Seacliff Mafia in its recent manifestation is Michael O'Leary (Godfather and Editor-in-Chief), Brian E. Turner (Technical Editor), Mark Pirie (Friend of the Family) and Niel Wright (Friend of the Family). The Seacliff Mafia produces the annual Christmas Surprise anthology, a gift for bookshops, friends and clients. The series was conceived and inspired by The Beatles who used to produce a single for their fans at Christmas time. But the Seacliff Mafia doesn't quite stop there. Its tentacles are long and strong and extend outwards to all corners of New Zealand and in-between.

The Seacliff Mafia first began in the 1970s when the Earl of Seacliff lived in the coastal Otago village of Seacliff and incorporates anybody, anywhere who has been published by ESAW plus the many founding members like Bryan Harold and the rest of the 'Harold/Bailey Gang', Juanita Ketchell, David Eggleton, Martin Schanzel, Robin Swanney- McPherson, Peter Olds, Sandra Bell, Brian Hare, Nigel Yates, Paul Joseph, Winsome Aroha, Bill Dacker and many others. Like all good families we all protect and look after one another, and beware any who cross us. The Seacliff Mafia has been involved in many surreal and Dadaesque performances including 'Stomach Cabaret' (1974), 'Reggae Mortis' (1978), the 'Moon Over The Manse' (I's seen da Moonbow), right down to the present day 'Winter Readings' in Wellington, which celebrate the 'popular artist/music' reality of our lives. At one time in the 1970s artist and Family member Robin Swanney-McPherson replicated a costume worn by Dada artist Hugo Ball in which the Earl performed in a show in Dunedin. The Earl also baptised a Family member's child during a hangi at Seacliff.

The Search

Date of Publication: 2007
Publisher: ESAW
Category: Poetry

The Search brings together a collection of 'lost' poems and two stories unearthed from Mark Pirie's early folders, notebooks and journals (mostly handwritten and written between 1993 and1996). Together they form an interesting collection showing his early experimentation with form and style towards his own unique and prolific voice in contemporary New Zealand poetry. *The Search* poems usher in the influence of new generational movements like Grunge and hip-hop as well as older influences. Most of the subjects of the early poems involve Wellington and to complement the poems Pirie has added a section of new poems about Wellington and some 'fine photos by John Girdlestone illustrate the compact details of city life' (Owen Bullock, *Poetry NZ*). Many of Wellington's well known street people and personalities feature in Pirie's poems, including elegies for Robert Jones, Paddy O'Dowd and a tribute to busker legend 'Kenny'. This book will be of interest to people who have travelled to or lived in Wellington over the last decade, and can relate to many of the memories and places mentioned in the poems.

Seyb & O'Leary

Michael O'Leary met Wayne Seyb, who lived in Karitane, just north of Dunedin, in the early 1990s, when he was living in the next township of Seacliff. Seyb read O'Leary's novel *The Irish Annals of New Zealand* in one sitting on the busride home one evening. Seyb was so impressed with it that he said he would like to do some artwork based on the book. Seyb knew that Michael was also an artist as well as a writer and he suggested that they make the paintings together. This was an intriguing concept, for while Michael knew of collaborations between artists and writers such as McCahon and Baxter, and Hotere and Tuwhare, he couldn't remember any where the writer and artist both did the actual artwork together. While this may be commonplace now, in those days it was a new and exciting idea. Over a month or so they both did some working drawings based on the notion of producing one large painting for each of the five chapters of the book. Then they met together with the working drawings and began to work on the paintings themselves. This was carried out in the basement of the bookshop and art gallery that was run by O'Leary and fellow artist Bryan Harold. The bookshop was called 'O'Books' and the gallery was called 'O'oops'. Wayne and Michael worked on the paintings over several weeks and when completed had five paintings, each five feet by eight feet. They are on hardboard with a wooden frame around each one. The materials used include house paint and oil paint sticks. Wayne at the time was influenced by German Expressionism and this is reflected in the paintings, as is Michael's interest in Celtic and Polynesian/Māori motifs. Wayne Seyb's work continues to appear and be exhibited. A recent issue of the literary magazine, *Takahe*, featured his artwork.

Shake Speer's Faith

Date of Publication: 1998
Publisher: Original Books
Category: Poetry

O'Leary's poem ['Shake Speer's Faith'] is a masterpiece and an indubitable epic in many respects. It is magnificently organised in structure, from the 'Prologue in Heaven' to the 'Epilogue in Hell', which of course looks back to the *Book of Job* and *Faust*.

O'Leary's poem is an epic (or at least a short epic, an epyllion) because it deals with historical figures and events. There is no doubt that even at the end of the 20th century there is great sensitivity in many quarters to treatment of Nazi personalities in any but the most disapprobatory terms. However, O'Leary is justified in epicising Nazis, because that is exactly what every epic does. Who thinks Hector and Achilles were anything but thugs? What was Aeneas? Of all the historical figures in world history the one always put on a par with Adolf Hitler is Attila the Hun, a notable character in all versions of the great Teutonic epic: the Nibelungelied.

Concern may be felt that O'Leary relates himself in the persona of Rubesahl to his historical material. However, all writers of epic involve themselves and the views of their own age in their epics. The most obvious and extreme example is Dante, but it is true of all epic writers, even Homer, who makes fun of the Olympian gods and obviously does not personally share the values of his militarists. This is true, though Homer was in fact a series of redactors still working on the text as late as 300 BC. That's how all the early epics developed. The Nibelungenlied author is no different from Homer in the same respects. In fact he goes for laughs even more obviously.

This poem is in the Spanish manner in respect that it is written in an adaptation of the Quintilla, in Spanish metre, a verse of five octosyllabic lines of which no three consecutive lines may rhyme together.

People may wonder why O'Leary has written his epic in such a style as he uses, one given to long involute sentences. Again this is the authentic style of epic from Homer to Dante. O'Leary feels it matches Spenser's. In fact it is much more like Shelley's. Nobody has ever been able to punctuate Shelley's verse helpfully. Indeed Shelley didn't even try, leaving it to his friends (such as Peacock, who can't be said to have succeeded). O'Leary hardly bothers with punctuation anyway. But if you attend to the text carefully you will always find at any point that O'Leary's text hangs upon some point that precedes, though it may be a few good lines before. Also remember that all epics are prosaic.

O'Leary's epic may be difficult and may never be popular, but it is the summation of themes that have run through O'Leary's fiction and poetry for 20 years. That is why it is given these extended remarks. – *F W N Wright*

(From the Foreword to *Toku Tinihanga: Selected Poems 1982-2002*, HeadworX, 2003)

The Singing Harp

Date of Publication: 2004
Publisher: ESAW
Category: Poetry

The Singing Harp (a collection of Iain Sharp's performance pieces from his Globe Hotel reading days in the '80s) was his first collection of poetry since 1985. On the back cover, Sharp writing of poetry stated, 'The mania still [affected] him occasionally in the early hours of the morning ... Everything sings, he insists, if you listen hard enough. But this might be just a buzz in his failing ears.' The collection contained his performance masterpieces and audience favourites at readings such as 'Do the Splog', 'Ponsonby Strut' and 'The Poets', a comic ode to poetry: 'Poetry. Dear old poetry. Your dusty relics groan on forgotten shelves of secondhand bookshops - Wordsworth and Shelley bearded with cobwebs.' - *Mark Pirie*

> " "
>
> 'To those who were at the Globe readings, this book will resonate ... accessibility, wit, the occasional glittering image and imaginitive leap, a certain larrikin naughtiness at times and sometimes a deft use of rhyme ...' - James Norcliffe, *New Zealand Books*

Slips

Date of Publication: 2008
Publisher: ESAW
Category: Poetry mini series

Review of Mark Pirie's *Slips: cricket poems*

I discovered cricket in 1969. At the time, we lived in Otatara, south of Invercargill. The only access I had to test cricket (for the uninitiated, this means five-day games between nations) was via radio: 4YC out of Dunedin were broadcasting commentaries on that summer's tests between New Zealand and the West Indies. It wasn't a powerful station, and the only way I could get reception in our house was to put my radio on top of the metal toilet cistern, which amplified the signal. (It's possible this was inconvenient to other occupants of the house.)

Cricket is an old game which has developed a massive literature: not just the primary literature of statistics and match reports, but a secondary literature of fiction, poetry and plays. Mark Pirie has recently made a welcome addition to this literature with Slips, which is No. 21 in the Earl of Seacliff Art Workshop's excellent mini-series of poem booklets. Slips is dedicated to Harry Ricketts, another cricketing poet (and biographer), thus acknowledging its place in this literary tradition.

Mark knows whereof he speaks. My cricketing days are well past me, but my son played junior cricket up to the 2006/07 season, and several times, just as his team were packing up for the day, Mark would turn up with his senior team. The cover of Slips shows Mark poised to take a slips catch (again, for US readers, the slips are like extra shortstops who stand behind the batter and take catches off what in

baseball would be fouls).

All the poems inside are about, or at least allude to, cricket. These allusions range from the glancing to the highly statistical: 'Legacies and Cold Stats' and 'Fiery Fred' would delight any cricket historian, while the longest poem, '11 Ways of Being Dismissed', is based on a cricinfo article about unusual dismissals.

My two favourite poems in the book aren't so stats-heavy. 'At Browns Bay' is a beautiful love lyric, while 'The Pavilion', following a long literary tradition, uses cricket as a metaphor for life.

This book displays many of the virtues of Mark Pirie's poetry: humour, moving writing about grief and loss, and some classic last lines. I particularly like the final line of 'Joe', about a gentleman who starts distracting the scorer:

I watch his words aeroplane up and down his breath.

Whether or not you know your doosra from your googly, *Slips* is worth catching. - *Tim Jones*

(From Tim Jones' *Books in the Trees*, 14 April 2008)

> **" "**
>
> "Many thanks ... for *Slips* ... in which you have correctly caught the whole gambit in the life of a cricketer - fifth grade or Test Match.' – Don Neely, personal letter, 23 July 2008

"Sonnet for Victor O'Leary"

Date of Composition: 2008
Collection: *Paneta Street*
Anthologised in: *broadsheet: new new zealand poetry 1*

Michael O'Leary had often heard the name Victor O'Leary over the years but did not know that they were related. His sister, Clare, had been good friends with Sean O'Leary and one day Clare's partner, Cathy Ellis, worked out that Sean was related to their O'Leary family. Then Sean told us that the poet, Victor O'Leary, was his father. This made Victor Michael O'Leary's second cousin, and while Michael only got to know him briefly before he died in 2008 he was really pleased to learn that he and Victor were so close. Michael met Victor at his bookshop in Paekakariki and a photograph of them together taken by Victor's wife, Marianne O'Leary, is on the cover of the ESAW reprint (mini-book 14, 2007) of his 1958 poetry collection, 'The Sensual Anchor', first published by Louis Johnson's Capricorn Press in a 3-poets anthology with Peter Bland and John Boyd. Victor O'Leary was a member of the 'Glenco' group of Wellington writers in the early 1950s, another of whom was James K. Baxter. Before he died Victor gave Michael a copy of a letter from Baxter to Victor as well as a copy of an unpublished Baxter poem, which O'Leary has interwoven into the text of his new novel, *Magic Alex's Revenge*, needle-in-a-haystack style. The photo of Victor and Michael together was later used for the front cover of Mark Pirie's new chapbook poetry journal, *broadsheet: new new zealand poetry*. Richard Langston wrote a response to the photo in his unpublished poem 'Sunday':

> The two poets on the front of the book
> are dying -
> one, in fact is already dead.
> He can no longer feel the hand of his fellow poet
> resting on his shoulder.
>
> ...

Sunday is the most mortal day.
It is a violin's slow sad note.

1 October, 2008

Sounds of Sonnets

Date of Publication: 2006
Publisher: HeadworX
Category: Poetry

Sonnet Showcase

New Zealand poets have written sonnets since they have written anything at all in English. All our 4,000 poets probably contribute a few. Some have written and published whole books of sonnets, lately anyway. But I haven't noticed that we have had a national anthology of sonnets or even a substantial critical coverage of New Zealand sonnets. Maybe the sonnet is a side of our culture that has never got the recognition it deserves.

So a book of 25 sonnets each by the two most publicly active and enterprising contemporary New Zealand poets is a timely eye opener on one of our needlessly dark corners. In English the sonnet has come in two forms: the traditional form of Shakespeare, Milton and Wordsworth which held sway till 1915 you can say, and since then the modern sonnet which characteristically uses shorter lines, so is less verbose and avoids old-style rhymes, so is less cliched.

The present offering of sonnets well illustrates these points. Both poets can rhyme their sonnets: Michael O'Leary often enough to show he is proficient that way, Mark Pirie just once in this selection.

There was an attempt in the 19th century to make the sonnet a more down home conversational vehicle for the anecdote. Mark Pirie finds this approach highly congenial and is seen most typically and consistently himself in the sonnet whether the result is a confession or a character study.

Both poets use the sonnet for obituaries and satires.

Michael O'Leary's poetry is often highly personalised. He can convey emotion most convincingly. His sonnets showcase the very wide range of his technical skill and his interests. – *F W N Wright*

"Station to Station: a Cognac for David"

Date of Composition: 2002
Collection: *Make Love and War*
Anthologised in: *Taumarunui: Unlevel crossings of the literary kind*

Written during two of O'Leary's many trips by train from Wellington to Auckland on the Overlander. On this journey O'Leary decided to take a notebook with him. Each station along the route was the subject of an individual, impressionist poem: hence, 'Station to Station'. The first trip went as far as Taumarunui where O'Leary met Iain Sharp who wanted to interview him about his novel *Unlevel Crossings*. They spent an afternoon and evening in Taumarunui before returning by night train, O'Leary to Wellington, Iain to Auckland. Michael's friend Paddy Rainsford, of 'Saturday Night' fame, went on the last night train half way to Auckland and back with O'Leary, during that journey all the staff, including the drivers and train crew, signed a copy of *Unlevel Crossings* for him to mark the demise of the Northerner Express. 'Station to Station' was also the name of an album by David Bowie, and O'Leary remembers 'going to the "Serious Moonlight" Bowie concert in Christchurch and walking towards the venue and hearing the eerie synthesized sound of a steam engine sounding out loudly over the speakers. It was spooky, having just arrived from Dunedin on the Southerner about half an hour before the concert began.' But the 'cognac for David' reference alludes to the time in Auckland when Bowie was making the film 'Merry Christmas Mister Lawrence'. O'Leary's friend and fellow poet/musician Sandra Bell was working at the Ariashi Japanese Restaurant in downtown Auckland at the time, where Bowie used to go for an evening meal. At the time Michael was working at a labouring job on Queen Street and he knew he would not be presentable enough to enter, so he gave Sandra some money and asked her to buy Bowie a glass of cognac as an appreciation for his work. Michael wrote a note which stated: 'To the thin white Duke, from the fat black Earl.'

Straight

Date of Publication: 1984
Publisher: ESAW
Category: Fiction
Extract anthologised in: *Te Ao Marama* 3

New urban novel

Michael O'Leary, Ōrākei born and bred, has written a novel, *Straight,* in which he contrasts childhood memories of Auckland with the city as it is today.

His first novel, it is the celebration of the diverse elements of Auckland that make the city unique in New Zealand. O'Leary's first 17 years were spent in the state housing area of Ōrākei (Tautari Street). Brought up with a strong sense of Irish ancestry and an awareness of Māori issues, O'Leary says he remembers his mother singing Māori songs as she did the family washing in the old copper.

'Ōrākei is significant in that it has state housing amidst rich real estate,' says O'Leary. 'It has Bastion Point and is the centre of the Ngati Whatua people. There is a multi-cultural character about Ōrākei which sets it apart from other areas of Auckland. 'Growing up there has affected how I look at things, making me aware of cultural differences, racism, economic differences between the rich and the poor.'

O'Leary's schooling took place at St Joseph's School, Ōrākei Primary and Selwyn College. His story-telling knack started during school days when he used to write songs and short stories or tell tales to entertain local school children on the way home. Free time was spent mostly hanging around Ōkāhu Bay, playing with other kids from the neighbourhood.

In 1968, both parents died and O'Leary left Ōrākei to go and live with an uncle. He then lived in the South Island for six years doing a range of jobs, working for the Railways, in offices, doing labouring and roadworks jobs. He admits he has problems holding down regular jobs or anything that requires settling down. *Straight* begins with the train journey back into Auckland after the time away, the author's feelings dominated by 'melancholy and memory' as the city reveals new buildings and big changes, as the train passes familiar landmarks that trigger off images from the past:

> As we pass into Meadowbank I feel torn from every side by emotion and memory ... the train passes under the Ōrākei overbridge ... I can see the mysterious gin factory to the left ... I could never believe that's what it was when I was young because I thought all things like that came from overseas ... Ōrākei, I struggle to understand the meaning of the word, but the train is moving again for me. I can see the old sewer pipe we used to walk across to Parnell and back.

> Only now as I enter excitedly the outskirts of my childhood do I begin to understand Rangi's explanation of the ancestral proverb ... I catch a glimpse of ghetto-like Glen Innes spread out like a ragged carpet, spread out like an inaccurate map of my past, and I know I am almost home.

O'Leary's writing, first published in the early 1980s, includes *Ten Sonnets: Myths and Legends of Love, Surrogate Children* (with Sandra Bell and Brian Hare), *Grafton Cemetery, Gone West* (Waikumete Cemetery) as well as stories and poems in various journals.

Straight, his first novel, is significant because it deals with urban themes and confronts issues such as racism, class conflict and the stresses of people's relationships in the city.

'In New Zealand literature the urban novel has been neglected,' says O'Leary. 'Most New Zealand writing is how beautiful the countryside is, but few people have paid any homage to the city. I believe Auckland is big enough to warrant something written especially about it in celebration of its particular qualities.'

He believes this neglect ties into the conservative nature of the New Zealand character and the fact that New Zealanders are afraid to express themselves emotionally. 'We are a nation of snails,' says O'Leary, 'hiding away in rural literature which is not confronting. An urban environment forces people to inter-relate and express themselves, if an urban novel reflects that it cannot avoid being confronting itself.'

O'Leary's concept of a writer is a person who brings out matters not usually talked about. He thinks art and writing should challenge a pattern of life in New Zealand which shields and protects the Anglo Saxon view of life where 'all is duty'. Writers and artists have a role to play in breaking down barriers and helping people to emerge from tightly swaddled cocoons.

'I'm not into the sleepy stuff,' says O'Leary, 'literature should stir things up.' Also, there has been enough of the humourless and bleak 'man alone' theme in New Zealand writing. *Straight* is a positive attempt to counter these traditions. In it the main character comes from being isolated to joining a family network.

For O'Leary the writer's role is equivalent to that of a witch doctor, evoking, agitating, healing and providing an intensity other people cannot.

'In order to write differently, I believe you have to live differently,' says O'Leary. 'The conflict between being a writer, and working in a regular job is something always confronting me.'

(From the *Gazette and Inner City News*, Auckland, c.1985)

The Super Man

Date of Publication: 1988
Publisher: ESAW
Category: Fiction

Super high in the '50s

(Review of Neil Rennie's *The Super Man*)

This particular Super Man galvanised by aircraft rather than telephone kiosks was born in Helensville in 1933. He joined the R.N.Z.A.F. in 1952, learned to fly at Wigram, and was thrown out just before graduation. By then he had lost his virginity to an Older Woman, escaped marriage to a Younger Woman who lured him into making her pregnant, shot down her angry boyfriend while duelling in armed Harvards over Lake Ellesmere, and decided not to end it all by flying into the Christchurch-Dunedin express.

Fortunately, he had already met Super Woman: who is, of course, a History student at Canterbury University. They settle in Southland and we follow their jointly hectic fortunes through to 1958 when Super Woman saves Super Man from death following a Tiger Moth crash that is entirely his fault.

Anyone who remembers the Golden Fifties in New Zealand will find plenty to interest them in this novel. The flying background, both military and civilian, is detailed and accurate; so, too is the account of hardships, rivalries and triumphs in the exciting early days of aerial topdressing.

This is Mr Rennie's first novel and should not be his last. He already has two of the main qualities needed for success - the diligence to create an authentic setting and the imagination to invent dramatic incidents - although at present his characters are not always convincing when they speak to each other. The book is a well-made paperback and includes several excellent line-drawings, but Mr Rennie and his publisher both need to take a closer look at grammar.

Even so, *The Super Man* is a good read, easily commanding attention from first page to last and I commend it warmly to those who would like to see more television dramas set and made in New Zealand. The essential Tiger

Moths, Harvards, Cessnas and Fletchers still exist; huge areas of the South Island have not yet been ruined; and there are some under-employed New Zealanders.

The book could easily be transformed into an endless serial covering a fascinating decade in our past when farmers were prosperous and self-confident, well able to squash snotty little bank managers described by Mr Rennie with great relish in one of his most vivid scenes. Community spirit was strong, everyone had jobs, drank beer and/or danced for relaxation, and knew nothing of drugs or telly. We adored the Queen, climbed Everest, beat the Springboks, and feared Wales.

Moreover, pouring fertiliser from the air onto steep hillsides is difficult, dangerous, obviously useful, and highlights photogenic work that should enthrall viewers around the world. Better still, one of the principal characters is a nice Pommie who loves it here and another is a Māori pilot awarded the Victoria Cross during the war, though we won't learn this until he is dead. – *Vincent Orange*

Swing and Other Stories

Date of Publication: 2002
Publisher: ESAW
Category: Fiction

Review of Mark Pirie's *Swing and Other Stories*

As usual, Mark Pirie's done the hard work for us already, in the blurb:

> These stories ... represent a view of urban living in '90s New
> Zealand ... and while displaying some of the characteristics of
> 'grunge-lit' and 'new-lad writing' of the time, they remain robust
> enough to take on a character of their own .

I really like those labels, 'grunge-lit ... new- lad' writing. If they're reviewers' cliches, they're ones I hadn't encountered before. I guess my own reaction would be simpler. These stories are about a bunch of useless slackers whose only interests seem to consist of scamming people, going on the piss, and getting laid. They have no redeeming nobility, no sense of moral purpose, and are completely unedifying. They're also extremely funny.

Hunting for favourites is always a bit invidious, but I guess I liked the impromptu taxi-service one ('The Ride') best, as it offered some useful tips on how to make some quick cash on a late night in the city - if you have a borrowed car and no scruples - as well as exemplifying the kind of plotless *joie-de-vivre* which is one of Pirie's greatest strengths. I also enjoyed 'It's the Mornings that Piss You off the Most,' mainly because it shows Pirie trying to get in touch with his feminine side - i.e. trying to inhabit one of his *female* bottom- feeders for a change. It wasn't till the last page of the story that I even noticed, actually (it seemed a bit odd that a Pirie character should care about the colour of his thighs in the sunlight ... *Ooh, dodgy territory, Mark*, I was thinking, until I realised). The more deliberately surrealist stories, 'White Wash', 'A Man is Going to Start Installing Cable in this Suburb Soon,' work well enough individually, but they're not as fruitful a direction for Pirie, I feel. They only really spark into life the moment there's some dialogue or character assassination required.

On the strength of this book, I feel that Mark Pirie should certainly persevere with fiction: perhaps there's an immense slacker novel lying dormant within him, waiting to *arise* and blow *Trainspotting* out of the water. – *Jack Ross*

(from *Spin* 45 (2003))

> " "
>
> 'Swing is a serious book, commenting on the mid-1990s and free market society. Its primary subjects are young, urban dwelling outsiders in Wellington: stoners, fraudsters, a repo man, young flatters, alcoholics, sex workers and poets. This book also took its inspiration from a book by an earlier New Zealand writer: John Reece Cole'' only collection, It was so late and other stories, which deals with jazz culture in the 1940s.' – Helen Rickerby, *NZ Poetry Society Newsletter*

Ten Minutes to Midnight

Date of Publication: 1989
Publisher: ESAW
Category: Non-fiction

Review of Colin Lloyd Amery's *Ten Minutes to Midnight*

An excitable account of the author's 1986 attempt to bring a private prosecution against French agents Marfart and Prieur, aimed at preventing their imminent departure from New Zealand imprisonment to a tropical staging-post. Other material includes sketches of some of the leading players in the drama, murdered Greenpeace photographer Fernando Pereira among them, and some account of more recent events. Although not as full as other publications on the *Rainbow Warrior* bombing, no collection of books about that incident would be complete without this one. The questions it raises about the New Zealand legal system, in particular, will be of wide interest. – *Dale Williams*

(From *New Zealand Listener*, 12 March 1990)

> **" "**
>
> 'Colin Lloyd Amery has written a diverting footnote to the Rainbow Warrior affair. Offered as a legal treatise, this slim but engaging essay is Amery's account of how the French terrorists slipped the laws of New Zealand.' – Andrew Stone, *New Zealand Herald*

They Drank Kava

Date of Publication: 2004
Publisher: ESAW
Category: Poetry

Review of Moshé Liba's *They Drank Kava*

They Drank Kava by Wellington-based Israeli poet Moshé Liba is published by the Earl of Seacliff Art Workshop. Liba's sub-heading is 'An imaginary journey through a failed coup': to my mind he plots the progress of the recent Fiji coup led by George Speight pretty accurately. Not that Fiji or George Speight are ever mentioned by name. The country is just an 'archipelago in the Pacific Basin' while he ap- pears only as 'the bold Leader'. Throughout is the constant lament that the indigenous people have 'had enough of newcomers getting equal rights', and, in the best ballad tradition, the refrain 'they drank kava' - appears at the end of every page.

Poetry can often appear obscure or esoteric but this work engages one's attention immediately. The writing is lucid yet colourful; the gripes of the 'people of the land' against democracy, parliaments and other western cultural ideas, imposed on their own way of life, clearly stated. (Though it seems paradoxical that Christianity, a typically western religion, quite recently imposed on Pacific cultures, is accepted as part of their tradition.) But despite the unease of the indigenous people, the injustice meted out to Indo-Fijians lingers constantly in the background - as Banquo's ghost does in Shakespeare's *Macbeth*.

Yet while drama - and even tragedy - unfolds, Moshé Liba imbues his story with a touch of humour. The islanders' solution to every problem seems to have been 'they drank kava'. In those words he encapsulates the Scarlett O'Hara mindset, 'I'll think about it tomorrow', so prevalent among the inhabitants of tropical climates.

And despite the gravity of the situation, the repeated refrain tends to remind one of musical equivalents, e.g. Berlioz's use of the *idee fixe,* in *Symphonic Fantastique* or 'The partridge in a pear tree' from *The Twelve Days of Christmas.* It is perhaps ironic that an Israeli poet should present us with the dilemma of choosing between the indigenous and the new immigrants when his homeland has 'the Palestinian problem' ... just as our own has the tangata whenua flexing muscle against the dominant Pakeha population. Is he saying that these enigmas are only soluble by forgoing confrontation and sitting down quietly to talk and 'drink kava' or whatever? – *Bernard Holibar*

(From the *New Zealand Poetry Society Newsletter,* September 2004)

Tiger Words

Date of Publication: 2002

Publisher: ESAW

Category: Poetry

Contributors: Janet Bayly, Dinah Hawken, Hiona Henare, Julie Liebrich, Whare McColl, Michael O'Leary, Roma Potiki, Lindsay Rabbitt, J C Sturm and Denis Welch.

The title of *Tiger Words*, edited by Michael O'Leary, was the name given to a series of poetry readings held at Michael O'Leary's Pukapuka Bookshop, Paekakariki, during a visit by American golfer Tiger Woods to Kapiti early in 2002. Designed to provide an alternative event which highlighted the cultural activities, as opposed to sporting ones, of the Kapiti region, the Tiger Words afternoons proved popular. The concept of Tiger Words is not only a pun on the great golfer's name, but also refers to the nature of poetry itself. That is, a use of words which can be seen as beautiful - but may also be unpredictable and dangerous.

To...

Date of Publication: 2004
Publisher: ESAW
Category: Poetry

To... is Bill Dacker's first collection of poetry. Dacker is known primarily as an accomplished Otago historian and researcher. He has dealt primarily with the Māori history of the lower South Island. This collection shows another side to the analytical, objective skills demanded by scholarly writing. The publisher's blurb states: 'Intensely personal, alternately humourous and painful, these intimate and beautiful lyrics expose the difficult and loving nature of family life in varying stages of development and transformation. In many ways it is a personal letter **To** ... his children, his former wife, his whanau generally, attempting to explain and understand at one and the same time.' Included in this collection is Dacker's poem on David Gray and the massacre at Aramoana, and its after effects on the small town's community. Dacker's poem is one of the finest artistic responses to the tragedy, and deals with the horrific event in a much more complex and humane way to the Sarkies' film *Out of the blue*. – *Mark Pirie*

> " "
>
> 'These are solid somewhat old-fashioned poems deeply rooted in the South. There is a line drawing on the back cover of the book portraying the Dacker living room. I can best imagine these poems being read here by the poet to his whanau. The lights are low, the fire is flickering. I can almost hear his voice.'
> – James Norcliffe, *New Zealand Books*

"To My Mother"

Date of Composition: 1985

Collection: *Con Art: Selected Poems, Toku Tinihanga: Selected Poems 1982-2002, TAB Ula Rasa: New and Selected Poems*

O'Leary writes: 'This is a sad, beguiling sort of a poem, and despite its simplicity it is the most difficult for me to write about. It is me looking at an old photograph of my mother, who died when I was eighteen (as did my father), and trying to work out the feelings and thoughts I have about her several years later. My mother and I were very close and I think she over-protected me as a child because of various childhood illnesses I had.' The poem is written in an internal dialogue type of structure, asking questions and answering with further questions. The fact that many of O'Leary's girlfriends over the years have either been Māori or Polynesian women got him contemplating why he was more attracted to them and whether it was something to do with his mother being part Māori. His brother and sister, like O'Leary, grew up under her influence more than their father's influence, who was often away working nightshifts, or at the pub, or TAB.

Toku Tinihanga

Date of Publication: 2003
Publisher: HeadworX
Category: Poetry

Michael O

When I want to hear from you
I take you down from the shelf,

your selected poems *Toku Tinihanga*.
Your voice the confluence of the blood

of a providential NZ Irishman and the
barefoot wairua of Māori. The story

you are serious about is the old one,
made or unmade, no matter, so felt

in your poems it could only be love.
It failed in the south and made you

a weeping coat, a black wintercoat.
Mr Yates's photographs of you capture

the light and shade in your eyes.
But your hair still flows like ideas,

and your head sounds with wakes and tangi,
Irish jigs and haka, a mad party of the mind

where Hone Heke shakes hands with Baxter
and Hendrix, all aboard a train running

through your dreaming days. It's *Out Of It*.

Memory is a train speeding on.

That's where you dig,
where you bring it all back.

And I know to find you in the only
true place to find a writer: your words.

Richard Langston

Review of Michael O'Leary's *Toku Tinihanga: Selected Poems 1982-2002*

If you are looking for a well-presented book by a New Zealand poet at the peak of his powers, you could hardly go past this book, *Toku Tinihanga* - a collection of poems by Paekakariki poet, Michael O'Leary. In this book many of the things we've come to love about New Zealand poetry, from the rock 'n' roll tributes of Sam Hunt to the mystical Catholic insight and honesty of James K. Baxter, are brought together in a bi-cultural setting, with elements of autobiography, love and philosophy thrown in for good measure.

Despite the appearance of the rather wild looking man on the cover, there is a strongly traditional, sometimes conservative element to many of the poems, such as the epic fable 'Rubesahl'.

The book is in five clear sections, and some poems are translated into Māori. The second section contains love poems that appear to show a powerful and seemingly elusive love for an unnamed woman. What is so pleasing is the variety of poetic styles, from elegies and sonnets to haiku, verse and love songs with a flowing and easy command of all forms.

O'Leary's indulgence in puns is sometimes startling as in 'Tom Waits for no-one' and on a train to the Hutt Valley, 'the Ava gardener tends his plot'. However, these often lead to some quite brilliant beyond pun wordplays, such as the Irish pub called O'Ryan and Maher's (Orion and Mars). Amongst the truly memorable are such gems as:

Stalinesque architecture of Te Papa
We rest take a frugal repast for our supper

Or:

> You drowned and I wept like a river
> Then sailed home to a solitary life.

There are enough real moments of worldly vision here to keep one dipping into it forever. This book belongs in all collections of New Zealand poetry, and may well occupy an important place in our cultural history. – *Graeme Collins*

(From *Southern Ocean Review* 27, 12 April 2003*)*

Launch of Michael O'Leary's *Toku Tinihanga* and Mark Pirie's *Dumber*

And a book is launched! Off it goes from the safe harbour of the mind into the heavy seas of public scrutiny and criticism. Glasses clink. The important people sail about, conversing judiciously, while the unimportant examine their fingernails, nervously eavesdropping and trying not to say anything stupid. Right?

Wednesday, April 30, saw a different sort of launch which certainly lacked that special view up people's noses these affairs sometimes offer. Two collections of poetry were unveiled, one a retrospective of over twenty years' writing, and the other a new collection by a younger poet - an unlikely combination. Even more unlikely is that the publisher of each was the writer of the other, or vice versa, if you see what I mean. To be more clear, Mark Pirie's imprint HeadworX launched Michael O'Leary's impressive 159-page retrospective, and O'Leary's company, Earl of Seacliff Art Workshop, which has published poetry and literary fiction since the '80s, launched Pirie's fifth collection.

This auspicious occasion took place at the new Bizy Bee's bookstore on Manners Street in Wellington. This was the store's first book launch and owners Bob and Judith Burch were delighted with the event. Judith commented on her desire to encourage new writers, while husband Bob said simply and succinctly, 'I thought it was wonderful.' Lewis Scott, who magnanimously MC'd, told me he saw this launch as indicative of a new trend: 'The thing that happened tonight clearly represents a tangible point where NZ literature takes on a nuance of the shades of people that are walking the streets of Aotearoa today.'

Pirie's publishing interests focus on neglected poets and new poets who may fall through the gaping cracks in the mainstream market. He's developed a reputation, both through HeadworX and his journal *JAAM,* for discovering new talent and showcasing poetry that is representative of a very wide scope of our culture. Niel Wright, who introduced both poets, says of Pirie, 'His achievements in the past ten years have no match in our history.'

Pirie's book is a meditation, or anti-meditation really, on the 'dumbing down' he sees pervading our society and culture. The collection, fittingly titled *Dumber,* is book-ended by ironic poems addressed to God, and visits everything from sex to literature in between. His style, while patently individual and varied, takes cues from the beat poets, Henry Miller and the Kiwi Bloke, as well as formats that inherently preclude intelligent discourse, such as personal ads. The outcome challenges you to find where the dumb ends and the intelligent begins.

Last Days

A Raymond Carver blues

From where they're standing
the light is not so good. She walks
ahead, eschewing a smile. She
leads him on into shadow,
a certain blackness falling

at her feet. Then, later,
in the woods, they find a clearing,
and he spies a look of sadness in her eyes
as she takes him by the hand, and slowly
they make love for the last time.

Tomorrow, she will leave.
'Goodbye,' she'll say. 'Thanks. No, I
mean it...' At least that's what he
thinks she'll say as she drives away,
a new man already at her side.

In another city, in another life perhaps,
they'll exchange phone-calls, and
remember those 'old summer days', when,
married, a flower in her hair, a ribbon
tied to her dress, she awaited his soft hands.

The title of O'Leary's collection, *Toku Tinihanga,* translates as either self-deception or deception of others. Many of the poems will be familiar to his readers. What is remarkable is the care he's taken in selecting the poems and how they're organised within the book. Collected works can sometimes be daunting simply because they are a mass of poems with no apparent connection amongst themselves, organised chronologically or worse yet, alphabetically. This collection boasts sections that feel like chapters, which lend it coherence as well as a sense of sympathy or intimacy with the poet's perception of his own poems. The most striking feature of O'Leary's writing is his honesty - which makes the title a poem in itself. Niel Wright says in his Foreword to the book, 'This book of poems presents the most ready approach to a powerful writer who never falls into mediocrity and consistently shows a strain of genius.'

Saturday Night

(for Patrick)

I have been drunk! On each of Baudelaire's
Fancy wings have I flown.
On wine, poetry, and the tail-wing of virtue
Have I in drunken chariots gone.

Drink! Drink! Drink! With the nebulous goal,
To find the limitless mind and soul.
On! On! On! Through light, time, and sound
Too late! I fall to the ground.

Which I hit with a terrible smash
And as a Phoenix, turn to ash.
You ask, "Like the bird
Will you rise again soon?"
I answer, "Yes, Sunday, Monday,
Or maybe Tuesday afternoon!"

Both collections, as well as the latest edition of *JAAM*, are available at bookstores, including Bizy Bee's Bookstore. – *Amelia Nurse*

30 April 2003

(From the *New Zealand Poetry Society Newsletter,* June 2003)

Toku Tinihanga CD

Date of Release: 2003

Publisher: ESAW Sounds Division

Tracks: 'He Waiatanui kia Aroha', 'Saturday Night', 'Southerners Crossing', 'Just Like a Bird' and 'Us at the Funeral of John Patrick Kennedy - 1994'

Toku Tinihanga, the Earl's sole CD release, was recorded at Waimea Studios in Christchurch in late 2002 with the help and assistance of Trevor Bycroft. Bycroft composed and arranged the music as backing to Michael's spoken words. 'He Waiatanui kia Aroha', the longest track on the album, which is set to piano music, is O'Leary's poem sequence for his friend Winsome Aroha. A long extended version of the poem 'Us at the Funeral of John Patrick Kennedy - 1994' also features, with Michael in full flow reciting the poem in Māori. Two tracks on the CD, 'Just Like a Bird' and Southerners Crossing', feature renditions of Michael's song lyrics by the Dunedin-Irish band Blackthorn, composed and arranged by Paul and Patsy Ryan. The first song on the CD, 'Saturday Night', which is an electric blues number, later made its way on to the Australian CD-ROM journal *papertiger* in Mark Pirie's mini- anthology of New Zealand poetry, *50 Poems by 50 Poets*.

Tupelo Hotel

Date of Publication: 2004

Publisher: ESAW

Category: Poetry

Contributors: Emily Dobson, Robin Fry, Basim Furat, Michael Harlow, Moshé Liba, Harvey McQueen, Michael O'Leary, Mark Pirie, Jenny Powell, Helen Rickerby, Jack Ross, L E Scott, Iain Sharp, Moira Wairama and F W N Wright.

This anthology represents the work of poets who participated in the 2004 season of annual winter readings held at the Tupelo Hotel. This event was sponsored by HeadworX, ESAW, Kwanzaa - The Afrikan Shop and the Tupelo Bar, Wellington. The cover features another take off in their continuing series of photographs all taken by Kapiti Coast photographer John Girdlestone. This time they have 'covered' the Doors' album *Morrison Motel*.

"Universal Mind"

Date of Composition: 2000

Collection: *TAB Ula Rasa: New and Selected Poems, Toku Tinihanga: Selected Poems 1982-2002*

'Universal Mind' is a complex poem, inspired by Jim Morrison's song of the same name. O'Leary writes: 'It has a great line about: "Then you came along with a suitcase and a song, turned my world around / now I'm so alone just looking for a home in every face I see / I'm a freedom man"'. This is the effect that pop music and culture had on O'Leary's generation, at least those who 'haven't joined the 'right-wing ex-L.S.D. boys in Treasury / so afraid of their own past / that their illusions are complete.' O'Leary comments: 'I don't usually write direct social or political commentary so openly, but this is a complaint against those people in positions of power who make decisions on behalf of the rest of us but only see the world from their own viewpoint and circumstances.' The poem starts out innocently enough with a description of experiencing an eclipse of the moon with O'Leary's friend Moana when they lived together in Paekakariki. In part two a darker tinge to the poem emerges, looking at a bohemian past of drink and drugs opening only 'doors of deception' - this becoming the opposite of the reason why Jim Morrison called his band 'The Doors'. Then the 'third way' equals nothing but pretentious language poetry, linguistic gymnastics and clever word play, the sound and the fury of wind inside a letterbox signifying nothing.

Unlevel Crossings

Date of Publication: 2002
Publisher: Huia Publishers
Category: Fiction

Kia ora begorrah!

Meeting Michael O'Leary by train in Taumarunui seemed like a good idea at the time. All four of O'Leary's novels - *Straight (1985), Out of It* (1987), *The Irish Annals of New Zealand* (1991) and his new book *Unlevel Crossings* (Huia Publishers, $24.95) begin and end on trains. I don't know any living New Zealand writer who's a bigger railway enthusiast.

Taumarunui is midway between Paekakariki, where O'Leary lives, and Auckland, where I live. It used to be one of the country's busiest railway stations. Most New Zealanders know the chorus of Peter Cape's song 'Taumarunui on the Main Trunk Line'.

Cape's lyrics mention 'popping off to refreshments for a cuppa tea and pie'. When he wrote the song in 1957, Taumarunui's railway station was a bustling place. There's no refreshments area nowadays. There's not even a waiting room. Travellers wait outside on a bench, exposed to the wind.

Heading down on the morning train to meet O'Leary wasn't too bad. But getting home afterwards was a problem. Scheduled to leave Taumarunui at 2.30am, my northbound train was half an hour late. You really notice delays like that when you're freezing in the early hours of the morning with nothing to see but rusting railway lines.

Worse, lightning strikes wrecked some of the electric lines and the signal system on the way back to Auckland. The electric engine had to be replaced with a diesel. That meant another three-hour delay. I've no quarrel with Tranz Rail employees, who struck me as a decent bunch doing their best in difficult circumstances. But, to put matters mildly, by the time I got home I was thinking the little that's left of our railway system doesn't work well. Still, as O'Leary assured me, that's not a bad frame of mind in which to read

Unlevel Crossings. The erosion of public transport and other services for New Zealanders who aren't wealthy is one of the book's key themes.

The central character, Patrick Fitzgerald, sets out on a journey of discovery after working in a factory for 20 years. 'Fitz' isn't exactly an autobiographical creation, O'Leary explains. He's most like an alternative self.

O'Leary runs Pukapuka, a secondhand bookshop on the main street of Paekakariki. He's been on the Kapiti Coast for five years. But in the last three decades he's lived in many parts of New Zealand and taken on a wide variety of occupations from railway guard to road-worker.

Born in Auckland in 1950, he grew up in a state house in Ōrākei - now one of the city's most desirable locations. His childhood home was sold years ago and replaced by a flash condominium.

When he was 17, his father died from a brain haemorrhage. His mother, who was of Te Arawa descent, died less than a year later. O'Leary took a factory job but studied at night school for university entrance. Teachers encouraged his interest in writing.

'I'd always been interested in language,' he says, 'but it came mainly through the lyrics of pop songs. There weren't many books in our house. John Lennon's *In His Own Write* and *A Spaniard in the Works* were the first books I remember buying - they've always been a big influence.

'I went to university when I was in my early 20s. I know lots of writers and artists. But I often wonder what my life might have been like if my mother hadn't died or if I'd just gone on working in factories. The Fitz character comes out of that speculation.'

O'Leary began writing *Unlevel Crossings* in 1990. 'It took me 10 years to write the novel and another two to find a publisher.

'Most of the big publishing houses turned me down because of the experimental nature of some of the writing, before Huia decided to give me a chance.

'Before that, my friend Niel Wright brought out some instalments in small editions as "works in progress". Parts of James Joyce's *Finnegans Wake* first appeared the same way.'

Like Joyce, O'Leary is an irrepressible punster. It's typical of his approach to change the word ancestors to 'incestors' and to refer to extreme right-wing ideas filtering through a process of 'osmosleyis' (a fusion of the word osmosis with British fascist leader Oswald Mosley). Parts of *Unlevel Crossings* are straightforward. Others are so laden with puns, jokes, literary allusions and references to rock songs that they demand multiple readings.

It helps to know Māori too. Some of O'Leary's jokes are bilingual, such as the splendid piece of onomatopoeia in which the rattle of a railway carriage is described as 'karikiti kiraki'. 'Older people don't get the puns and allusions,' says O'Leary, 'but they like the parts about train journeys because it reminds them of the era when rail was still the main way of getting around the country.'

Partly *Unlevel Crossings* is a Joycean language experience and partly it's a literary and political satire, but I think it's also a down-to- earth book about recent changes in New Zealand society. The urban Māori element is important. So are issues like redundancy and what you do when you lose your job. 'I hope it appeals to 3½ million New Zealanders - to anyone with the money to buy it.' – *Iain Sharp*

(From *Sunday Star-Times*, 16 June 2002)

Review of Michael O'Leary's *Unlevel Crossings*

Whenever you hear that lonesome whistle blow, that tootle as a goods train rolls by off in the distance, and reflect for a moment on other journeys, other lives, destinations unknown, choices not made, destinies unfulfilled, and you become maybe melancholy, maybe maudlin, or maybe even unrelievedly happy at your lot, you are in a way entertaining the theme that is the mainspring of the action in Michael O'Leary's new novel *Unlevel Crossings*.

Unlevel Crossings is both a journey of self-discovery and a paean for our once-proud, now-rustbelt, railway system. In this novel, the state of a New Zealander is crossed with the state of New Zealand Rail. *Unlevel Crossings* is an account of both an individual and a society in a state of transit and transition over the past decade or so. In its view- point and its methods it is a bicultural novel about fringe-dwellers. It is a book of many voices, but above them all rises the authorial voice.

Poet, playwright, publisher, novelist, scribe of the marginalised, Michael O'Leary is a writer above all interested in the possibilities of language in all its variety: sending words into slangy, eccentric orbits is one of the things he does best. *Unlevel Crossings* is the story of an outsider trying to make sense of the world, struggling to make different realities match up. It is about intersections and exchanges and transport. It is a splendidly droll novel, memorably comic in its unlevel absurdities, its crossover jesting.

Which is not to say that it is all easy going. Though there are many incidental pleasures there are also many frustrations and obscurities. These are best skimmed over, to be rewardingly dwelt on by those with the inclination for romans a clef. Stick to the essentially straight-ahead narrative and you will be whisked engagingly along, clickety-click, clackety-clack.

Patrick Mika Fitzgerald is a forty-something factory worker in Auckland who is made redundant, whose mother dies, and who loses his home - all around the same time. He decides to pursue a dream he has had, a vision of a beautiful woman's face at the window of the Southerner train; she is waving to him.

Much given to daydreaming, footloose Fitz heads South - by rail - encountering a rogues' gallery of characters, some of whom appear and disappear in the turn of a phrase. The texture of the novel weaves straight realism with word associations, streams of consciousness, rivers of fantasy: 'When they asked (Fitz) questions he answered them in dreams and visions.'

Echoes of the modernist literary canon - quotes and phrases - mingle with the vulgar vernacular, along with echoes of the rock and roll canon, such as snatches of song titles from the likes of the Beatles, the Rolling Stones and U2. *Unlevel Crossings* borrows something of its circular structure and its freewheeling puns from James Joyce's *Finnegans Wake* - a notorious novel, widely shunned by the masses for its obscurantism yet attracting its own loyal following. Early James Joyce, that is the writer of the short stories and of *Ulysses,* is also an inspiration for much of the powerfully eloquent lyricism, especially mood pieces about the landscape. At other times though, O'Leary is as wilfully garrulous as George Bernard Shaw at his most expansive, bailing us up in thickets of whimsy.

A long middle chapter, 'Yellban Apocryphal', which imagines Wellington as phantasmagorical, a kind of Nighttown in the manner of Ulysses, is a tour-de-force of loquacious absurdity, rising to a manic pitch of implausibility. Attending a party at a student flat in deepest Wellington, Fitz encounters a quarrelling, disputatious crew much given to undergraduate humour. There is perhaps something a bit sour about this succession of relentless music hall zanies, these giggling, squiggling cartoons who leap and cavort like tipsy leprechauns for page after page. No wonder Fitz has a nervous breakdown and has to be carted off to hospital. Are these twerpy stooges real, or are they figments of this drug-fuelled innocent's imagination?

The 'Yellban Apocryphal' section delivers wild poetry readings, wilder parties, choreographed chaos, ad-libbed craziness. We meet amongst others: Abel Ard ('absinthe makes the heart grow fonder'), Selcordna ('he seems to speak a kind of Eastern European Esperanto') and Viv Bagnolet ('she's a hard case, that Viv'). These misfits are lively but you can see their creator's hands pulling the strings; they are the creatures of his wilful bidding; he is the pasha of their implausibility, the sultan of their caprice.

And though he is also the Dickens of their denouements, we remain much more interested in and convinced by Fitz, the gormless hero who is able to grow and develop as a result of his encounters and ordeals, his increasing self-knowledge.

And in a way the novel only really gathers steam after Fitz escapes from Wellington and its distractions. As Fitz travels by ferry across Cook Strait the narrative begins to deepen and gain in significance. Fitz encounters someone able to tell him the truth about his father's back- ground and help give his life some coherence. Threads begin to draw together. Ultimately the real shape of the novel is a composite: it is part be-bop beatnik, part lyrical travelogue, part joke-fest. Above all, its verbal music reminds you of jazz, as 'stray horns blow mournfully in mists.'

The southern journey is richly evocative. The author is loath as ever to let an opportunity for a gag slip by - 'A large sheep with short, thick wool waits to be Sean ... it's the blokes who are nervous round here!' - but it's the exhilaration of the trip that really gets your attention, the train 'bursting out into sunshine and wet ferns and fronds of the bush above Deborah Bay', and the arrival in Dunedin: - 'to him the station seemed a magical place with its beautiful bluestone outerwalls and its tiled concourse with the stained glass windows of the Blessed Virgin train ...'

The journey south is also a journey into Māoritanga - with the observations on the differences between the main islands Te-Ika-a- Maui and Te Wai Pounamu; the account of the train which is a moving marae; and ultimately Fitz's meeting with the woman of his dreams, Hinengaro Te Riro i He, who 'inherits Fitz's dream reality' and crosses over into mystical union with his wairua.

Apotheosis is reached in Dunedin and environs as neo-Nazi Wagnerians plot revolution and Fitz saves Hinengaro from their machinations. In league with new-found friend Paul Te Ariki Calvert, Fitz completes a process of self-discovery.

Above and beyond the many gigglesome walk-on characters - such as Haki Maroke Kuha the self-proclaimed New Right Maori Messiah, and Herr Frisch alias Wilfred von Oven the Nazi war criminal - what we savour, besides Fitz's growing awareness, is the author's poetic celebration of the New Zealand landscape, dark and magnificent: the precise and evocative description of an Otago snowstorm; the succession of days fading away into a series of tranquil nocturnes, their evening calm broken only by the mournful wail of a distant choo- choo train. – *David Eggleton*

(From *JAAM* 19, May 2003)

Wellington years

An earl of our times

'Wellington's an entire new phase to me. I've never spent much time here. I've always thought of it as a railway station and a port between Auckland and Dunedin. I love it. It's a kind of a quirky place.'

Writer and publisher Michael O'Leary has recently moved to the capital, and at the beginning of the year he opened ESAW (Earl of Seacliff Art Workshop) bookshop in Featherston Street.

Wellington will get a mention in one of O'Leary's novels for the first time, in *Unlevel Crossings*, his fourth.

He describes it as a long-term project, and a big one in comparison to his earlier works. 'It's a good metaphor for what I've written so far.' With the novel *Out of It* he started out writing a novel about a cricket test match.

'But half way through I got impatient and turned it into one-day game and finished it off!' There's a pause while we recover from laughing. 'This one will be a five-match test series.'

O'Leary says his main thrust in life is to be a writer. To date he has published nine books: three novels, two non-fiction and four poetry and prose. But as a child of a working-class family growing up in state housing area of Ōrākei in Auckland, books in the household were non- existent. 'We were too busy out fighting and playing and having a good time.'

However he has always loved stories, and drew on the oral traditions of his Irish and Maori ancestry, making up stories and telling them to other children. 'The kids used to say 'who told you that?' I said I made them up and they didn't believe me.

'It's in my blood. I don't know where it comes from, but I'm very grateful that it's there.'

At school he was more interested in the Beatles and the Rolling Stones than in books. The only two books he remembers reading are John Lennon's *In His Own Write* and *A Spaniard in the Works*. It wasn't until the age of 21 that he started to really read.

He himself finds it difficult to accept that the Michael O'Leary who got an A+ for an essay on Samuel Beckett at the University of Otago a couple of years ago and the Michael O'Leary who got 23 per cent for School C English are the same person. 'I've always felt any success I had was undermined somehow by a feeling that I wasn't meant to have that success. My parents died when I was young and it's like I've been given some consolation prize at the expense of their death. If they'd never died I would never have got beyond the state house and factory job.'

After studying part-time at Auckland University, O'Leary moved to Dunedin in 1974, where he began to write, and his work was published in various journals. He lived at Seacliff, and it is here he adopted the self-styled persona of 'Earl of Seacliff'. 'I'm an Irish Earl which is different to the English Earl. It's an important distinction. They were all killed, or exiled from Ireland. I've come back to haunt the English!'

Six years later he moved back to Auckland where he researched and wrote two booklets, *Grafton Cemetery* and *Gone West,* for the Auckland City Council Parks and Recreation Department. By this time he had also had his poetry published and had completed his first novel. With the knowledge he garnered publishing the cemetery booklets he decided to set up his own publishing firm, The Earl of Seacliff Art Workshop, and has published his own writing and that of others ever since. To give the enterprise a financial base, he set up Parimoana Bookshop, first in Kingsland and later in Queen Street.

On my arrival O'Leary thrust a slim book of poetry into my hands, *Loud Quiet Song* by John Ellis, his first publication for six years, 'I'm cranking everything up after being in abeyance.' Concentrating on university work took precedence, but now having completed a degree in literature and Maori Studies at the University of Otago, he wants to flex the publishing arm of his business again.

He says he has often published people who are not published by the mainstream; their writing has then gone on to become acceptable. For example works by David Eggleton, and New Zealand's first gay novel, *Passion,* by Glynn Parker. 'A lot of people I have published have subsequently become well known or well off or both.'

O'Leary sees his own writing as in that vein, in terms of being not acceptable to established publishers, 'I don't do it out of any perverseness, it's just what I am.' He describes the writer's role as halfway between magician and priest, giving expression to what other people feel or think, whether it's for entertainment or enlightenment or learning.

His main motivation for this bookshop is for it to be a specialist literary bookshop, concentrating on modem first editions and older rarer literary works. 'I would like it to be a focal point for people interested in literary things.' It is time to close the bookshop, and together we take the old-fashioned elevator with its mechanical dial indicating the flours back down to street level. As we part I mention that the shop is bright and cheerful compared to most second-hand bookshops where you are usually poking around in the dark. 'Write about it,' he advises, as he braces himself against Wellington's autumn chill. – *Kathy Dudding*

(From *City Voice,* 10 April 1997)

Encounters with the Earl

On my first trip to New Zealand I met Michael O'Leary three or four times. I'm not sure of the sequence. A bit like a pedestrian after an accident. I think the first week we were officially (Cath Kenneally & I) guests of Writers & Readers Week & staying in a fairly plush new building on the harbour's edge. The second week we were unofficial guests - staying with Greg O'Brien & Jenny Bornholdt. Two of the occasions were - characteristically, I think - a little unnerving. Michael suggested we kill some time one day looking at an exhibition of New Zealand art - probably at the Wellington City Gallery. I'm sure it wasn't at the old neoclassical building that I remember the Art Gallery of Wellington to be.

At this stage the Festival was up & running: I hadn't read yet but had probably put in an appearance or two - to see Ciaran Carson for example, I remember, & to go to some writers' parties, meeting Enzensberger, & Wellington names: Chris Price, Fergus Barrowman, Damien Wilkins, Elizabeth Knox & others.

Well the art was interesting enough of course & there was plenty I wanted to pay attention to: names I knew but which I had only seen in reproduction, or had never seen at all.

Michael was muttering darkly about Maori rights & their representation in exhibitions generally & in official New Zealand's representations of itself. Most Australians at least know that New Zealand has a different & better history in this area than Australia does. I nod & listen. Finally, Michael, who has been including me as an ally in his projections of himself & his views, makes a suggestion. This inclusion or enlistment is generous of course & I don't demand to see the manifesto I seem to be signing up for. It is also a little coercive & overbearing, though O'Leary, whom I like & find amusing & informative, is not heavy-handed in the matter. The fish likes the fisherman who reels him in gently, whose line persuades with small tugs & easings- off. Maybe that is what is happening. His suggestion, though, is that we should urinate together on a particular assemblage of stuff - one of the exhibits - that he finds a particularly egregious example of this Pakeha misrepresentation. Together we look at the work, a fairly dismal pile on the floor. Michael's idea has some obvious merit as practical criticism. Am I, too, not an anarchistic lefty bo-ho free spirit rebel - a poet after all - in the manner of Ginsberg & Bukowski & Baxter & Rimbaud et al? Michael is about to unzip. Am I not with him in this - it will be a major & appropriate statement of our position & besides maybe nobody will notice till we're gone? Michael is somehow able to exert a sense of enormous expectation, his expectation.

Do I know enough to justify this action? Aren't I here as a guest of New Zealand? Isn't this going to be a major scandal & embarrassment, involving a bunch of individuals needing to step in & soothe waters, with lots of apologies & forgiveness all round? I am sure to look like an idiot - not even the sort of idiot in fact that I hide within my outwardly sensible self. Someone other entirely. Serious people will have to intervene, on the grounds, basically, that I'm a fool. I tell Michael I'm not sure it's a good idea, but also that I'm running on empty & won't be able to help if he wants to go ahead. This last seems a less satisfactory option, I can tell. Michael broods on the altered equation he must now deal with. Solo, then? I move to stand & wait at some distance while the Earl ruminates, Napoleon on St Helena. It is the international & fraternal dimension that had been its attraction for

Michael, that had most recommended the act. And so Michael comes away, unfulfilled.

Later that same day - or was it a day or two later - the morning of the day I was to read ('An Hour With Ken Bolton' - a big event for me, if not for Writers & Readers Week), O'Leary & his friend Iain Sharp meet me to take me for a drive out of Wellington. How far will we go is the question. The answer that will best satisfy Michael O'Leary is, The further the better, turn up the music, let's get a bottle!

There was a feeling of 'incipient road-movie' about the situation & this only increased as we drove. Maybe the Earl had other Australians in mind - Brett Whitley? Bob Adamson? - or had in mind references to alcohol & excess in early poems of mine. I think he is hoping I will somehow 'do a number' - the year the guest poet turned up late, drunk & dishevelled, crazed of expression, fired-up to lash out at all forms of order & conformity. That would do. Trailing police cars even.

My memory now is of speeding along freeways, with anecdotes (of escapades, of jokes, pranks, great victories) going back & forth between Michael at the wheel & Iain in the back seat, me beside the driver, laughing with a developing caution compared to the gusto of my companions. A crazed pilgrimage seemed on offer. The car might easily break down. No, I didn't think we should really go on to the next town or, really, that we need, could really do justice to, another bottle of scotch. Etcetera.

If paranoia hadn't coloured my recall it would probably transpire that we had mostly talked about music we liked (the Earl's taste was more pop than mine, but okay, & nice to share as the scenery swept by looking one moment 'very New Zealand' at others like generic Europe or Australia), & about poetry & literature generally, & politics. But I was mightily relieved when we turned around & I sensed the Earl resigning himself to not being at the centre of any storm of controversy. Of course, as well as being relieved, I was unhappy to be disappointing him. A second time. A big disappointment. That he was bearing manfully.

We got back in time & I managed to focus so that the 'hour with KB' - mediated by Greg, who made it easy - went well. Michael, Iain, Greg & Jen, & Cath & I had a night of yabbering & laughing later that night. I was much more able to joke with the pressure off. Iain & Michael, I remember, were talking about their first encounters with the name 'Bill Manhire'. 'Manhire', whom they'd never met. Was it an odd-job company, hire-a-man, sort of thing? A male escort agency? Iain maintained that he had thought it might be a Maori name - Man-hir-e. The Earl joked about his reviewing practices. A number of books he had reviewed unread. This was a revelation to Iain, who had commissioned many of these articles for the *Sunday Star-Times*. The Earl was pleased. The reviews had sometimes seemed a little arbitrary, but always in an informed & lordly way.

Ever since I have never been sure that Michael hadn't been pulling my leg the whole time. Or maybe he was prepared to enjoy it at that level but to run with the action if I'd been the wilder, braver spirit that maybe he had wanted me to be.

Cath & I were in New Zealand again in 2006 - Auckland first & then Wellington. And I met the Earl again - he & Mark Pirie had organised a reading for us in addition to our more 'official' gig at Wellington City Gallery. It was a very pleasing thing to do: the audience were varied & interested & we got to hear Mark Pirie, a writer I'd been in contact with a lot since the '96 trip but had not met in person. And Dinah Hawken, whom Cath & I had known since '96 & seen a little in the meantime (whose books we'd been reading over the years), was also on the bill. The Earl was great. This time he was a statesman-like presence whose MC-ing of the reading was both generous & careful & brought the best out of the readers & prepared the audience. A dream run.

Six months later the Earl's press offered to publish something of mine in their mini-series. How's that? – *Ken Bolton*

"While My Guitar Violently Wails"

Date of Composition: 1999

Collection: *TAB Ula Rasa: New and Selected Poems, Toku Tinihanga: Selected Poems 1982-2002*

Anthologised in: *JAAM 21 "Greatest Hits", White Album Readings*

Destructive power is the opposite to creative power, although O'Leary thinks they move along a continuum rather than being mutually exclusive. This poem was inspired by the attack on George Harrison by a fellow Liverpudlian who had got it into his mind that the Beatles were evil witches. Harrison had become particularly security conscious after John Lennon's murder and lived in what was thought to be a safe and isolated mansion. The Beatles self-titled 1968 'White Album', to which O'Leary and Mark Pirie paid tribute on its 40th anniversary at last year's 2008 Winter Readings, was at once a particularly inspirational piece of writing, both in lyrics and in music. But, like a lot of things that uplift the spirits of people it can also suffer other interpretation. The song 'Helter Skelter', a joyous ride in a children's playground, became a sinister sign for Charles Manson's murderous rampage. Harrison's own masterpiece on the 'White Album' is alluded to in the poem's title and there are echoes of Shakespeare as well as post-Beatle Harrison and Lennon songs.

White Album Readings

Date of Publication: 2008

Publisher: ESAW

Category: Poetry

Contributors: Gemma Claire, Evelyn Conlon, Bill Dacker, Marilyn Duckworth, Rob Hack, Richard Langston, Will Leadbeater, Harvey Molloy, Michael O'Leary, Mark Pirie, Harry Ricketts, Helen Rickerby, Nelson Wattie and F W N Wright.

2008's Winter Readings celebrated 10 years of HeadworX Publishers in Wellington, and was also a tribute to the 40th anniversary of The Beatles' 'White Album', with the Beatles' music played at the readings. 2008's winner of the Earl of Seacliff Poetry Prize, Will Leadbeater, came down from Auckland to read. This was a rare chance to see Will Leadbeater read in Wellington. The cover of the anthology was a take- off of the plain white cover effect of the Beatles' 'White Album'.

Winter Readings

Winter Readings (2003-2008) was a series of live poetry readings in Wellington (influenced by rock music and the Globe Hotel readings in Auckland in the 1980s). The readings were organised mainly by HeadworX, ESAW, Poetry Archive Trust, and Kwanzaa - the Afrikan Shop and featured many prominent New Zealand poets as well as new and up-and-coming poets. Each year an anthology was published and featured a take-off of an album cover. Tributes were made to U2, the Doors, the Rolling Stones, Oasis and the Beatles. Before the rock tribute concept took hold, the first anthology and readings were dedicated to the memory of art writer and bookshop proprietor Neil Rowe in 2003. The rock tribute readings began in 2004 at Tupelo Bar, then moved on to St John's Church and finally, the City Gallery. Their inception proved popular (with audiences of 50-80 people) provoking the following responses, including a tribute to Michael from Robin Fry.

A Tribute to the Earl of Seacliff - Michael O'Leary

Michael O'Leary, the Earl of Seacliff, is a familiar figure to everyone who attends poetry launches and readings in the capital city, with his long grey hair and beard and with the warmth of his manner.

I made Michael's acquaintance when I began attending the Winter Readings series of events organised by the Earl and his friend, Mark Pirie (with help from Niel Wright). These two poets are financially savvy, satirical and very politically aware. They entertain us and stir us up - a partnership that really works, and works up a following with new and inventive ways of honouring poetry and the difference between fashionable writing and good writing whomever it comes from.

The products of Michael's Earl of Seacliff Art Workshop and Mark's HeadworX are of high quality, immaculately copy-edited and attractive to handle. ESAW's mini series, the *Poetrywall* anthology, and Mark's broadsheets from The Night Press are recent innovations that allow poets to see their work in print and their readers to be able to afford them.

The expanding popularity of these committed and hardworking poets has the feel of a writing whanau, united in friendship, loyalty and common aims of *in*clusiveness rather than *ex*clusivity.

As a published author of theirs, I learnt from them a bit more about how things work in our tight little circles of publishing and about the breadth of interest Michael O'Leary shares with Mark Pirie and others. These committed people are an asset to our capital city. They give great hope to new and established writers who quickly perceive that 'though there is plenty of room on the (poetry) bus' to quote Michael Harlow, the front twenty rows are usually reserved.

One of their main interests is pop culture. It shows in the photo shoots for their book and anthology covers and the music that weaves through their winter readings.

When I was young(er) I was almost unaware of the deep emotional channels pop songs reach with their universal themes of love/loss/ longing etc. My own favourite pop songs were ones that related closely to my own feelings and experiences at the time. 'I see those harbour lights' being one, would you believe it, expressing the loss of leaving New Zealand for the UK, then making the journey in reverse five years later, by ship, of course, compounded by the loss of a first love which I threw carelessly away.

However tough or worldly we are, or others might think us to be, no one, I believe, is untouched by pop culture or pop music. Surely even the most discerning classicist in music of my generation could not for long have remained indifferent to the rhythms and voice of Elvis and the myriads of imitators his music has spawned.

But I digress ... back to Winter Readings where I first met the Earl...

Winter in Wellington wouldn't be the same without these poets' carefully crafted launches and events. For now they remain here in the capital city. It's to be hoped that here they'll remain and long continue. – *Robin Fry*

Michael O'Leary

Poetry nite had by all
Poets & listeners, wall to wall
A good nite had
It was fun
I felt & heard their
presence
One to One

Steve Carter

(From *Poetrywall: Anthology of the Poetrywall*, ESAW, 2007)

Winter Readings at Tupelo

Listen to me
I am a stranger
in this place
just listen:
It is my first time
in a pub.

I was born

to be a puritan.
I was raised
in the Kibbutz
as a Spartan.

I was told
a man is born
to work -
no drink
no smoking
no cards
no drugs
no fooling around
only work.

I am here a stranger
in this palace of smoke
in this temple of beer and wine
I am a Spartan.
Listen to me, just listen:
I am here a stranger in this place.
I am here, now, twice:
the first time
and the last!

Wellington, 20-6-2004

M. Liba

(From *My Country, the World, - and Me,* Cyberwit.net, India, 2009)

Women's Conference

Words that hurt, words that heal

I have been a feminist activist for many years, learning along the way just how difficult the communication between women can be. As communication is my field of endeavour, I have found myself writing and talking, across the years, mostly for and to women: for ten years, I wrote (on a voluntary basis) for the iconic feminist magazine, *Broadsheet*. For that magazine, I helped create and run conventions, seminars and workshops, all focused through feminist thought.

Similarly, my novels and short stories are created through a feminist perspective, a perspective I am unable to change because feminism, when understood, irreversibly changes most women - and even some men.

This was the background to my volunteering to be part of the 2005 Women's Conference in Wellington. The conference, titled 'Looking Back, Moving Forward' was the brainchild of ex-Labour MP Margaret Shields, herself an active feminist in the '70s and early '80s.

I applauded the intent to gather together women who had been part of those active years of feminism, and to try to appeal to 21st century young women. So it was that I found myself part of the wider collective of women constructing this new conference. My first specific task was to create a newsletter which would be electronically sent to a comprehensive mailing list. Its main task was to chart our progress and encourage registration - or at least, an expression of interest in coming to the conference.

The task was not difficult, but by the time I came to put it together, I had lost the heart to do it because meetings of the collective were rife with argument and dissension. Feelings were wounded. Hurtful charges of racism and other ignorances were levelled at first one woman, then another. I worried that whatever I wrote, these ugly aspects of the work would get in the way.

But fortunately, I live in Paekakariki, home also to the Earl of Seacliff Art Workshop and the inimitable Michael O'Leary. Stopping at his excellent bookshop one morning, he gave me a copy of his latest book of poetry, which

I was delighted to have. At home, reading it, I came across a verse in one of his poems which reminded me of the central tenet of my feminism. It spoke so simply and forcefully that I realised here was the focus through which I could achieve my task. After getting his permission, I made the verse the keynote of my newsletter, which gave significance and depth to it.

This is the verse:

> She gives me the gift
> Only a young woman
> Can bestow ...
> The strange healing,
> and holding up of a mirror
> The touch of the goddess ...
> And no matter how humble
> His or her beginnings have been
> That gift of love, of aroha*

The newsletter succeeded in its task, the conference was held and very well attended. Thank you, Michael, for your poetry and your clear, warm, respectful approach to life in this world. – *Sandi Hall*

* From *Make Love and War* (HeadworX, 2005)

Wrapper

Date of Publication: 1992

Publisher: ESAW

Category: Poetry/Fiction

Contributors: Sandra Bell, Kim Blackburn, Jenny Bornholdt, Paki Cherrington, Bill Dacker, Karen Denby, Yvette Dentory, Grant Duncan, Kim Eggleston, David Eggleton, Riemke Ensing, Pamela Gordon, Kai Jensen, Judith Laube, Trixie Menzies, David Merritt, Mike Minehan, Piet Newlands, Rewa J.R.H. Norris, Gregory O'Brien, Con O'Leary, Peter Olds, Bob Orr, John Pule, Albert LIvinston, Refiti, Bruce Ringer, Elizabeth Smither, Alex Staines, Robert Sullivan, Hone Tuwhare, Jenny Vuglar, Richard Wasley, Richard Wilcox, and Sonja Yelich.

Review of *Wrapper* edited by Michael O'Leary

The last year or two has seen a burgeoning of locally produced literary magazines. There has been *Boomer: The Otago University Literary Review* which in 1991 spread its net wider and into the non-university community, from Super 8 have come *The Psychopathology of Everyday Life* and *My Friendships With Famous People* and threatening imminent arrival are *Boomer* 1992 and another Super 8 number, *Snafu*. But the latest local magazine to hit the streets is *Wrapper*, a collection of poetry from writers throughout New Zealand.

The focus of *Wrapper* is on previously unknown writers but a few better known names appear - Hone Tuwhare, Elizabeth Smither, Greg O'Brien, David Merritt, Riemke Ensing, David Eggleton, and Jenny Bornholdt.

Wrapper has not had a hasty genesis, stagnating for several years in various cities, in the back seats of assorted cars, being electronically transmitted (disease-like) from Hamilton to Coromandel and back, collecting dust in all the best dustbowl areas of New Zealand, snoring in the back of O'Books, Dunedin, travelling in the dark insides of satchels, Gladstone bags, cardboard boxes, plastic things and all this under the nurturing hands of five editors. The brainchild of Michael O'Leary it was initially collated by himself and the help of a nebulous and much pondered over kind was received from Ben Patrick and Grant Duncan. After their effort waned, Dave Merritt took his turn at the helm and managed to turn it from page to page into words on a screen, he dutifully tossed it on to Jeffrey Pettis who toiled over it, sweated on it, juggled with it and handed it back to Dave M. At this point, three and a half years after the initial collating, things were looking dangerously as if something might come of it all and suddenly, to much clamour and surprise, it was noted that the Literary Fund deadline was hard at hand and with an intense, grunty contraction out popped the magazine as it can be witnessed in various bookstores and etc throughout the nation. The lengthy lead in time has borne fruit with *Wrapper* being a cornucopia of fine poetry. Very little in this collection seems to be filling space, and that is no mean feat given the amount of space-filling poetry that is written in this world.

So congrats to the many headed ed, although at a glance it appears that some of the better known poets have handed in what might be described as not quite their most brill stuff. You know what I mean, thinking that this publication isn't *Landfall* (t'ank god for dat, I hear yon murmur) they don't hand in their absolutely best stuff, hot off the press… But this effect could be the result of a lot of the lesser knowns having contributed *very good* stuff… At the launching Michael O'Leary commented that several of the writers who were completely and safely anonymous at the beginning of the compilation procedure have since gone on to wider acclaim, and so *Wrapper* provides a glimpse of several writers at a germinal stage of their, if one can use the word without conjuring an image of something running wildly downhill at a great pace, careers.

It has much to be recommended and one can only either review everything in it or nothing in particular, since to say I liked this and I liked that is to imply that the unmentioned (unmentionable) was not liked as much. But then the question of one reviewers taste is moot to say the least. I mean who cares what I like and what I don't, after all I know that I'm opinionated without malice, but do you? Probably not. So I liked David

Eggleton's piece, dense and evocative are a couple of adjectives that spring to mind; Kai Jensen's Insulting a Cat tickled my fancy; adjectives for Dave Merritt's pieces - wry, deft; Kim Eggelston fine, clear images; etc.

I can't conclude without mentioning that Wrapper is very ... well put together, it looks a fine publication, with woodcuts by Nigel Brown and drawings by Greg O'Brien gracing its pages. Can be bought at O'Books in the Octagon. – *Critic book reviewer*

(From *Critic,* c.1992)

Zubu

Zubu is a character O'Leary sometimes uses in his adventures of two tigers, Zubu and Sambo. They appear in his poetry and are the main characters in the children's story 'Te Moemoea o Te Rau Tau'. The tigers also have a large part toward the end of O'Leary's novel, *Magic Alex's Revenge*.

Encores

Letters to the Editor

Thank you Michael - Earl of Seacliff - for bringing poetry to the public at an easily affordable price, and for venturing beyond the inner circle for your clients. There is a lot of unrecognised talent in all fields outside the main centres. May your good work continue for many years to come.

Rosalie Carey

Paddy on the railways .

A whole wave of young men around Waitati and Seacliff joined the NZR in 1975. The S9 track gang was run by a lanky ganger, John Capell. The grade 2 gangers were from men who had once worked in the Far North and on the South Otago line before they were pulled up.

Michael O'Leary worked from Port Chalmers. The gang travelled on a lumbering green bus. Other times the gang travelled on the red jigger, ripping around the bends. The running ganger was myself, David George, and old friends Paul Murchie, Flint and Chris Hall formed a part of the gang. One day the Inspector of Permanent Way Jimmy Richards berated Flint for wearing two coats. 'How can a man work wearing two overcoats!'

Like a marching army there were times of intense boredom and then feverish activity. Derailment of wagons occurred frequently with night call outs. Sometimes the gang would line up along the track with crowbars and pull the track into line.

Michael eventually had to choose between the railway gang and a writing career. Though the latter won the toss, the track and railways continue to fascinate him.

David George (At Paekakariki on the way back south after attending a reunion at Jerusalem on the Whanganui River to launch the book *The Double Rainbow* by John Newton about the relationship between poet James K. Baxter's commune and the local iwi, Ngati Hau.)

26 April 2009

Appendix: Questionnaire for Small Press publishers by Michael O'Leary

What was your initial reason for getting involved in publishing - please try to think of this in the spirit of what you were thinking and doing at the time.

I realized that my writing would not be acceptable to commercial or conventional publishers. This situation continues even today with my fourth novel, *Unlevel Crossings*, currently doing the rejection rounds. It has been the same for my poetry, although my first two books of poetry were published by Lancaster Publishing and Martian Way Press respectively. Most of the other writers I have published were in a similar situation and my decision to be a publisher was influenced a lot by watching writers who I thought were talented not being able to get their work in print because they weren't in vogue.

In 1984 I had a job with the Auckland City Council writing and preparing for publication two books on Auckland cemeteries. I used the knowledge gained at this time to set up the Earl of Seacliff Art Workshop. My original concept revolved around the idea of setting up a factory in one of Auckland's industrial areas like Penrose. From this site many artists, writers etc. would spend their days and nights working on projects, much in the way a conventional factory operates, except the final product would be an art work or a book rather than a car or a refrigerator - this somewhat fanciful dada/surrealist notion was the genesis of ESAW. In fact, at the time David Eggleton and I were carrying out a limited version of this concept. Four days a week, we were making various artifacts, and the remaining three days we would go into downtown Auckland to sell them on the streets - this was in the days when such things were illegal, an added incentive for us!

Who or what was your main influence behind your decision to publish? These may include literary or non-literary influences.

My main influence to be involved in literature came through two rather different avenues. As a young person my main inspiration came from the '60s pop music, in particular the lyrics of the Beatles and the two books of prose and poetry by John Lennon. As I wrote in the poem 'Flip Side to the Ballad of John and Yoko', written when Lennon was shot, 'Your songs and books helped me discover, in myself, what all the education in the world, could not, that I could write and illustrate my own story.' Later I came under the influence of James K. Baxter, Marcel Duchamp, Oscar Wilde and James Joyce all of whom have left their mark on the way I do things as an artist, writer and publisher. I have always been driven by a sense of destiny, an intensity of passion and belief, and the need to make a positive contribution to 'life', the fact that we all fall short of the glory of God I see as being not my fault but my humanity.

The fact that the muse has lead me to some illicit and dangerous places is just part of the fate of an artist.

In your choice of authors was the main consideration for inclusion philosophical, literary or pragmatic?

A mixture of all three, sometimes all on the same project.

'...and if there is still a number of commissioned works which seem to have been dreamed up by a sabotaging office-boy on an LSD trip, there are now each year a growing quantity of books which worthily add to our literature.' - Professor J.C. Reid from an article introducing New Zealand Books in Print, written in 1968. I interpret Reid's assessment as an indication of the rift between the acceptable 'worthy' literature as endorsed by academia, and the new wave of sabotaging office boys and girls who at that time commissioned publishers to put out their works, or simply published things themselves, and in many cases the work of their friends. Comment on this quote in relation to the 'Vanity Press' vs 'Real Publishing' debate.

I feel that this 1968 quote is significant because it draws the demarcation line between what is seen as acceptable and what is not in literary terms, and by implication makes academia the final arbiter over what is 'worthy' and what is not. As a publisher it has always been my policy that the author knows best. Thus, the poets and writers whom I have published have always been free to present to the world their work of art the way they want it to appear without editorial interference from me (although I have always made myself available if people want my opinion or advice). The fact that some of the drug-addled office boys of the sixties have become the conservative academics and latter- day critics and protectors of public taste in literary matters, is ironic indeed.

As far as the argument over vanity publishing goes, I am of the mind that all publication can be considered a 'vanity' in the sense that someone is arrogant enough to feel that they have something worthwhile to say, outside their immediate circle, and that it is being set down for posterity, is indeed a vanity. So the argument is one of whose vanity is more credible or readable or better-presented, rather than a shallow, indeed vane, assertion about 'standards'! Or, to put it another way, in the matter of literature - 'Vanity, Vanity; all is Vanity!'

Initially, was your focus outwardly cosmopolitan or inwardly New Zealand looking, and how has this emphasis changed over the years?

My emphasis has been on the cosmopolitan nature of New Zealand/Aotearoa, and because most of my publishing has been carried out in cities, my emphasis has been urban-focused.

What were your methods of printing and distribution as a publisher? Did you receive any financial or other assistance from either public organisations, or private sponsorship?

Most of ESAW publications were printed by an Auckland commercial printer, The Print Centre, up until about 1990. In the same period distribution was done by Brick Row Publishers. Since then both publishing and distribution has been erratic and various. For example, *The Irish Annals of New Zealand* was printed by the University of Otago Printery and primarily distributed through my Dunedin bookshop, O'Books.

Thus far I have received only one publishing grant, from the NZ Literary Fund to assist with the publication of *Wrapper*. (I have received two small grants to assist with my writing as well.) Auckland University Students Association funded *The City Assails*. Whitireia Polytech helped with both *Waiting for a Train of Thought* and *Nine Seasons*.

How much of your publishing was commissioned and paid for (either fully or partially) by the author? Was your operation helped by the voluntary work of friends and family?

About half and half of my publishing was the way my system operated. Finance has always been a difficulty. At one stage I was grinding concrete for twelve hours a night and running a bookshop during the day to pay for the publishing I was doing (during the '80s in Auckland). I have always treated equally the work offered to me for publication, whether paid for by the author or by myself, although some things would obviously not have been done if the author had not been able to fund it - however that would have been a decision based on financial rather than literary grounds.

I have always been blessed with many people around me who have been willing to put time and energy into my many projects over the years. Whether it is my extended whanau, the Seacliff Mafia (whose tentacles are long and varied), or the authors themselves, people have embraced the concept of shared work and my debt and gratefulness is with them.

What has been the cost to you personally in terms of time, money and resources, of being involved in publishing in New Zealand? You may consider this in relation to more difficult areas such as relationships with friends, family etc. also.

Much of the last twenty years of my life has been dedicated to these things. The cost to me has been the sacrifice of more conventional aspects of goals and achievements that may be the ambition of other men in our society. However, I knew very early on that dedicating my life to being an artist, in whatever form that took, was going to mean a certain amount of difficulty and isolation. I accept that this is why I haven't got a wife and a family in the ordinary sense, or a good career - I accept that my lack of business acumen has lead all my ventures into financial ruin and me into huge personal debt - or high-paying job, why I can't buy a house and to a large extent have to remain vulnerable to the obvious insecurities inherent in such a lifestyle. However, I have many close friends and supporters who believe in my work as much as I do myself, and who are prepared to help me despite my short- comings. Ka pai to mahi tatau, no reira.

Where do you place yourself and your achievements as a publisher (and as a writer if applicable) in the history of the modern-day New Zealand literary scene? Do you feel that your contribution has been adequately acknowledged.

I feel that as a publisher my achievements lie somewhere in the middle of the field. Apart from obvious exceptions, the number of publications I have produced is comparable to similar operations. I have been attentive to aesthetic aspects of book production as well as literary ones, and feel the books I have produced look good. I feel that the 1992 anthology, *Wrapper,* is yet to be recognised for its true value, and the novel *Passion* (1990) - New Zealand's first locally published homosexual novel, which unfortunately got bogged-down in issues that had more to with gay politics than actual literary merits.

As for my writing career, I feel that even though its taking a long time my achievements are beginning to gain recognition, and my recent inclusion in both the *Oxford History of New Zealand Literature* (2nd ed.) and the *Oxford Companion to New Zealand Literature* attests to this fact. As to the future I will continue to pursue my artistic career in whatever form that takes.

(*Editor's Note:* This self-interview from 1999 is a response to a questionnaire that Michael O'Leary sent to small press publishers that year. Michael published the responses he received from small presses in his book, *Alternative Small Press Publishing in New Zealand (1969-1999)*. Michael decided, however, not to include his self-interview in the book. It is published here for the first time. Since Michael wrote this response, ESAW has published over 100 titles.)

ESAW Bibliography

List of Publications

The Earl of Seacliff Art Workshop/Miracle Mart Receiving (1984-2009)

Non-fiction

Amery, C. *Ten Minutes to Midnight* (1989)

Derby, R. *Take a Seat and Rest a While: Kapiti Streetscapes, a Visual Dialogue* (2004)

Hare, B. *Peregrinations of a 'Priest': An Autobiography of a 'Nobody'* (2006) Maloney, P. *From Makarewa to Motueka: A Wonderfully Blessed Life: Some*

Memories of My Life and Times (2008)

O'Leary, M. *Scrapbook of the Earl of Seacliff Art Workshop and Michael O'Leary*

(1998)

Turner, B.E. *The Gospel According to Brian: The Damnation of Christ* (2009)

Humour

O'Shaughnessy, M. & Blunt, I. *The Arraignment of Dr Ley* (1989)

Fiction

Cherry, Frances. *Gate Crasher & Other Stories* (2006)

- *Out of Her Hair* (2009)

Coogan, Patrick. *What Colours a Pakeha* (2004)

Eggleton, D. *After Tokyo and Other Stories* (1987)

Entwisle, P. *Elaine and Other Stories* (1992)

Moynihan, Isa. *Here & There, Now & Then* (2007)

O'Leary, M. *Straight* (1984 1st ed., 1985 2nd ed., 2007 new ed.)

- Out of It (1987)
*- (with Corbett, K.) (Tongan and English translation). Hala e Kolo ni Mo
Ha Lanu (1987)*
- The Irish Annals of New Zealand (1991, 2001 new ed.)
- Magic Alex's Revenge (2009)
Parker, G. Passion (1990)
Pirie, M. *Swing and Other Stories* (2002)
Rennie, N. *The Super Man* (1988)
Turner, B.E. *The Road Goes On* (2003)
- A Day for Waving (2004)
- Dreamers (2006)

Poetry and Song Lyrics

Alexander, R. *Museum of Lost Days* (2008)
Bell, S. *postcards from Friedrichshain, notes from Pomerania* (2006)
Bellaney, P. *The Rooster Crows* (2005)
- A whistling woman, a crowing hen (2006)
Berengarten (aka Burns), R. *Manual - the first 20* (2006)
- Manual the second 20 - Holding the darkness (2007)
- Manual the third 20 - Holding the sea (2008)
Bernhardt, J.C. *The Deaf Man's Chorus* (2006)
Beyer, T. *City Limit* (2006)
Bolton, K. *Three Poems* (2007)
Butterworth, K.P. *fluid* (2006)
Campbell, M. *Resistance* (2005)
Carey, R. *Autumn Leaves* (2007)
Chan, J. *the smell of oranges* (2003)
- Becoming Someone Who Isn't (2007)
- These Hands Are Not Ours (2009)
Cherry, F. *Stories I've Told* (2007)
Claire (aka Rowsell), G. *Uncivil Servant* (2007)

Dacker, B. *To...* (2004)

Daube, J. *Tradesman's Run* (2006, 2008 2nd ed.)

Duncan, G. *Away With Words* (1986)

Ellis, J. *Loud Quiet Song* (1997)

Fisher, J. *The Sun is Darker* (2003)

Fry, R. *Inside It* (2006)

Furat, B. *The Moon That Excels in Nothing but Waiting* (2006)

Hare, B. *From and for Jesus* (1998)

Herrero-Kidman, A. *Pages for the Stage* (2004)

Jensen, K. *Hans Urlich Rudel and His Stuka* (1989)

Laube, J. *Limbo Dancing* (1987)

Leadbeater, W. *Jubal's Lyre* (2008)

Liba, M. *The Estuary of Komo: A Lament for the Children of Gabon* (2004)

- *They Drank Kava: A Journey Through a Failed Coup: A Ballad* (2004)

Lipschutz, M. *The Break of the Twig and the Fall of the Leaf* (1987)

McPherson, H. *Travel and Other Compulsions* (2004)

Olds, P. *Music Therapy* (2001)

- *The Mad Elephant* (2006)

- *Reaching for the Baxters* (2007)

- *Graffiti* (2008)

O'Leary, M. *Ten Sonnets: Myths and Legends of Love* (1984)

- *Before and After* (1987)

- *Livin' ina Aucklan'* (1988, new ed. forthcoming)

- *(with Bill Dacker) Kia Aroha* (1992)

Flip Side of the Ballad of John and Yoko (broadsheet, 1999 2nd ed.)

- *He Waiatanui kia Aroha (in association with the Fernbank Studio)* (2001)

- *Doomsblay* (2004)

O'Leary, V. *The Sensual Anchor* (2007 2nd ed.)

Paterson, A. *Incantations for Warriors* (1987)

Plumb, V. and Wiedemann, A. (English and Polish translations) *Doppleganger* (2006)

Pirie, M. *The Blues* (2001)

- *Dumber: Poems* (2003)

- Bullet Poems in four rounds (2004)
- The Ballad of Courtney Love (broadsheet, 2004)
- The Angel Bus: Songs 1992-1994 (2004)
- Poems for Poets: Dedications and Elegies (2004)
- Two Poems: An Impression the Sea (2004)
- Giving Poetry a Bad Name: Selected Early Poems (2005)
- London Notebook (2005)
- Wellington Fool (2006)
- The Search: Poems and Stories (with photos by John Girdlestone) (2007)
- Slips: cricket poems (2008)
Proops, R. *Guild of Scavengers* (2006)
Riddell, R. *Elegy in Memory of Barry Mitcalfe* (1987)
- How to Eat a Hot Dog on the Main Street of Thames (1990)
Romaniuk, J. *The Quest* (1990)
Scott, L.E. *Poems for Gwen* (2004) Sharp, I. *The Singing Harp* (2004)
Smither, E. *Gorilla/Guerrilla* (illustrated by Greg O'Brien) (1986) Tait,
P. *Ain't No Cat* (1989)
Turner, B.E. *Pocket Book Pomes* (2005)
Wattie, N. *Early Egypt and the Late Egyptians* (2006)
Wright, F.W.N. *Only a Bullet Will Stop Me Now* (2004 2nd ed.)

Anthologies

Henshall, R. (ed.). *The City Assails: New Auckland Writers* (1987)
*Mahones: Four Poets: Bill Dacker, Michael O'Leary, Mark Pirie and Iain
Sharp* (2005)
O'Leary, M. (ed.). *Wrapper* (1992)
- Waiting for a Train of Thought: Whitireia Writers (1998)
- Nine Seasons: Whitireia Writers (1998)
- Tiger Words: Paekakariki Poets at Pukapuka (2002)
- (with Pirie, M.). *"Greatest Hits": An anthology of writing 1984-2004* (in
association with HeadworX/JAAM) (2004)
Pirie, M (ed.), *Bookmarks: Winter Readings at Bizy Bee's* (2003)
- Tupelo Hotel: Winter Readings 2004 (2004)
- The Manuka Tree: Winter Readings 2005 (2005)

- Poetrymath: Winter Readings 2006 (2006)

- Poetrywall: Winter Readings 2007 (2007)

- (with Claire (aka Rowsell), G.) Poetrywall: Anthology of the Poetrywall (2007)

- The White Album Readings: Winter Readings 2008 (2008) Seacliff Mafia. *Christmas Surprise* (2005-ongoing)

Various. *Sonnets: Wellington Sonnets by Prize-winning Entrants in the Wellington Sonnet Competition 2008* (2008)

- Poets of Mana: Porirua poets (2009)

Recordings ESAW Sounds Division

O'Leary, M. *Toku Tinihanga* (CD, 2003)

Art Books

Brown, Nigel. *Black Frame: Work 1964-87* (1988)
O'Leary, M. (with Wayne Seyb). *Seens from the Irish Annals* (1993)
Yates, Nigel. *Dunedin: An Essay* (1993 2nd ed.)
- Notes from Underground (2007)

ESAW Poetry Prize Winners

2007 Evelyn Conlon
2008 Will Leadbeater
2009 Jill Chan

Michael O'Leary - Published Work

Non Fiction

2009 *G'Day Country Redux* (with David McGill) (Silver Owl Press)

2004 *Central Cluster Claims: The Upper Whanganui Iwi District* (CFRT)

2003.*Ngā Take Motuhake a Rangitāne* (CFRT)

1996 *History of the National Bank, Te Aro Branch* (Private)

1985 *Gone West* - History of Wakamete Cemetery, Auckland (Auckland City Council)

1984 *Grafton Cemetery* - Auckland - History (Auckland City Council)

Fiction

2009 *Magic Alex's Revenge* - Novel (completes the *Dreamlander Express* trilogy with *Unlevel Crossings* and *Straight*) (ESAW)

2007 *Straight* - Novel (new ed.) (illustrated by Greg O'Brien) (ESAW)

2002 *Unlevel Crossings* - Novel (illustrated by Greg O'Brien) (Huia Publishers)

2002 *Te Moemoea o Te Rau Tau* - Children's Story (Te Tahuhu o te Matauranga)

1999 *Michael O'Leary Stories: Short Stories & Other Prose*, archival copy (Original Books)

1999 *Out of It* - Novel, new ed. (Original Books)

1997-

1999 *Aucklana Livinia Pluralla; Dream Reality; Sow of Hades; South; Long Dazed Journey Into Night; Yellban Apocryphal; Float the Notes, Take the dAy Train* (Gradual publication of chapters as 'Work in Progress' of novel *Unlevel Crossings)* (all through Original Books)

1997 *The Irish Annals of New Zealand* - Novel, Celtic script version (Original Books)

1997 *Noa / Nothing I* - Short Stories (Original Books)

1991 *The Irish Annals of New Zealand* - Novel (ESAW, 2001 new ed.) (adapted for the theatre by Simon O'Connor and performed in Wellington in 2001)

1987 *Hala e kolo ni mo ha lanu* - Children's Story (translated into Tongan by Kahoa Corbett, illustrated by Lena Patience) (ESAW)

1987 *Out of It* - Novel (illustrated by Gregory O'Brien) (ESAW)

1984 *Straight* - Novel (illustrated by Gregory O'Brien) (ESAW, 1985 2nd ed.)

Literary Criticism

2007 *Alternative Small Press Publishing in New Zealand: 1969-1999* Literary History/Publishing History (Steele Roberts)

2002 *Alternative Small Press Publishing in New Zealand: 1969-1999* Literary History/Publishing History, archival copy (Original Books)

1999 *It's All in the Mind You Know* - Essay on Samuel Beckett
(Original Books)

Poetry

2008 *Paneta Street* (HeadworX)

2007 *Sounds of Sonnets* (with Mark Pirie) (HeadworX)

2005 *Mahones: Four Poets: Bill Dacker, Mark Pirie and Iain Sharp*
(ESAW)

2005 *Make Love and War* (HeadworX)

2004 *Doomsblay* (ESAW)

2003 *Toku Tinihanga: Selected Poems 1982-2002* (HeadworX)

2002 *Taumarunui: Unlevel Crossings of a Literary Kind* - Poetry/
Diary (illustrated by Michael O'Leary) (Original Books)

2001 *He Waiatanui kia Aroha* (in association with the Fernbank
Studio) (ESAW)

2001 *TAB Ula Rasa: New and Selected Poems* (Original Books)

1999 *Ka Atu I Kopua: New Poems 1979-1999* (Original Books)

1999 *Flip Side of the Ballad of John and Yoko* - broadsheet, new ed.
(ESAW)

1998 *Shake Speer's Faith and Other Poems* (Original Books)

1998 *Livin' ina Aucklan'* (illustrated by John Pule) new ed.
(Original Books)

1997 *Con Art: Selected Poems* (Original Books)

1992 *Kia Aroha*, with Bill Dacker (ESAW)

1989 *Livin' ina Aucklan'* (illustrated by John Pule) (Miracle Mart Receiving) (new ed. through ESAW forthcoming)

1987 *Before and After* - Poetry and Prose (Miracle Mart Receiving)

1984 *Undiscovered Voyage* (with Litia Alaelua) (Private)

1983 *Ten Sonnets: Myths and Legends of Love* (Martian Way Press)

1981 *Surrogate Children* (with Sandra Bell and Brian Hare) (Lancaster Publishing)

1980 *Flip Side of the Ballad of John and Yoko* - broadsheet (Private)

Recordings

2003 *Toku Tinihanga* CD, poems set to music - Waimea Studios, Christchurch (ESAW Sounds Division)

1995 *Twilight City, Just Like a Bird, Potatoes, Fish and Children, Southerners Crossing:* 4 songs recorded by Dunedin Irish band Blackthorn - Green-Eyeland Studio - Dunedin

1980s Nice Nazis tape

As an Editor

2004 *"Greatest Hits": An Anthology of Writing 1984-2004 - JAAM 21*: Anthology of New and Established Writers Taken from JAAM/HeadworX/ESAW Publications (in association with HeadworX/JAAM) (ESAW)

2002 *Tiger Words: Paekakariki Poets at Pukapuka* - Poetry Anthology (ESAW)

1998 *Waiting for a Train of Thought: Whitireia Writers -* Anthology (ESAW)

1998 *Nine Seasons: Whitireia Writers -* Anthology (ESAW)

1992 *Wrapper -* Anthology of New and Established Writers (ESAW)

As an Artist

2009-

2002 Contributed many art works to ESAW, *JAAM*, HeadworX, *broadsheet* and Original Books publications: including cover art, plus pieces for some of the Winter Readings anthologies and works in Kapiti Arts Trail.

2002 'A Helen Clark Retrospective' at One Eye Gallery, Paekakariki.

1994 Collaboration show with Christchurch Artist, Wayne Seyb – toured Dunedin, Timaru, Gore, Wellington, Paekakariki

1991 ONE-MAN Show at Blue Angel Gallery, Auckland.

O'Leary Appearances in other works

'News 20 May', Sandra Bell, in *Surrogate Children* (Auckland: Lancaster Publishing, 1981).

August 6th, Ken Bolton (Adelaide: Little Esther Books, 1999).

'Michael O'Leary', Steve Carter, in *Poetrywall: Anthology of the Poetrywall*

eds. Mark Pirie and Gemma Claire (aka Rowsell) (Paekakariki: ESAW, 2007).

Flesh and Blood, John Harvey (UK: Heinemann, 2004).

The Treadmill Tapes by David McGill (Paekakariki: Silver Owl Press, 2007).

'February 8th, 2003', Mark Pirie, in *Two Poems: An Impression of the Sea* (Paekakariki: ESAW, 2004).

'The Earl of Seacliff Travels from the Octagon to Tokyo', Jenny Powell.

'Green Viva', Iain Sharp, in *white horse black dog: sport fifteen* (Wellington: Sport, 1995).

'The Nevertheless Incredibly Happy Poem', Iain Sharp, in *The Singing Harp* (Paekakariki, ESAW, 2004).

'Poets at Paekakariki', Nelson Wattie.

For You: Poems/stories dedicated to Michael O'Leary/ ESAW

'The Earl of Seacliff', J D Bowen.

'On ESAW's 25th Anniversary', Jill Chan.

'O'Books', Bill Dacker, in *To.* (Paekakariki: ESAW, 2004).

'Bards of Paekakariki', David Eggleton.

'Blood on the McCahon' and 'The Rake', Pamela Gordon.

'The Final Rebirth', Brian Hare, in *Surrogate Children* (Auckland: Lancaster Publishing, 1981).

'Sunday' and 'Michael O', Richard Langston.

'The Earl of Publishers', Moshé Liba, in *My Country, the World, - and Me* (India: cyberwit.net, 2009).

'Adolf the Spider' and 'Watching a Friend on the "Southerner" Speed Through Seacliff Heading North', Peter Olds, in *The Mad Elephant* (Paekakariki: ESAW, 2006).

'My Bro: The Earl of Seacliff', Tricia Pink.

'Visiting Graves', Mark Pirie, in *London Notebook* (Paekakariki: ESAW, 2005).

'Thoughts in Remuera', Mark Pirie, in *Poems for Poets: Dedications and Elegies*

(Paekakariki: ESAW, 2004); and in *Just Another Fantastic Anthology: Auckland*

in Poetry ed. Stu Bagby (Auckland: Antediluvian Press, 2008).

'Labouring' and 'With or without', Mark Pirie.

'The Man at the Sea', L.E. Scott.

'Don't go past me with your nose in the air', Hone Tuwhare, in *New Zealand Listener*, 1 October 1990; and in *JAAM 21: "Greatest Hits": An Anthology of Writing 1984-2004* eds. Michael O'Leary and Mark Pirie (Wellington: JAAM Publishing Collective in Association with HeadworX/ ESAW, 2004).

Anthology Appearances by Michael O'Leary

50 Poems by 50 Poets: Recent New Zealand Poetry ed. Mark Pirie (Brisbane: papertiger media, 2004).

Bookmarks: Winter Readings at Bizy Bee's ed. Mark Pirie (Paekakariki: ESAW, 2003).

Boomer (Dunedin: OUSA, 1991).

The First Wellington International Poetry Festival Anthology eds. Mark Pirie, Ron Riddell and Saray Torres (Wellington: HeadworX, 2003).

Che in Verse eds. Gavin O'Toole and Georgina Jimenez (UK: Aflame Books, 2007).

ESAW Christmas Surprises (Paekakariki: ESAW, 2003-ongoing).

Just Another Fantastic Anthology: Auckland in Poetry ed. Stu Bagby (Auckland: Antediluvian Press, 2008).

JAAM 21: "Greatest Hits": An Anthology of Writing 1984-2004 eds. Michael O'Leary and Mark Pirie (Wellington: JAAM Publishing Collective in Association with HeadworX/ESAW, 2004).

Mahones: Four Poets, with Bill Dacker, Mark Pirie and Iain Sharp (Paekakariki: ESAW, 2005).

The Manuka Tree: Winter Readings 2005 ed. Mark Pirie (Paekakariki: ESAW, 2005).

Manukau in Poetry eds. Bernard Gadd, Bruce Ringer and Melissa Steiner (Manukau City: Hallard Press, 2006).

Other Voices 2 ed. Bernard Gadd (Auckland: Brick Row/Hallard Press, 1991).

Pacific Voices ed. Bernard Gadd (Auckland: Macmillan, 1989).

Poets of Mana: Porirua poets (Paekakariki: ESAW, 2009).

Poetrymath: Winter Readings 2006 ed. Mark Pirie (Paekakariki: ESAW, 2006).

Poetrywall: Winter Readings 2007 ed. Mark Pirie (Paekakariki: ESAW, 2007).

Sounds of Sonnets, with Mark Pirie (Wellington: HeadworX, 2006).

Spirit of Kapiti [Kapiti Poems 8] (Wellington: Steele Roberts, 1999).

Surrogate Children, with Brian Hare and Sandra Bell (Auckland: Lancaster Publishing, 1981).

Te Ao Marama 3 ed. Witi Ihimaera (Auckland: Reed, 1993).

Tiger Words: Paekakariki Poets at Pukapuka ed. Michael O'Leary (Paekakariki: ESAW, 2002).

Tupelo Hotel: Winter Readings 2004 ed. Mark Pirie (Paekakariki: ESAW, 2004).

Voyagers: Science Fiction Poetry from New Zealand eds. Mark Pirie and Tim Jones (Brisbane: Interactive Publications, 2009).

Sonnets: Wellington sonnets by prize winning entrants in the Wellington Sonnet Competition 2008 (Paekakariki: ESAW and Wellington Writers Walk Committee, New Zealand Society of Authors, Wellington Branch, 2008).

Whetu Moana: Contemporary Polynesian Poems in English eds. Albert Wendt, Reina Whaitiri and Robert Sullivan (AUP: Auckland, 2003).

The White Album Readings: Winter Readings 2008 ed. Mark Pirie (Paekakariki: ESAW, 2008).

Poems/Articles/Reviews published in (print periodicals):
Art New Zealand, broadsheet: new new zealand poetry, Craccum, Critic, Dominion Post, JAAM, Metro, New Zealand Listener, Paekakariki Xpressed, Pilgrims, Poetry NZ, Printout, Rambling Jack, Samoan Observer, Saoirse, Snafu, Sunday Star-Times, Tango and *Valley Micropress.*

O'Leary Film/TV appearances
Lord of the Rings, Via Satellite, Pictures: The Burton Brothers, and several other films as an extra.

Off the Rails, TV series, about New Zealand Rail presented by Marcus Lush.

O'Leary Readings/Public performances
Michael O'Leary conducted many poetry readings and artistic happenings throughout the 1970s, including a performance piece in Dunedin dressed as Dada artist Hugo Ball, reading at Mt Crawford Prison in Wellington with John Bailey and Paremoremo Maximum Security Prison in Auckland with Hone Tuwhare.

O'Leary performed regularly at Globe Hotel, Auckland, in the 1980s, and in many other readings throughout the 1980s around Auckland with several poets including Bob Orr, Iain Sharp, John Pule, Gregory O'Brien, Grant Duncan, Sandra Bell etc.

O'Leary has also been involved in many other readings and performances throughout the land in various bars/cafes/art galleries with a wide variety of other poets and artists up to the present day. David Eggleton and O'Leary did innovative street art, performance and theatre during the

1980s in Auckland and they also used to busk together, along with John Pule at the same period. In 2003, O'Leary was invited to take part in the First Wellington International

Poetry Festival organised by Ron Riddell and Saray Torres.

O'Leary performed regularly alongside Mark Pirie at Winter Readings, Wellington, 2003-2008. Together the two poets hosted the readings and presented new and established New Zealand poets from around the country to Wellington audiences.

List of Related Sources

A Comprehensive Bibliography of Michael (John) O'Leary, 1950- as Author, Editor and Publisher, compiled by F.W. Nielsen Wright (Wellington: Cultural and Political Booklets, 2000).

A Portrait of Two Artists: Count Geoffrey Potocki de Montalk, 1903-1997, Michael O'Leary, 1950-: Bibliographies, F.W. Nielsen Wright (Wellington: Cul- tural and Political Booklets, 1997).

An Irish Annal of Aotearoa: A Psycle Drama, Simon O'Connor (Wellington: Original Books, 1997).

Earl of Seacliff website (www.earlofseacliff.co.nz[1])

HeadworX Publishers website (http://headworx.eyesis.co.nz)

Hone Tuwhare: A Biography, Janet Hunt (Auckland: Godwit, 1998).

'Winter Readings at Tupelo', Moshé Liba, in *My Country, the World, - and Me*

(India: cyberwit.net, 2009).

The Long Forgetting, Patrick Evans (Christchurch: Canterbury University Press, 2007).

Michael O'Leary's Finger, Works for the Screan (i.e Screen) and Stage, Martyn Sanderson, Rachel Donaldson, Michael O'Leary and class mates (Wellington: Original Books).

New Zealand Book Council Profile on Michael O'Leary (http:/www.bookcouncil.org.nz/writers/olearymichael.html)

---

1.   http://www.earlofseacliff.co.nz

Oxford History of New Zealand Literature in English ed. Terry Sturm (Auckland: Oxford University Press, 2nd edition, 1998).

Oxford Companion to New Zealand Literature eds. Nelson Wattie and Roger Robinson (Auckland: Oxford Univeristy Press, 1998).

Peregrinations of a 'Priest': An Autobiography of a 'Nobody', Brian Hare (Paekakariki: ESAW: 2006).

Poetrywall: Anthology of the Poetrywall eds. Gemma Claire (aka Rowsell) and Mark Pirie (Paekakariki: ESAW, 2007).

Scrapbook of the Earl of Seacliff Art Workshop and Michael O'Leary (Paekakariki: ESAW, 1998).

Taumarunui: Unlevel Crossings of the Literary Kind, text and illustrations by Michael O'Leary; with additional material by Iain Sharp ... [et al.] (Wellington: Original Books, 2002).

Yesterman Among Tui-Cymbalists: Poems, Notes and Essays, F.W. Nielsen Wright (Wellington: Cultural and Political Booklets, 2009).

Online Publications by Michael O'Leary

Featured in *Blackmail Press 6* ed. Doug Poole (http://nzpoetsonline. homestead.com/index6.html)

Featured in *ESAW Christmas Surprise* e-Books (www.earlofseacliff.co.nz)

Featured poems in *Manukau in Poetry* online anthology (http://www.manukau- libraries.govt.nz/poetry/)

'Hone Tuwhare: A Personal Memoir' in *Ka Mate Ka Ora* on-line journal, ed. Robert Sullivan, Issue No. 6, September 2008 (http://www.nzepc.auckland.[2] ac.nz/kmko/06/ka_mate06_oleary.asp)

'Sonnet for Victor O'Leary' in *broadsheet: new new zealand poetry* on-line PDF journal, ed. Mark Pirie, Issue No. 1, May 2008 (http://headworx. eyesis.co.nz)

Sample poems on HeadworX website (http://headworx.eyesis.co.nz)

Poems on nzepc (New Zealand Electronic Poetry Centre) online poetry archive (http://www.nzepc.auckland.ac.nz)

---

2.   http://www.nzepc.auckland/

Poems in *Voyagers: Science Fiction Poetry from New Zealand* eds. Mark Pirie and Tim Jones (Brisbane: Interactive Publications, 2009)

Notes on Contributors

Winsome Aroha is a long-term friend of Michael O'Leary's and the subject of a number of his poems, including the poem sequence 'He Waiatanui kia Aroha'.

Sandra Bell (a writer/musician) became well-known in the Dunedin and Flying Nun music scene of the 1980s. She has lived more recently in Germany and is now back in New Zealand. In 2000 she released her Berlin solo album *City of Sorrows* (with help from Bill Direen). She has had poetry published in anthologies and in the three-poet volume, *Surrogate Children* (with Brian Hare and Michael O'Leary), in 1981. In 2006 ESAW published her mini collection, *postcards from Friedrichshain, notes from Pomerania*.

Ken Bolton works at the Experimental Art Foundation in Adelaide, South Australia. He writes poetry and art criticism. He does a little publishing via Little Esther Books and also runs the Lee Marvin Readings.

J D (June) Bowen is a retired librarian and late-comer to composing verse. In the course of her career as a librarian she has been privileged to meet many New Zealand writers including Keri Hulme, Janet Frame and Owen Marshall, but Michael O'Leary lingers in her mind as the most charismatic personality.

Alistair Te Ariki Campbell (1925-2009) moved to New Zealand on the death of his parents in 1933. A prolific author, he has published four novels, a radio play, and 18 collections of poems, including most recently *Just Poetry* and (with Meg Campbell) *It's Love, Isn't It?: The Love Poems*, both from HeadworX. His many awards, including the Pacific Island Artists' Award and an Hon DLitt (from Victoria University of Wellington), culminated in an ONZM in the New Year's Honours, 2005, and Prime Minister's Award for Literary Achievement in Poetry, in 2005. He died in August 2009.

Rosalie Carey is a teacher of oral communication and drama, a professional actress of stage and screen, a public speaker, fund-raiser and writer in a variety of genres. She has had published nine books as well as articles and poems in anthologies and publications such as the *New Zealand Listener,* the *School Journal* etc

Gemma Claire was born in 1983. She lives in Auckland, where she is training to be a New Zealand Sign Language Interpreter.

Jill Chan has published three collections of poetry: *The Smell of Oranges* (Earl of Seacliff Art Workshop, 2003), *Becoming Someone Who Isn't* (ESAW, 2007), and *These Hands Are Not Ours* (ESAW, 2009), which was awarded the 2009 Earl of Seacliff Poetry Prize. She currently edits the online magazines *Poetry Sz: demystifying mental illness,* and *Numinous: Spiritual Poetry*, and *Best New Poems Online.*

Two of the earliest major influences on the musical career of Graeme Collins were provided by his grandmother Bessie Collins. These were the old pedal organ she owned and the Clutha-Mata Au River that flowed past her place at Beaumont, Central Otago. Then, in the early 1960s, he became aware of the Beatles. In 1964 he bought the first Beatle concert ticket sold in New Zealand and so went to their Wellington concert. These were the paths to his key role as a member of the bands Dedikation, Human Instinct, the Underdogs and Dragon. In his later years he was deeply involved in the conservation movement, fighting the open cast goldmining at Waihi and the building of a dam on the Lower Clutha. Graeme continued to write music and poetry until his untimely death in 2004.

Geoff Cush's first short story, about two cowboys making love on a freight train, appeared under the pen name Steve Stack in the British gay magazine *VULCAN*. He is a novelist, playwright, travel writer and reviewer whose work has been published and performed in Britain, France, New Zealand and Morocco. Originally from Wellington, he is currently living there again.

Bill Dacker is a researcher and writer who has published books (*Te Mamae me Te Aroha, Mahika Kai*), written reports, and been a key participant in the creation of exhibitions, videos and DVDs, primarily about the history of Kai Tahu Whanui in the south of Te Wai Pounamu but also about the fate of Maori political prisoners in Dunedin. He has also been involved with researching and reporting on environmental histories and current environmental issues in the south. His poetry has been published by ESAW in anthologies (*Wrapper* and *Mahones*, plus three Winter Readings anthologies) and in his own first collection, *To....*

Kathy Dudding is a Wellington poet, artist and filmmaker. She works for the New Zealand Film Archive.

David Eggleton lives in Dunedin. He is a poet and writer whose articles, reviews and essays appear on a regular basis in a variety of publications. He has published a number of books of fiction and non-fiction, and his most recent collection of poetry is *Fast Talker*, released by AUP in 2006. His collection of short fiction, *After Tokyo*, was published by ESAW in 1987. He has been an assiduous reader of the Earl's oeuvre over many years.

Rangi Faith (born in Timaru in 1949) is a poet, editor and critic who has been widely published in New Zealand. He is author of *Unfinished Crossword* (Hazard Press 1990), *Rivers Without Eels* (Huia Press 2001) and *Conversation With A Moahunter* (Steele Roberts 2005). He edited *Dangerous Landscapes* (Longman Paul 1994). He works as a writer and tutor in Rangiora, North Canterbury, and is presently completing a new book of poetry.

Linzy Forbes is a Porirua writer and publisher.

Coming from a background of theatre, broadcasting and journalism, Robin Fry was born in 1932 in Palmerston North. She is a graduate of Victoria University of Wellington and the Royal Academy of Dramatic Art (London). Author of three poetry collections *Weather Report* (Inkweed, 2002); *Daymoon* (HeadworX, 2005); and *Inside It* (ESAW, 2006), Robin

Fry won the open section of the NZ Poetry Society's International Competition in 2008 and in 2001.

Bernard Gadd (1935-2007) was a noted educator, anthologist and writer. His poetry has been published widely, including in *Landfall* and the *New Zealand Listener*. He wrote 15 collections of poems as well as essays, plays, fiction and non-fiction, edited

several anthologies, and co-edited the haiku-related *Kokako* journal. In 2004 he won the *Bravado* poetry contest and *Takahe* cultural studies essay contest. In 2007 he was included, with Michael O'Leary and Mark Pirie, in *Che in Verse,* an anthology to commemorate the 40th anniversary of Che Guevara's death.

David George is a poet from Central Otago.

Michael Gifkins wrote his weekly column in the *Listener* for six years in the late 1980s. Widely known as an author, commentator and critic, he conducts an international literary agency from Auckland. He remembers Michael O'Leary as perhaps the most idiosyncratic yet reassuring presence on the literary scene at the time.

Pamela Gordon lives in Dunedin and is employed by the Janet Frame Literary Trust to manage the Frame estate. She previously taught linguistics and English language at Otago University and Semyung University, South Korea. She had some poems published in the 1980s and very occasionally still performs her own poetry.

Rob Hack was born in Invercargill in 1953 which he vacated three years later for Niue. Of Rarotongan and Kiwi blood he has enjoyed well over 30 jobs in New Zealand and Australia since leaving Tawa college in 1970. For the last three years he has studied writing and especially poetry at Whitireia Polytechnic completing a BAPPA and will publish a collection of poems this year. He lives in Paekakariki.

Sandi Hall is a writer who has been happily captivated by living in Aotearoa for 36 years.

Brian Hare was born and raised in Auckland and his early life was influenced by family tragedy and disruption. He began to look into alternative ways of living from his teenage years and he took all the 'trips' that were on offer in the late 1960s/early 1970s. Eventually he settled in Seacliff in Otago and became a student at the teacher's college and a married man with two daughters. But his internal search lead him away from these social 'certainties' and the rest of his life was spent exploring various dream/realities that meant he was at one moment a pious born again Christian, the next one of the devil's emissaries. Brian was a writer and poet of some insight and stature, and in 2006 ESAW published a memoir, *Perigrinations of a 'priest'.* Brian Hare died in 2008.

Lee Harris was working as a journalist for the *Otago Daily Times* at the time of writing the piece on the Earl's O'oops Gallery contained in this book.

Siobhan Harvey's work has appeared in magazine and anthologies such as *Landfall*, the *New Zealand Listener*, *Meanjin* (Australia), *Poetry NZ* (featured poet: issue 33) and *Snorkel*. She works as a New Zealand Society of Authors mentor, teaches creative writing at the University of Auckland and writes for the *Listener* and the *Press* (Christchurch). She is the editor of *Our Own Kind: 100 New Zealand Poems About Animals* (Godwit, 2009).

Bernard Holibar is a Wellington writer and reviewer.

Tim Jones is a Wellington author. His most recent books include the short story collection *Transported* (Vintage, 2008), the poetry collection *All Blacks' Kitchen Gardens* (HeadworX, 2007), and the fantasy novel *Anarya's Secret* (RedBrick, 2007). He recently co-edited *Voyagers: Science Fiction Poetry from New Zealand*, with Mark Pirie (Interactive Publications, Brisbane, 2009). His blog, *Books in the Trees*, from which the review in this book was taken, is at http://timjonesbooks.blogspot.com[1]

Richard Langston's three books of poetry are *Boy, Henry, Come See the Blue,* and *The Newspaper Poems.* He is working on a fourth, 'Shark Fin Soup

---

1.   http://timjonesbooks.blogspot.com/

and Other Poems', which is scheduled to be published by Fitzbeck in 2009. He is a reporter for TV3's *Campbell Live* programme.

Will Leadbeater was the poetry reviewer for the *New Zealand Herald* from 1980-88 and has published four collections of poetry. He writes: 'Over the past few years I have judged competitions for I.W.W. and in 1975 I won an American Poetry Competition judged by Donald Hall. For several years in a row, I was invited to three schools by the "Writer's in Schools" programme.' In 2008 he was awarded the ESAW Poetry Prize for his collection *Jubal's Lyre*.

Moshé Liba (a retired diplomat) is a lecturer, writer, playwright, poet, painter and sculptor. Writing in several languages, he has published 55 books, including text- books, children's books, theater play, brochures, and albums (11 of them in New Zealand), including 26 books of poetry (2 of them with ESAW). During his stay in New Zealand (1999-2004) he was Adjunct Professor in European Literatures at the University of Auckland, board member of the New Zealand Academy of Fine Arts, and of other literary and fine arts associations. As a painter and sculptor he has presented 47 solo exhibitions and participated in more than 300 group exhibitions.

David McGill is preparing to travel research his 43rd New Zealand social history in the august company of Michael O'Leary. Both share a love of train travel as well as pop music trivia centred on the Beatles. This reductive journey of *Two Men on a Train* in the faint carbon prints of his 1985 publication *The G'Day Country* draws inspiration from *Three Men on the Bumble*.

Born in Tauranga, **Heather McPherson** did the most important things of my life in Christchurch: finished BA, had a baby, joined Women's Lib and the Women's Art Movement, came out as a lesbian, started Spiral Women's Arts magazine in the adventurous Aotearoa tradition of small press publishing (Michael who published my last book of poems a distinguished continuer). Have just revisited Christchurch and with a friend made a pilgrimage to Ursula Bethell's grave in Rangiora, tidying it and taking flowers. As Sappho said: 'Someone in some future time will think of us.'

Harvey McQueen has published six volumes of poetry and co-edited *The Penguin Book of New Zealand Verse* (Penguin, 1985). His *New Place* is the only modern anthology of 19th century New Zealand verse.

Hedley Mortlock is a book reviewer

Michael Morrissey has published 19 books - 10 books of poetry, four of fiction and edited five anthologies of poetry and prose. He was the first writer-in-residence at the University of Canterbury in 1979 and the first New Zealand writer to participate in the University of Iowa's International Writing Programme. He has been writing a book review column for *Investigate* magazine for ten years during which time he has reviewed some 500 books.

Andrea Mudry is a Canadian writer and researcher who was on a year's sabbatical in New Zealand at the time of writing the review contained in this book. Her most recent book, *World Enough and Times,* addresses the issues of aging.

Emma Neale lives in Dunedin, where she works as an editor and freelance writer. She has published three collections of poetry and four novels and in 2008 edited *Swings and Roundabouts: Poems on Parenthood*. Neale was the inaugural recipient of the NZSA Janet Frame Memorial Award for Literature in 2008.

Amelia Nurse is a Wellington writer. She works for Radio NZ. She read at *The Manuka Tree* Winter Readings in 2005.

Born in Matamata in 1961, **Gregory O'Brien** is a general cultural odd-jobs-man. He has curated art exhibitions for City Gallery Wellington and elsewhere, and written widely on various topics. Recent books include a collection of poems, *Afternoon Of An Evening Train* (2005), and a forthcoming one, *Little Oneroa*; as well as a book about New Zealand painting for youngish people, *Back and Beyond*. A collection of short fiction, *The Prose Years*, is also in the pipeline.

Peter Olds was the 2005 recipient of the Janet Frame Literary Award for a poet. His books include *It Was a Tuesday Morning: Selected Poems* (2004) and *Poetry Reading at Kaka Point* (2006). He lives in Dunedin..

Clare O'Leary is a documentary filmmaker, she is Mike's youngest sister and has been interviewing him over the last 12 months for a documentary about his life and work. Clare is currently making a documentary about the poet Hone Tuwhare and also has another project in development about the Wellington artist, Gordon Crook.

Michael O'Leary is a poet, novelist, artist, performer and bookshop/art gallery proprietor. O'Leary's career as a literary publisher covers twenty years. He has worked under two main imprints: The Earl of Seacliff Art Workshop (ESAW) and Miracle Mart Receiving (in 1987), procured from Gregory O'Brien in a corporate raid common during that time (for a seven figure sum).

Vincent Orange is a Christchurch book reviewer.

Mark Pirie is a Wellington poet, publisher, anthologist, critic and editor of *broadsheet: new new zealand poetry*. He is the most prolific author of the Earl of Seacliff Art Workshop with around a dozen titles that he has written or edited. Poets Group, Christchurch, have just published his verse novel, *Tom*. He recently co-edited *Voyagers: Science Fiction Poetry from New Zealand*, with Tim Jones (Interactive Publications, Brisbane, 2009).

Jenny Powell is a Dunedin writer who has published three individual and two collaborative collections of poems. Her next collection, *Viet Nam: a poem journey* is to be published by HeadworX.

Steve Rendle is a Wellington-based journalist.

Joan Rosier-Jones is a writer-cum-creative writing tutor with five novels to her name. She is also author of *So You Want to Write* and *Writing Your Family History,* and occasionally dabbles in journalism.

John Quilter is a Wellington bookseller.

Trevor Reeves was born in Dunedin in 1940, which is where he now lives. He started writing in the mid-1960s and has had work published worldwide. His published books number eight and include four books of non-fiction. He founded Caveman Press in 1971, publishing writers worldwide and Square One press in 1986, publishing local history books, biography, autobiography, architecture, poetry etc. The literary magazine, *Southern Ocean Review*, which he edits and publishes, is on its last issue, at #50.

Jack Ross's latest novel *E M O*, the last in a trilogy made up of *Nights with Giordano Bruno* (2000) and *The Imaginary Museum of Atlantis* (2006), came out from Titus Books in 2008. He has also published two collections of short fiction, as well as several volumes of poetry. Other books include the AUP audio/text anthologies *Classic, Contemporary* and *New NZ Poets in Performance* (2006-8), edited with Jan Kemp.

Martyn Sanderson is an actor, scriptwriter, poet and grandfather born on the way to Westport and now living in Otaki. An erstwhile drinking mate of the O'Leary, he is now a mere friend and admirer.

Elizabeth Smither has published 15 collections of poetry as well as novels and short stories. In 2008 she was awarded the Prime Minister's Award for Literary Achivement in Poetry.

L E Scott is an African American jazz poet and world traveller. His work has been published in most of New Zealand's literary magazines, as well as US magazines such as *Essence, The Black Scholar, Obsidian* and *Chelsea.* Scott has also had a number of collections published, the latest of which is *Speaking in Tongues*, published by HeadworX (Wellington) in 2007.

Iain Sharp was born in Glasgow in 1953, but he has lived in New Zealand (mostly in the Greenlane, Ellerslie and Penrose region of Auckland) since he was eight years old. He has worked for many years as a librarian and journalist. His biography of nineteenth-century artist, explorer and Victoria Cross recipient Charles Heaphy was published by Auckland University Press in October 2008.

Elizabeth Smither has published 15 collections of poetry as well as novels and short stories. In 2008 she was awarded the Prime Minister's Award for Literary Achivement in Poetry.

Guy Somerset was books editor of *The Dominion Post* between 2003 and 2008 and is currently arts and books editor of the *New Zealand Listener*.

Roger Steele is a partner of Steele Roberts Publishers, whose first book was *Dedications* by JC Sturm (1996) and second was *Shape-Shifter* by Hone Tuwhare. The firm continues to publish literature, history, and other intriguing aspects of Aotearoa New Zealand culture.

Anne Tucker is a Wellington poet and reviewer.

Brian E. Turner started writing in 1978 and is a prolific and successful playwright. A number of plays have been performed in back alley theatres in NZ and overseas. His plays often deal with unusual aspects of life and consciousness, and present interesting challenges for producers and casts. He has published three novels and is Technical Editor for ESAW.

Ron Ward is a book reviewer.

Nelson Wattie is a Wellington poet, book reviewer and translator. He co-edited *The Oxford Companion to New Zealand Literature,* with Roger Robinson.

Dale Williams is a book reviewer.

F W N Wright is the author of the epic poem *The Alexandrians* (in 120 books, published from 1961-2007). He lives in Wellington.

Hamesh Wyatt, a priest and drama tutor, was for a number of years the poetry reviewer for the *Otago Daily Times*.

Joe Wylie was a book reviewer for *Takahe* magazine in Christchurch when he wrote the piece contained in this book.

About the Author

Michael O'Leary is a poet, novelist, publisher, performer and bookshop proprietor who has been a magnetic figure for many other contemporary New Zealand writers. He writes in both English and Māori; and his diverse and prolific work in poetry, fiction and non-fiction explores his dual heritage: Māori on his maternal side and Irish Catholic on his father's as well as his mother's. Born in Auckland in the year of the Tiger 1950, he was educated at the universities of Auckland, Otago (Dunedin), and Victoria University (Wellington). His Earl of Seacliff Art Workshop imprint (inspired by Andy Warhol's 'Factory', the Beatles' Apple label, and John and Yoko's 'Plastic Ono Band'), which he founded in 1984, has published some of his own prolific output, as well as many other New Zealand writers. This press has also featured books by writers from other countries, including the first versions of Richard Berengarten's series, *Manual*, in four mini-books (2005-2009). The 240-page A-Z compilation, *25 Years of the Earl of Seacliff* (ed. Mark Pirie, 2009), documents Michael O'Leary's versatile and influential oeuvre. Michael O'Leary is a trustee for the Poetry Archive of New Zealand Aotearoa (PANZA), a charitable trust dedicated to archiving, collecting and promoting New Zealand poetry. He now lives in Paekakariki, north of Wellington.

Read more at https://books2read.com/michaeloleary.